Lost and Found

Making and remaking working partnerships with parents of children in the care system

Edited by
Judith Masson
Christine Harrison
Annie Pavlovic

University of Warwick

LONDON AND NEW YORK

First published 1999 by Ashgate Publishing

Reissued 2018 by Routledge
2 Park Square, Milton Park, Abingdon, Oxon, OX14 4RN
711 Third Avenue, New York, NY 10017, USA

Routledge is an imprint of the Taylor & Francis Group, an informa business

Copyright © Judith Masson, Christine Harrison and Annie Pavlovic 1999

All rights reserved. No part of this book may be reprinted or reproduced or utilised in any form or by any electronic, mechanical, or other means, now known or hereafter invented, including photocopying and recording, or in any information storage or retrieval system, without permission in writing from the publishers.

Notice:
Product or corporate names may be trademarks or registered trademarks, and are used only for identification and explanation without intent to infringe.

Publisher's Note
The publisher has gone to great lengths to ensure the quality of this reprint but points out that some imperfections in the original copies may be apparent.

Disclaimer
The publisher has made every effort to trace copyright holders and welcomes correspondence from those they have been unable to contact.

A Library of Congress record exists under LC control number: 98055930

Typeset by Manton Typesetters, 5-7 Eastfield Road, Louth, Lincs, LN11 7AJ, UK.

ISBN 13: 978-1-138-33513-4 (hbk)
ISBN 13: 978-1-138-33515-8 (pbk)
ISBN 13: 978-0-429-44395-4 (ebk)

LOST AND FOUND

Contents

List of contributors vii
Introduction ix
Table of cases xvii

1 Recreation and promotion of partnership through action research 1
   Christine Harrison and Judith Masson

2 Legal issues: partnership with parents and children's rights 27
   Judith Masson

3 Working in partnership with parents of children being looked after: issues of theory, research and practice 49
   June Thoburn

4 Young people, being in care and identity 65
   Christine Harrison

5 Partnership with parents of children in foster care or residential care 91
   David Berridge

6 Rebuilding partnerships with parents of looked-after children 105
   Judith Masson and Christine Harrison

7 Partnership and leaving care 127
   Nina Biehal

8	The experience of making contact with birth parents in adoption *Alan Burnell*	145
9	Partnership and contact: issues for management *Brian Waller*	155
10	Searching for lost parents *Annie Pavlovic*	167

Appendix: useful addresses   197
Bibliography   199
Index   213

List of contributors

David Berridge is Professor of Child and Family Welfare at the University of Luton. He has been a social researcher for approaching 20 years and was formerly Research Director of the National Children's Bureau and Research Fellow at the Dartington Social Research Unit. His recent publications include *Children's Homes Revisited* (1998, with Isabelle Brodie) and *Foster Care: A Research Review* (1997).

Nina Biehal has carried out research on user involvement, leaving care, runaways from residential and foster care and on preventive services for teenagers. She is currently a senior research fellow in the Social Work Research and Development Unit at the University of York.

Alan Burnell is a qualified social worker with 20 years' experience in work with children and families. For 10 years he worked as counsellor at the Post-Adoption Centre in London, exploring with individuals issues relating to contact and reunion in the context of adoption and fostering. He was director of the Post-Adoption Centre until the end of 1997 and is now a founder member of Family Futures Consortium, a voluntary organization specializing in attachment formations within families.

Christine Harrison is currently a lecturer in social policy and social work at the University of Warwick, where she teaches on qualifying and post-qualifying social work programmes. She has extensive previous experience as a social worker and guardian ad litem and is consultant to staff in a hostel for women offenders. Her current research interests include assessment in child care and child protection, feminist perspectives in social work and young people in the care system.

Judith Masson is Professor of Law at the University of Warwick. She was a co-director of the 'working in partnership with "lost" parents' project. She has specialized in sociolegal studies of children, families and social work, conducting research into step-parent adoption, wardship and the representation of children in care proceedings, and working on the Department of Health's implementation programme for the Children Act 1989. She is currently undertaking research on emergency intervention to protect children.

Annie Pavlovic graduated in sociology from the University of Warwick. She has wide experience as a researcher in sociolegal and social work-related projects, particularly on the probation service, the adoption contact register and relationships between siblings. Between 1993 and 1996, she was a full-time research fellow on the "lost" parents' project. She has lectured in social policy and is currently a lecturer in sociology at Nene University College, Northampton.

June Thoburn is Professor of Social Work at the University of East Anglia, Dean of the School of Social Work and Director of its Centre for Research on the Child and Family. She has written widely on family support, child placement and child protection. Her recent studies in these areas involve children of minority ethnic origin.

Brian Waller was Director of Social Services for Leicestershire County Council from 1988 to 1997. Between 1996 and 1997, he was also the Chair of the Children and Families Committee of the Association of Directors of Social Services. Currently he is Visiting Professor of De Montfort University and director of Homestart UK.

Introduction
Judith Masson, Christine Harrison and Annie Pavlovic

> The essence of partnership is sharing. It is marked by respect for one another, role divisions, rights to information, accountability, competence and value accorded to each individual input. In short each partner is seen as having something to contribute, power is shared, decisions are made jointly and roles are not only respected but are also backed by legal and moral rights. (Tunnard, 1991)

This book is a collection of essays focused on the theme of partnership with parents in social work practice with children and families. It developed from an action research project, funded by the Joseph Rowntree Foundation, on 'working in partnership with "lost" parents' conducted by Judith Masson, Christine Harrison and Annie Pavlovic at Warwick University between 1993 and 1996. Through teaching activities associated with the implementation of the Children Act 1989 we had become aware that there were many parents who had lost contact with both their child and their child's social worker after their child had entered the care system. These were the 'lost' parents of the study. To label these parents as lost is perhaps misleading; they are perhaps better described as forgotten or discarded. Their role as parents of children in the care system was undervalued and their opportunities to maintain a relationship with their child were limited or absent. Consequently, there was generally no reason for social workers to stay in touch with these parents. For parents, already burdened with poverty and ill-health, active discouragement or the lack of any support readily undermines their attempts to remain in contact with both their child and the social worker.

Partnership with parents has become an integral part of social work with children and families living together or apart. Inevitably, it concerns many other people involved in the care of children and providing advice to individuals. As a way of working, partnership permeates all aspects of relationships with parents and children, including relationships with those providing care in place of parents. Consequently, the issues discussed in this book are of relevance to all those working directly or indirectly with children, parents and other relatives; amongst these are social workers, including those in training and those who train them; family placement workers, carers and residential workers; team managers and policy makers in local authority social services departments; guardians ad litem, court welfare officers and lawyers acting for children or parents; and children's rights officers and advisers working in voluntary agencies which support families and children.

The Children Act 1989 sought to establish a new balance between families and the welfare agencies within which parents were given greater recognition. Whilst children were looked after by a local authority social services department, parents now retained their parental responsibility, even where children had been made the subject of care orders. New obligations were imposed on local authorities to consult and consider the views of parents and children in relation to all decisions about care. These more extensive duties to work in partnership with parents applied to 'lost' parents as to others, but many social workers felt daunted by this and uncertain about how to proceed to reinvolve parents. It was the aim of the project to find out whether and how the local authority's responsibilities towards these parents and their children could be undertaken

The majority of children and young people who enter the care system spend a relatively short period of their life there. This has been the case particularly since the late 1980s, because greater emphasis has been given to social work to achieve the early restoration of children to their families. However, a significant number of children, over 2000 each year, do not return during their childhood. As a group, these children in long-term care have been overlooked, especially in relation to their needs to maintain links with their families. A number of factors have contributed to this marginalization, including beliefs about the negative effect of contact on finding and maintaining stable foster placements, the failure to recognize the significance for children's development of links and knowledge about identity, and the displacement of long-term work with children through organizational priorities, particularly child protection concerns.

It might be assumed that changes in the Children Act and the new emphasis on involving parents would mean that, in future, parents will not become lost. However, experience from the project suggests that such optimism is misplaced. Loss occurs both *before* children enter the care system when the relationship between parents breaks down and *after* entry to care. The numbers of divorces involving children under the age of 16 years continues to rise and an increasing proportion of children are born to unmarried couples whose relationships are generally thought to be no longer-lasting than those of married couples. Some at least of the factors that in the past have undermined parental involvement in the care system continue to exert a powerful influence and new factors can be identified. The parents of children in the care system continue to experience enormous disadvantage and discrimination in their lives. Despite attempts to refocus children's services, child protection still dominates both social services department priorities and the caseloads of individual social workers. The shortage of suitable placements means that children are often placed inappropriately and in a succession of placements, making it difficult for parents to establish relationships with carers.

As part of the project, the research team arranged workshops to explore with the participating social workers the existing research, relevant knowledge and current practice issues. All of the areas discussed arose directly from the work practitioners faced in trying to establish a working relationship with parents of looked after children. Two of the contributors, Alan Burnell and June Thoburn, were members of the advisory committee for the project and, as such, regularly took part in discussions of themes emerging from the research. They helped to shape both the research and the workshops with participating social workers. The other contributors were known to the project team through their work. David Berridge and Nina Biehal were both engaged on studies directly relevant to the concerns of social workers involved in the 'lost' parents study. Brian Waller, as a Director of Social Services and Chair of the Association of Directors of Social Services Children and Families Committee, was well placed to consider the implications for social work management of the research findings.

In this book the ideas presented in the workshops and emerging from the research itself have been developed to present current understandings of the role of parents and the ways that they may be helped to contribute to the well-being of their children in and after care. Directly related to the research, the chapters also discuss the social, political, organizational and practice dimensions of working in partnership with children, young people and their parents. They are relevant to finding 'lost' parents and attempting to rebuild working relationships with them, to keeping hold of parents who may be in danger of becoming lost, and to sustaining relationships with them.

The opening chapter of the book gives a synopsis of the 'working in partnership with "lost" parents' research project: its aims, methodology and findings. It demonstrates that, while demanding, work to re-establish working relationships with 'lost' parents of children in long-term care can be successfully undertaken and can bring important benefits for all concerned. This work is complex, requiring considerable efforts on the part of individual workers and recognition from management. There are tensions between the perspectives of social workers, carers, parents and young people, varying over time, that must be continuously negotiated. A partnership approach demands that conflicts are worked with rather than avoided, as happened in the past. The exclusion of the weaker parties' voices, frequently those of parents and young people, has limited understandings of the well-being of young people in care.

A major incentive for the research project was the legal and philosophical changes generated by the Children Act 1989 and its implementation during the early 1990s. Whilst legal change may be prompted by research and provide a framework for intervention in the lives of children and their families, implementation may have unintended as well as intended consequences. In particular, it may have little significance or effect if retrospective application in relation to children and young people in long-term care is not recognized by managers and practitioners as important and where parents and children are powerless or lack the information necessary to challenge this. In Chapter 2, Judith Masson gives detailed consideration, not just to the relevant legal provisions of the Children Act 1989, but to what these might mean for children, parents and workers attempting to translate them into progressive practice. Roles, responsibilities, rights and how these can be fulfilled and exercised, together with the conflicts and tensions which will inevitably arise, are fully explored.

The fullest implementation of the provisions of the Children Act applying to children being looked after by the local authority is dependent on the kind of working relationships which can be forged between practitioners and parents, and between practitioners and children and young people. The concept of working in partnership is further developed in the chapter by June Thoburn, which concentrates on situations where there has been alleged or known child maltreatment; these are often regarded as the most conflict-laden and least conducive to working in partnership with parents and families. Drawing on recent research studies, the author identifies the principles which underpin partnership-based practice and highlights the very difficult circumstances which many parents of children in the public care continue to experience. The vital contribution that working in partnership with family members, including parents and young people, can make to effective social work practice is established. As well as exploring the ways in which partnership-based practice can be promoted, the chapter underlines how important valuing a parent is to this process and that much can be achieved where there is an active commitment to this work.

The value that parents have for children and young people being looked after, and the contribution that parents can make to their child's well-being, are also recognized in Chapter 4. Whilst the inception of the 'working with "lost" parents' research project lay in the legal changes embodied in the Children Act 1989, a practice imperative can be found in the plethora of research which preceded it. In particular, shifting views about child development, the nature of attachment and about the care of children away from their birth families have led to a reappraisal of the significance of family, culture and community for children in the public care. This chapter contrasts orthodox approaches to child development with more recent accounts which have emphasized the broader social and political determinants of individual identity. Drawing on young people's own stories, Christine Harrison demonstrates how difficult their lives have been before, during and after care and suggests that promoting a positive identity is the right of every child being looked after.

Most children who become looked after experience foster care; some also experience residential care. A small, but nonetheless significant, minority experience multiple residential and foster care placements. For all parents of children and young people being looked after, the need for working partnerships also applies to foster carers and residential workers. In Chapter 5, David Berridge outlines current knowledge about foster and residential care, focusing on issues relating to working in partnership. Recognizing the changes that have characterized professional attitudes to the active involvement of parents when their children are being looked after, the diversity of definitions and understandings of partnership is explored. The findings of research about when, how and why parents' involvement with their children in foster or residential care has occurred are considered and evaluated. While this highlights both the benefits and the difficulties which are associated with parental involvement, the need for a better understanding of the complex issues involved is also argued.

Chapter 6, by Judith Masson and Christine Harrison, again draws directly from the 'working in partnership with "lost" parents' research to show how partnerships can be rebuilt and the obstacles to this process can be overcome. When practitioners begin to contemplate finding and rebuilding a relationship with a parent of a child in public care who is currently lost, they must also contemplate how the parent became lost and the impact this may have had on them. This may also mean confronting the inheritance of practice informed by a substantially different value base and poor or even discriminatory practice. Although there is great diversity amongst children who are looked after and their parents, the research project identified a number of common themes from children's histories which constituted barriers in the process of restoring a working relationship. These and other contemporary ideological and practical barriers are considered, together with the ways in which social worker participants in the research struggled to overcome them.

Many of the children included in the research project were young people approaching the point where they would leave care for some sort of independence. Over the three years of the project a number of them did indeed leave care. Though longed for, this did not often bring them the sense of freedom they anticipated, and it frequently brought to the surface their lack of supportive family or other significant relationships. Nina Biehal draws on longitudinal research with care leavers and discusses the potential for working in partnership with the parents of young people leaving the care system and critically evaluates the implications of this. Patterns of leaving care are examined, together with patterns of family contact. The diverse meanings of partnership are explored and the associated form, aims, benefits and limitations of partnership are examined. The conclusions emphasize the need to maintain a working partnership with parents throughout the time a child is being looked after and the need simultaneously to work in partnership with young people.

The legal status of adopted children, and their birth parents, is different from that of looked-after children and the obligations for social services departments to work with parents do not apply. Nevertheless, in other ways, there are strong parallels, and the experiences of both groups of children before and after entry to public care may be similar. For example, both fostered and adopted children may have experienced a high level of disruption in their lives before and after coming into care, including the breakdown of a placement intended to be permanent. There are similarities in their needs also, particularly for the development of a strong sense of personal identity and the significance to this of knowledge about personal and family history; all children have memories which cannot be ignored. In Chapter 8, Alan Burnell reviews the contribution that knowledge from the field of adoption can make to re-establishing partnership with the parents of children who are looked after. He underlines the vital importance of mediation and support for carers, children and parents if the potentially painful process of making contact with a parent is to be beneficial.

Establishing partnership-based practice with 'lost' parents, like working in partnership more generally, is not only an issue of practice for individual social workers. There are organizational factors and managerial responsibilities which are also crucial if progressive practice is to be actively promoted. Brian Waller, in Chapter 9, considers organizational and policy dimensions, all of which are relevant to working in partnership. Departmental policy and guidance, staff development and supervision each have an important role, not just in giving explicit messages to parents, children and carers about what they should be able to expect, but in providing encouragement, support and resources to workers. They are also important in shifting the attitudes, beliefs and values that have in the past contributed to the exclusion of parents and other family members.

Some parents are lost before their child enters the care system, some soon after; others, without help or support, attempt to stay in contact for a considerable period before eventually giving up. Whenever and however parents become lost, few social workers feel confident or skilled in finding a parent whose whereabouts are unknown, particularly when years have passed since the last contact with them or where there is little information in a child's case records. Annie Pavlovic's chapter aims to provide the knowledge needed to begin the search for a parent or other family member. It carefully assembles the sources of information, from publicly held records, which provide the starting point, and works through the various routes that can be taken when social workers have decided that they want to search for a parent. Whilst some parents can be difficult to find, more often they are surprisingly easy to locate. For a parent, being found can have diverse ramifications about which a worker embarking on a search can only speculate. The process of searching raises ethical issues, and the chapter also acknowledges that there may be good reasons why some parents do not want to be found, for example in cases where a mother has escaped from domestic violence.

The chapters in this book acknowledge that partnership with parents, or for that matter children and young people, is easier to aspire to than to achieve. The discussions about partnership raise questions about the distribution and redistribution of power between professionals and those with whom they work. Despite changes in law, policy, practice and the recognition of the necessity for anti-disciminatory practice, the barriers to achieving partnership have proved enduring and difficult to overcome. Some of these barriers are social and political, effectively disempowering parents whose lives frequently remain permeated by discrimination and disadvantage. Other barriers are constructed through limitations in policy, resources and practices which both fail to counteract this level of disadvantage and continue to devalue parents and the contribution they can make to their children's well-being. While not underestimating either these difficulties or the complexity of practice involved, the different chapters also provide incentives and positive examples of what can be achieved.

Many people other than the authors of the separate chapters have contributed to furthering the idea that working to make or remake partnerships with the parents of children and young people in the care system is a crucial way of safeguarding and promoting the well-being of those being looked after by a local authority. The editors wish to record their appreciation of Barbara Ballard, formerly of the Joseph Rowntree Foundation, who on behalf of the Foundation supported the project from its inception through to dissemination. Thanks are are also due to all those who participated in the research process: the members of the advisory group; those who gave presentations at the workshops; the social workers who took part in the study by discussing their cases and showing the barriers which faced them in establishing partnerships with 'lost' parents and how they tried to overcome them; and the children, young people and parents whose lives were the focus of the study, particularly those who talked to the researchers about their experiences of the care system. Without the partnership of all these people it would not have been possible to show that working relationships between social workers and lost parents can be remade. Special thanks also go to Nihid Iqbal who, as secretary to the research project, transcribed interviews, arranged workshops and organized the production of this volume.

In respect for the privacy of those whose experiences have informed the research and practice referred to in this book, names and some identifying features have been changed. Individuals or their next of kin have consented to the inclusion of birth, marriage or death certificates.

Table of cases

Berkshire C.C. v. B. [1997] 1 FLR 171
Gaskin v. U.K. [1990] 1 FLR 167
Gillick v. West Norfolk and Wisbech Area Health Authority [1986] A.C. 112 H.L.
R. v. Derbyshire County Council ex parte K. [1994] 2 FLR 653
R. (Mrs) v. Central Independent Television plc [1994] 2 FLR 141 C.A.
Re B. (minors) (care order: contact) [1993] 1 FLR 543 C.A.
Re C. (disclosure) [1996] 1 FLR 797
Re F. (contact: child in care) [1995] 1 FLR 510
Re M. (contact: welfare test) [1995] 1 FLR 274 C.A.
Re M. (a minor) (care order: threshold conditions) [1994] A.C. 424 H.L.
Re O. (contact: imposition of conditions) [1995] 2 FLR 124 C.A.
Re T. (termination of contact: discharge of order) [1997] 1 FLR 517 C.A.
Re W. (medical treatment: court's jurisdiction) [1993] Fam 64 C.A.
Re Z. (a minor) (freedom of publication) [1996] 1 FLR 191 C.A.
W. v. Essex C.C. [1998] 3 All E.R. 111 C.A.
X. v. Bedfordshire C.C. [1995] 3 All E.R. 353 H.L.

1 Recreation and promotion of partnership through action research

Christine Harrison and Judith Masson

Introduction

In 1997, there were just under 52 000 children and young people being looked after by local authorites. Although 9000 had spent only a relatively brief period in the care system, there were over 19 000 who lived away from their families, in state care, for more than three years. Amongst those who become looked after in any year, 8 per cent, 2400 children, although not readily identifiable, we know will not return home during their childhood. It is for all these children that there should be acute concern about maintaining links with their families and communities, knowledge about identity and culture, and how they understand their personal histories.

Prior to the Children Act 1989, where children remained in long-term care, little attention was sometimes given to maintaining links with their families of origin. In 1986, Millham and colleagues published their influential study, *Lost in Care*, which revealed a dismal picture of children's lives in care, cut off from families, friends and communities, and without a clear plan for their future. The research highlighted the importance of swift and active social work intervention in the period immediately after reception into care if children were to be restored to their families. It underlined the crucial role of contact with family in facilitating early discharge from care. Subsequent research by Millham and colleagues focused attention on family contact for children in the care system long-term (Millham *et al.*, 1989). In practice, less attention was given to the role of the family for the minority of children who would not return home. For these children, family relationships, rather than being promoted, were actively or passively discouraged. Formal termination of contact was routine in some authorities. In others, informal methods – placing children at a distance, and siblings separately, providing no financial support for visits, not disclosing children's whereabouts and doing nothing to counteract an environment hostile to visiting – were just as effective in destroying relationships (Millham et al., 1989).

Accumulating research in the 1980s contributed to a wholescale re-evaluation of the care of children away from their families (Fox Harding 1991; DH, 1991a; Cretney and Masson, 1997). Parents were recognized as having an important contribution to make to their separated children's welfare; links with the wider family, community and culture were seen as vital for children's well-being. The Children Act 1989 embodied these new understandings in provisions relating to parental rights and responsibilities, local authority powers and duties and children's rights, striking a 'new balance' (DH, 1989b, p.iii) between the family and the state. The key provisions of the Act and their implications are discussed by Masson in the next chapter.

The legislation was welcomed; considerable enthusiasm was engendered through a massive programme to educate and train practitioners for the new environment of child care and the challenges it would present (Masson, 1992). Nevertheless, it has proved difficult to shift the entrenched approaches in social work practice and social services departments. Initial enthusiasm is, of itself, insufficient to reshape attitudes, values, policies and practices in ways which lead to enduring change (Laming, 1998; Cheetham and Kazi, 1998; Select Committee on Health, 1998). In particular, family support services have remained lamentably underdeveloped in the face of pressures for child protection (Audit Commission, 1994; Dartington Social Research Unit, 1995).

More difficult even to contemplate has been the application of Children Act principles and provisions to children already in the care system and their families. In these situations implementing the Act necessitated re-directing efforts, often towards goals which had previously been dismissed, confronting the consequences of past social work practice and changing the perspectives of workers and carers, not all of them convinced of the merits of change. The idea that new legislation is not retrospective provides a convenient justification for doing nothing different in cases already held. But laws which give new rights rarely limit them to those newly affected by them, at least where the responsibilities apply to public bodies rather than individuals. For example, when access to birth records was introduced it applied to anyone who had been adopted, not just those adopted since 1975.

Translating the principles encompassed by the Children Act into policy has made demands on managers; the development of children's services plans provides a focus for service improvement and co-ordination (DH, 1998). For social workers, partnership provides a challenge, even for those committed to the empowerment-based practice which is the pre-requisite of any real, as opposed to euphemistic, degree of partnership. Social, political and organisational factors as well as legal imperatives, profoundly influence practice and present workers with dilemmas and pressures which have to be skilfully navigated. In relation to 'lost' parents this was particularly challenging because workers were often struggling with the inheritance of bad or discriminatory practice.

The conception of the project

It was within this context that the idea for the 'working in partnership with "lost" parents' project was conceived. This was an action research project designed to identify how and in what ways working partnerships could be developed between social workers and the parents of children in long-term care who were not currently in contact with their child or the social worker. That this was an issue, that such cases existed and that social workers were uncertain about how to proceed became obvious to us as we spoke to them during the course of teaching and training. Not everyone was convinced of the need for the research or by its aims. Early presentations about the project to some management teams evoked the response that this was 'opening up a can of worms' and protests that it could never have been intended that the Act would be applied in this way. Other responses, from social workers and team managers already attempting to find family histories and family members for children being looked after, were positive. Indeed, these people were keen to share their dilemmas and successes and anxious to participate in a project which would explore and support the work they were trying to do with young people in their care. Alan's social worker brought to the project both her positive experiences in tracing and recontacting lost family members and the determination to attempt to improve the circumstances of young people for whom past decisions, taken with the best of intentions, had left negative legacies.

Alan

Alan was received into care as a young baby because of the seriousness of his mother's mental health problems. His father, who was not married to his mother, visited Alan at the residential nursery where he was placed but was given no encouragement to remain involved with his son. Alan's father disappeared; no record was kept of his full name and the only information recorded was that he was thought to be from Nigeria. Alan's mother came from the Caribbean. At the age of 6 years, Alan was made a ward of court; under the Children Act 1989 he became the subject of a deemed care order.

Concern that Alan would be traumatized by his mother's behaviour led to the termination of her contact with him. Alan was placed transracially in a predominantly white area, some distance from the multiracial area where his mother lived. The placement was regarded as stable although it did not meet all of Alan's needs. His social worker became increasingly aware of the impact on Alan's identity of his separation from family, culture and community, and lack of knowledge about his background. Alan became more vocal about the racism he was experiencing; his worker who had been involved in the termination of his mother's contact began to re-evaluate this. Working with Alan, she began the task of re-establishing contact with his family. She traced two half-brothers. Alan's mother's mental health problems continue, but with the support of his brothers Alan can cope with this.

Finding Alan's father was more difficult because of the paucity of information the social worker held. However, an advertisement in the black press containing the father's Nigerian family name drew a response from paternal cousins and opened up another dimension of Alan's identity. Indirect contact was made with Alan's father, who had returned to Nigeria; father and son exchanged correspondence. Sadly, the father died before a meeting could take place. Both Alan and his social worker regret some of the decisions taken about Alan's early life, and Alan is angry about the care provided for him. The relationships which have been restored have enabled Alan to have some knowledge of and pride in his family and cultural heritage; they also help him to offset the racism he continues to experience.

More detailed discussions confirmed that there were many children in local authority care for whom loss of living parents was an issue or who had lost contact with other people significant to them, like brothers and sisters. In the course of these preliminary discussions, it also became evident that there were other children and young people experiencing similar degrees of loss following an order freeing them for adoption which had not led to an adoption order. For these young people many similar issues arose but the partnership obligations of the Children Act do not apply to their parents who in law are *former parents* with limited legal recognition. For this reason children who had been freed were not included in the study.

For us the emphasis was not just on research, but also on action, and on trying to ensure that the benefits of the Children Act were given detailed consideration for all looked after children. If working partnerships could be established in these most inauspicious circumstances, where the parent was literally 'lost', then the perceived difficulties in working with parents would appear less severe. In addition, the experience, knowledge and skills derived from restoring working relationships with 'lost' parents, and from the perspectives of parents, children and social workers involved, would yield lessons of wider relevance to child care practice.

The project aimed to draw directly on the work of a small number of teams, where one or more team member was committed to the principle of working in partnership, held a relevant case or cases and wanted to participate in the research. Through this, there could be an exploration of ways in which links with 'lost' parents could be re-established and of what facilitates or frustrates the establishment of working partnerships. The progress and outcome of the work would be evaluated with the inclusion of the perspectives of parents and young people as well as social workers. In an attempt to reconcile some of the tensions between research and practice in social work (Adams *et al.*, 1998) the research team involved participating social workers in the development of the project by responding to needs which they expressed. The essential foundation for the action–research orientation of the project was the identification of positive practice through collaboration with research participants. The project provided support, consultancy and training from the research team and external contributors, for practitioners taking part in the study. Social work participants appreciated the support given to their practice at a time when many social workers have been undermined and deskilled by both organizational change and increased proceduralization of practice (Langan and Clarke, 1994).

The broader context of research and practice

The Children Act 1989 obligations and the requirement to extend them to children who had been in care before its implementation provided the banner for the research project. However, the rationale and practice imperatives extended well beyond this legal framework and were derived from a wealth of research, knowledge and personal accounts that have offered significant challenges to social work policy and practices in child care. This included research not just in child care or social work but also from related fields, for example feminist theory, identity politics, queer theory and postmodernism. Within the field of child care and child development, new understandings have precipitated a re-evaluation of the care of children away from their families. Views about attachment, permanence and the significance, form and extent of contact with parents and other people important to the child have been repeatedly revised over the last two decades. At the heart of everything lies the child, his/her sense of self, place in the social world and well-being.

Neither law reform nor exhortations for change, however impassioned, will necessarily shift the long-established policies and practices in child care and welfare. However, changes are more likely to occur if workers and managers understand the reasons for them. This understanding is enhanced through knowledge of relevant research being set in the context of practice. Evidence continues to accrue about the impact of multiple disadvantage and oppression in the lives of those in receipt of welfare services, in relation to gender, poverty, 'race', disability and sexuality. There is also evidence that welfare and social services have failed to take sufficient account of this and have thus, albeit inadvertently, compounded discrimination in their interventions with children and their families (Ahmad, 1990; Langan, 1992; Barn, 1993; Barn *et al.*, 1997; Booth and Booth, 1994). Feminist writers, for example, in social work and related fields have continued to centralize gender in debates about child protection (Milner, 1993), domestic violence (Mullins, 1997; Mullender and Morley, 1994; Mullender, 1996), child sexual abuse (Kelly *et al.*, 1991, 1995; MacLeod and Saraga, 1988; Hooper, 1992), child contact arrangements (Hester and Radford, 1996) and racism in the lives of black women (Wilson, 1993; Mama, 1989).

The impact of these and other forms of oppression has also been described where children become looked after, are identified as being in need, or are on child protection registers. It is families 'overwhelmed and depressed by social problems that form the greatest proportion of those assessed and supported by child protection agencies' (Dartington Research Unit, 1995, p.22). Racism, both in the lives of black children and families and through welfare agencies, compounds this. Racism may have a particularly negative impact on black children and those of mixed parentage who enter and remain in the care system (Banks, 1992; Barn, 1993; Ince, 1998).

Until relatively recently, little concerted attention has been paid to the quality of the lives of children and young people in the care system (DH, 1995; 1998), particularly when compared to other areas of child care such as child protection (Stevenson, 1992). While most children and young people in local authority care will return to their birth families (Bullock *et al.*, 1993a), for the proportion who remain looked after, long-term care has frequently been characterized by instability, disruption and, sometimes, abuse (Utting, 1991). The negative effects on their health, education, self-esteem and identity have proved enduring (Stein and Carey, 1986; Biehal *et al.*, 1992a; Broad, 1997; Ince, 1998); young people who have been in the care system are overrepresented in the populations of young homeless, young unemployed and those in custody (Select Committee on Health, 1998). Additionally, evidence suggests that 'disabled children experience patterns of care which would never be tolerated for non-disabled children' (Morris, 1995). Inadequate planning, in and beyond care, have long been a concern; the risk of losing contact with parents, siblings and other family members is known to be very high. The development of the DoH's *Looking after Children* recording system (DH, 1995; Ward, 1995) and *Quality Protects* (DH, 1998) are responses to this catalogue of concerns, although on their own they will not guarantee high-quality care.

Where parental involvement is concerned, research evidence suggests that in the past parents were frequently marginalized and their contribution to their children's identity and development was either undervalued or viewed as a destabilizing influence (Masson, 1990). This particularly characterized approaches to permanency planning for children and young people from the mid-1970s which, when rehabilitation was not speedily achieved, focused on termination of contact and long-term fostering or adoption. Permanency arrangements often failed to provide the intended stability. It proved difficult to find placements; breakdown rates for both adoption and fostering were similar, rising to almost 50 per cent after five years for boys placed when aged between 8 and 11 years (Fratter *et al.*, 1991). Despite these problems, child care agencies approached decisions about children's entry to the care system with the assumption that it provided better care.

Work undertaken by Jenkins and Norman (1972) drew attention to filial deprivation, a concept which captured the range of emotions experienced by parents separated from their offspring. Feelings of guilt, inadequacy and distress undermine parents' intentions to maintain contact with their child and social worker. Although this is well recognized, attempts to counteract it have not been sustained. Parents, particularly mothers, experiencing considerable disadvantage have felt powerless to convince social workers that they continue to care about their children and could, if given the opportunity to participate, make a significant contribution to their well-being (Family Rights Group 1986; Fisher *et al.*, 1986; Monaco and Thoburn, 1987; Farmer and Owen, 1995).

Family contact is the key to discharge from care (Millham *et al.*, 1986); contact and knowledge of family of origin are crucial to a child or young person's development while in long-term care (DH, 1989a). Over recent years, the significance of maintaining links has been recognized, challenging the view that security and positive sense of identity for children in long-term care lie in the severing of connections and placement for adoption. Although there is inadequate quantitative evidence on the benefits of contact (Quinton *et al.*, 1997), maintaining contact through direct or indirect means may contribute to the stability of placements (Fanshel and Shinn, 1978) and reduce the rate of foster home breakdown (Berridge and Cleaver, 1987; Fratter *et al.*, 1991). It is now widely accepted that there are many routes to permanence (Triseliotis, 1985; Thoburn, 1985, 1990) and that children can maintain attachments to a number of adult/parental figures (Schaffer, 1990; Fratter, 1996). This is reinforced by cross-cultural studies that show that, in societies where substitute care is valued and esteemed, children's attachments are less likely to be viewed as competitive (Wozniak, 1993). At the same time, approaches to the concept of partnership which have arisen from an analysis of disadvantage and the distribution of power have urged practitioners towards a more empowerment-based model (Rees, 1991; Platt and Shemmings, 1996; see also Chapters 3 and 7 in the present volume).

The partnership project

The research team, the authors and Annie Pavlovic, research fellow, had backgrounds in social work, law and sociology; the composition of the advisory group reflected practice, research and agencies representing users. Its role was significant in acting as a sounding board in relation to the development of the research. The group's advice was particularly valuable in relation to methods and ethics.

The project adopted an explicitly action–research method allied with anti-oppressive research values and characterized by a combination of levels of intervention and participation, where partnership was both the focus and the method of study. Like all methodologies, action research is not without problems relating to ethics, access and analysis. When the dimensions of class, gender, 'race', sexuality and disability are also piled on the scales, maintaining the balance between action and research becomes an even more precarious, but nevertheless vital, political exercise (Humphries, 1994).

The need to generate and maintain positive reciprocal research relationships influenced every stage of the process (see Figure 1.1). Research, action and evaluation interacted so that the project developed in repeating cycles over a three-year period. The data collection comprised a combination of interviews with practitioners, children and parents; documentary analysis of case files; and feedback from training workshops which punctuated the project. Additional material was gained through a hypothetical case study and discussions associated with the provision of consultancy.

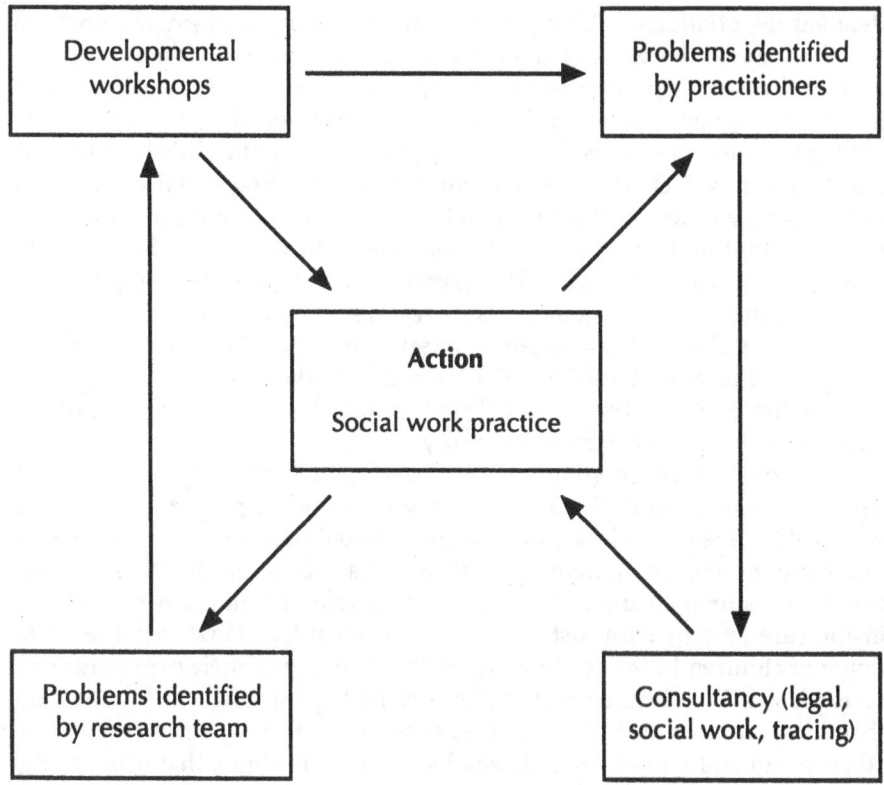

Figure 1.1 The research process

The following criteria were used to identify cases for inclusion in the study:

- children being 'looked after' (that is, accommodated or under care orders);
- no contact between at least one parent and the child; and
- no contact between parent and social worker.

Social workers and teams were recruited through both 'top-down' and 'bottom-up' strategies. The project was publicized through articles in *Community Care* and *Adoption and Fostering* (Masson and Harrison, 1993; Harrison and Masson, 1994), presentations at conferences and through social services inspectorate regional meetings. A total of 25 directors of social services were approached with details of the project to be distributed to team managers and practitioners. Separate from this, social workers from four other authorities approached the project directly, requesting involvement. More detailed negotiations followed to gain the necessary agreements with all social workers who expressed an interest and their employing authorities. A formal research participation agreement was drawn up, clarifying the roles and responsibilities of both the participating social workers and their authorities and the project team. Responsibility for the direct work and planning for each child remained with the case-holding social worker. All of the social workers participating held at least one relevant case and some indicated that up to 50 per cent of their workload comprised looked-after children who had lost touch with a parent. The prospect of being provided with training and consultancy was very welcome and also acted as an incentive for obtaining managerial consent. In some cases, concerns about past poor or discriminatory practice led social workers or their managers to harness the power of the project. This inevitably influenced the sample of children and social workers in the study.

There were 62 children and young people, 31 boys and 31 girls, aged between 6 months and 17 years at the beginning of the project. Of these, 37 were white, five were black and 20 were of mixed parentage, most with one white parent and one parent of African or Caribbean origin. No attempts could be made to ensure a representative sample: the numbers of children in the care system with lost parents is not recorded. However, the wide range of children in the study allowed the diversity of their experiences to be explored. The children were older and had spent longer in public care than most children in the looked-after population; three-quarters were over 10 years old and four-fifths had been looked after for more that three years; 25 children had spent at least three-quarters of their lives in the care system. Amongst the group there were those who had had no parental contact for many years, some whose family contact had ended recently and others where limited contact was continuing but appeared to be at risk.

The children were being looked after by 10 local authorities in England with differing political, economic and child care priorities. Five, including two London boroughs, were metropolitan areas and five were shire counties. The rate of looked-after children per 10 000 population was high for one authority, middling for five, low for two and unavailable for two (DH, 1996, p.11).

Overall, 50 social workers, 45 women and five men, participated in the study; during the study 10 left and 10 others became involved when responsibility for a child in the study was transferred to them. There were both newly qualified and experienced practitioners, most from teams covering the full range of child care, including child protection and duty, and others from long-term children and families teams. In total, there were practitioners from 17 teams, seven of which had at least three team members participating, but in six others a sole social worker joined the study.

Team participation was particularly valued because of mutual support and greater opportunities for taking issues forward through team discussions. Although several team managers actively encouraged involvement, on reflection greater efforts on the part of the researchers to include managers within the project would have been advantageous. Maintaining the sample was problematic. Staff turnover in the departments involved led to the transfer of children to workers who had not volunteered for the study and had not attended the early presentations and training.

The components of the research

The social workers were interviewed three times. An initial unstructured, case-specific interview allowed the 37 practitioners involved at the beginning of the project to give their own understanding of when, why and how children had entered and remained in the care system, how parents had become lost, and what difficulties the practitioner anticipated or concerns they had about restoring a working relationship with them. A second, more structured, interview with the 38 social workers then holding a study case aimed to chart development in the child's circumstances and locate this within a broader organizational context. The final interview, with 31 social workers, structured and by telephone, updated the child's current circumstances and explored the practitioners' experiences of participation in the research in relation both to the study cases and to their work more generally.

Many hours of research time were spent reading volumes of case files containing the agencies' accounts of children's lives. This located the legal, organizational and social dimensions of parental loss, reflected the dominance of particular values, and gave important clues for future work to reinvolve parents. The data were analysed both qualitatively through thematic exploration and quantitatively using SPSS (Statistical Package for the Social Sciences). This allowed comparison with existing research and published statistics and provided the depth which comes only through the detail of individual life histories.

Five training workshops were staged during the project, each addressing a different theme that had been identified as a problem by the practitioners or the research team. They covered such issues as making the first contact with a parent who had been formerly lost, partnership and contact where there had been sexual abuse, and issues for black children in the care system. Consultancy was provided at the request of individual social workers or teams. This covered tracing parents in 12 cases, legal issues in eight cases and social work issues in 10.

Towards the end of the study, arrangements were made via the social workers to interview nine young people whose ages ranged from 11 to 20 years; four were black or of mixed parentage. Six mothers and three fathers (all white) were also interviewed to obtain their detailed accounts and perspectives. The young people's interviews allowed them to give a narrative account of their care and broader life experiences, highlighting the meanings they placed on these. Similarly, semi-structured interviews with parents focused on their past and current circumstances, in particular the impact on them of social work and the consequences of losing a child to the care system.

The children and parents involved in the study

Knowledge of children's lives before care came from the social services department records and the first interviews with social workers. It was rare for the interviewed social workers to have been involved at this stage; indeed, many were unclear about the details of this part of the child's life, and some could not give an accurate account of the child's parentage or legal status. In part, this was due to inadequacies in files, but some social workers had given insufficient attention to delving into existing case records. The detailed work done by the researchers meant that in some instances they had a fuller understanding of the case history than the social worker or their manager.

For 50 children, their entry to the care system had occurred in the context of concerns about ill-treatment, 25 were considered to have suffered neglect, 23 physical abuse, eight sexual abuse and eight emotional abuse. Ill-treatment by a parent or step-parent was a factor in the admission of 31 children. Whilst the perpetrators were mostly men, mothers, even those who had separated or were themselves victims of abuse, appeared to have been held responsible for failure to protect their children. Behavioural difficulties contributed to entry for 13 children, including a crying baby of a lone mother whose first foster placement broke down for the same reason, primary school-aged boys presenting challenging behaviour and adolescent girls in conflict with their parents. The circumstances of parents undermined their inability to provide care; eight mothers had severe mental health problems, four parents were physically too ill to care and three, including two lone parents, had died.

Two children in the study had been compulsorily removed at birth; at least 15 other mothers had also experienced such action in relation to a sibling of the child in the study. Two other children had remained in the maternity hospital, for reasons which were unclear, after their mother's discharge. Removal at birth is the strongest indication of a woman's failure as a mother and the worst possible basis for partnership with social work or health professionals. Contrary to what might be assumed, the women in these circumstances had similar feelings to those of other mothers and continue to care about their children. Jill's mother made repeated visits over eight years to the social services district office to enquire about her well-being, particularly her education, and left small gifts and cards for her without any encouragement. A similar pattern was found for three of the four mothers who lost their child at birth.

Before they entered care, 32 of the children and young people had already lost contact with a parent, usually their father in the context of the breakdown of the parents' relationship. Most of these children had been very young when this happened and it appeared that few of the fathers had continued to be involved in their children's lives after parental separation. There were instances of mothers ending contact to protect their children from their fathers and also of fathers with care excluding mothers to punish them. Some fathers had not sought contact, stating their belief that this was better for their children.

While in care, 50 children lost contact with a parent, most commonly their mother. There were few cases of formal termination of contact, rather contact faded owing to lack of encouragement or active discouragement. Some case files clearly recorded the difficulties placed on parents who were expected to arrange visits via social workers who were hard to contact and to see their children either in social services offices or in unwelcoming foster homes. Indeed, overcoming these barriers was a test of their commitment to their children which, not surprisingly, many failed. The context for the negative approach to mothers' contact was often a plan for adoption or a decision against rehabilitation. There were also cases where protection of children from abuse by fathers or exposure to mothers with mental health difficulties was an issue.

Of the children in the study, 56 had full, half- or step-siblings, but of these, 25 entered care alone. There were eight sibling groups, totalling 17 children, in the study, but only three of these had remained together throughout their time in care. There were striking differences between care histories, relationships with parents and attitudes to parental involvement amongst siblings. For many children, being looked after meant the loss of a sibling through separate foster placement, and 14 children lost a sibling through adoption. Children were also aware that they had lost opportunities to develop relationships with siblings born after their entry to care.

The majority of the children, 43 (70 per cent) remained in care after their initial entry; 11 (18 per cent) had three or more periods in care. Those with more than one entry included a wide range of patterns of care: for example, those who had a series of short admissions immediately preceding their most recent entry and others who had returned home after a lengthy stay, only to be readmitted much later. A small number had yo-yoed in and out of accommodation until the local authority initiated court proceedings.

A total of 22 children entered the care system without court proceedings; care orders and wardship had been used for 39 children and one young woman was never formally accommodated but supported in 'foster care' by a section 17 payment; 37 of the children were fostered, four with relatives and a brother and sister with a former neighbour. Three were currently living with their mothers, seven were in residential placements. None of the black children or the white children were transracially placed, but 11 children of mixed parentage were placed with white families and six were in residential care. A review of legal status at the end of the study indicated that eight children were still not subject to any order and 40 were the subjects of care orders, including deemed care orders. In all, 12 had ceased to be looked after, 10 on reaching the age of 18 years, one following the discharge of a care order and another on leaving accommodation at age 16 years.

Care histories

The children had had a wide variety of experiences of the care system. Remarkably, given the findings of other studies, 26 had had only one or two foster placements or, more rarely, one residential and up to one foster placement. File recordings indicated that adoption had been planned for at least 10 children but was not achieved for various reasons, including the breakdown of the placement or the prospective adopters' marriage, the financial implications of adoption and the failure to identify an appropriate placement. However, some of the foster placements became de facto adoptions in the context of attenuated social work involvement. There were 19 children who had very unsettled lives in care, with four or more foster placements or three or more residential placements. At least five of these children also experienced the disruption of an adoptive placement. Assessments and plans were not always evident from the children's files; it was not always clear how or why a decision was reached that a child would remain in care rather than return home. Similarly, recording of service provision was lacking. There was some evidence of reasons which could have made rehabilitation difficult; for example, a risk of further abuse was noted for 11 children. Rehabilitation had been attempted, unsuccessfully, for 12 children.

However, for the majority the current social worker was uncertain about the reasons for their admission and unconvinced that they had needed to remain there. Some suggested that, with a different intervention or more family support, the child could have been cared for in their family.

Children missing from the study

The sample only included one child with severe disabilities, a boy of 8 years who had entered care following a hospital admission with 'shaken baby syndrome'. Since Morris (1995) has estimated that over a quarter of children cared for away from home have disabilities, their absence requires comment. There are several possible explanations: first, that disabled children are less likely to lose contact with parents; second, that issues of parental involvement are not taken as seriously for them; third, that partnership may be ruled out where a parent is believed to bear some responsibility for a disability. The study design which relied on social workers to identify and bring forward suitable cases may not have facilitated the inclusion of disabled children for any of these reasons. However, it should not be assumed that the findings have no relevance to disabled children and their parents.

Parents

The children and young people in the study had between them 51 mothers and 54 fathers, but three fathers and two mothers had died before their child's entry to the care system. The identity of seven fathers was not known. Immediately prior to entry to care, 34 mothers and 14 fathers, including seven couples, were living with their children; 14 of the mothers were caring for the children as lone parents and 20 were living with a partner; only two of the fathers were lone parents. Far more detail was recorded in the files about parents with care, usually mothers, than absent parents, usually fathers. Whether parents were together or separated, social work records almost always focused on the mother. Often there appeared to have been no attempt to contact absent fathers when the child originally entered care, even where he had parental responsibility.

What was recorded about the family circumstances of the parents reflected deprivation and disadvantage; poverty, poor housing and mental health difficulties were common. Although these and other factors, particularly domestic violence, are now well recognized as precipitating social services intervention, their significance in undermining parenting was not well appreciated at the time. Action which might have countered the impact of these factors, especially for mothers, was not taken. Case recording is partial; it relates to what the social worker has done or been told and is recorded for specific purposes. It constructs the official story of a child's life, the parent's character and the rationale for the intervention. The interviews with both parents and children revealed some contradictions and different understandings of events, but these parents had come to accept that, when their child entered care, they had had severe difficulties in coping and needed help.

Key findings of the research

Hypothesis testing is not the aim of qualitative research, which does allow a detailed exploration of events and their meaning for individuals. The longitudinal and interactive nature of the project generated a range of findings relating to the processes by which parents are lost and found, the experiences of children and parents, and the work necessary to restore relationships with social workers and within families. The findings relate both to the study cases and to workers' practice more generally. Practitioners stated that the understandings they had gained through participating influenced how they approached other work, particularly with families whose children had recently entered, or were at risk of entering, the care system. But the project neither sought nor was able to test whether this was the case. Organizational factors proved critical, not just directly through, for example, non-allocation, but also in terms of the climate within which practitioners felt they were working.

Finding parents

Most parents could be found relatively easily; only for a few was the search time-consuming and involved. Out of the 41 mothers who were lost, it was possible to locate all but seven. Out of 46 lost fathers, seven could not be found because they were unidentified and the whereabouts of another 12 remained unknown. This suggests that loss of parents is often more ideological than real. In the case of 12 mothers and six fathers, no social worker action was required to find them (see Table 1.1); these parents came forward seeking knowledge about and involvement with their children. That this happened was incidental to the research, it was clear from case files that such approaches regularly occur. The research appeared to be significant in terms of encouraging a more positive response from social workers, which helped to ensure that parents were not lost again.

Most of the parents who were contacted responded positively to the approach. For their part, social workers had a more positive view of parents whom they had met. Negative impressions gained from files were often displaced through personal contact, particularly where parents were coping in their lives. This contact provided a foundation for establishing working relations, but did not guarantee that relationships would remain unbroken

Table 1.1 Summary: finding parents – who got in touch?

	Mothers	Fathers
Social worker initiative	19	11
Parent's initiative	12	6
Contact by child alone	1	1
Other agency	1	–
Unknown	1	1
Not lost	8	5
No attempt to contact	7	20
Deceased	2	3
Unidentified	–	7
Total	51	54

in the future. For six of the 20 children whose relationship with a parent was renewed, it was not being maintained at the end of the study, but it should not be concluded from this either that nothing had been gained or that the parent–child relationship had no future. Overcoming the barriers posed by the length of separation, children's trauma before and in care, parents' difficult lives and geographical distance was bound to be difficult.

Young people were instrumental in putting the search for parents on the agenda. They asked their social workers at reviews and other times about their families, revealing the importance for them and their development of information and understandings about their past. These requests were a powerful motivating force for the search, and for participation in the study. Two main factors, both related to development, contribute to adolescents speaking out about these issues. Their development itself brings to the fore questions about identity and, as they get older, young people become more able to make demands of their social worker. Two parents were found by their children acting without social work support, suggesting that, where there needs are unmet, young people will take action. These young people were at considerable risk, both through absconding and in approaching strangers in their attempts to find parents. All these findings raise questions about the adequacy of social work provision earlier in young people's lives and the consequences of failing to give attention to the promotion of identity.

Where social workers made approaches to parents, they usually sent letters (for examples, see Chapter 10 of the present volume) but some used intermediaries or made direct contact at the parent's address. Considerable care was taken over the process; the passage of time meant that lives had diverged and recognition could not be assumed. A gradual sharing of information through telephone calls or the exchange of videos prepared the way for meetings. This also minimized the danger of both parents and children being overwhelmed by the intensity of their first meeting. Renewed relationships between children and parents were not the only result of the search for parents. Even where these did not develop (and there was no assumption that they would) the majority of children gained something which enriched the picture they had of their families and their histories (see Table 1.2). Nine children obtained photographs, letters or other forms of information, 10 met a parent or relative on at least one occasion, and two were able to establish a relationship with relatives who made a commitment to them. The social workers of the 21 children for whom, at the end of the study, there were no clear gains had been less active in searching for, contacting and reinvolving parents.

Table 1.2   End of project summary of the results for children of trying to re-establish partnership

Results	Number of children
Information/photos/letters	9
Meetings with parents or relatives	10
Regular visits to 'lost' relatives	2
Renewed relationship with 'lost' parents	14
Renewed relationship with 'lost' parent, not maintained	6
Unclear at this point	14
Little or no positive development	7
Total	62

The experiences of parents

Interviews with parents indicated that the systems which had operated were not easily reversed. The disempowering effect of previous exclusion permeated parents' subsequent relationships with their child's social worker, exacerbated by the difficult lives many parents still had. Although parents remained concerned about their children some appeared to feel that they needed permission for any new development in the relationship with their child. Others distrusted social services so much that they started proceedings for contact orders without discussing matters – the approach which departments had often used in the past.

Parents who were found conveyed their exceptional pleasure in having news of and, especially, seeing their children. They were 'over the moon'; 'it was really lovely'. To know that a child was looked after and had turned into a healthy young woman 'lifted the whole world off my shoulders'. But parents' intense emotions at the possibility of renewed relationships did not prevent them recognizing that their children's needs and wishes could be different from their own. Parents themselves spoke of their children's need to have a full understanding of their history, demonstrating agreement with social workers on this. The parents interviewed acknowledged that contact had to depend on what their children, now grown almost to adulthood, wanted. Where contact had been re-established, some parents looked forward to their child leaving care. They did not want social services involvement in their relationship with their child, or at least they felt they needed 'some freedom with their child'. Where there was still no direct contact, it was unclear whether relationships would be able to develop when the social worker stopped passing letters or information between a parent and child.

None of the parents interviewed were familiar with the term 'partnership' to describe the relationship between parents and social worker. One said that it was important to 'share things about the child' and another who was reluctant to become involved in their child's life said of the social worker, 'She's a nice woman, very informative. If there's anything I don't want to hear I can stop her.'

Parents needed to feel that they were listened to and that their views were respected. Some commented that they felt foster carers' views were privileged over their own or that social services only contacted them because they wanted something. One mother whose son had started to spend weekends away from his residential home with her felt that the social worker was pleased about this because it was a way for them 'to get [my child] off their backs'. Irrespective of the form contact took, parents, like social workers, were generally unclear about what role they could have in their children's lives.

Reinvolving parents in children's lives

One way of looking at parental involvement was to record their invitation to and participation in formal meetings relating to their child's care, such as reviews, and their consultation at other times. Despite being found, the majority of parents were still not invited to their child's reviews. Of the 17 parents who were invited, only one refused to attend, although some missed reviews on occasion or stopped attending them. Another 16 parents, 13 mothers and three fathers, received information about reviews but were not directly invited to them. There were also eight parents who were continually sent details of reviews, as a way of keeping a channel open, despite their complete lack of response to the social worker. Amongst the parents who were interviewed there was generally little knowledge about the review system, and consequently they had not asked about reviews. Parents who had no information about reviews were given only very limited information about their child. This group included 10 parents who had re-established contact with their child; three of these did not maintain this contact. Even where parents were involved in reviews they tended to be the recipients of information rather than participants in the decision-making process. In contrast, there were social workers who made the considerable efforts required to promote active participation by parents, for example preparing them before each review, providing transport and giving parents time to discuss concerns about themselves as well as about their child. The parents who were treated in this way were positive about their child's social worker and the care provided for their child.

Children's perspectives on working with parents

The children interviewed had many ambivalent and conflicting feelings about the things that had happened before, during and after care which necessarily had an impact on their views about their family. Understandably, not all wanted renewed contact; nevertheless they yearned for fuller information about their histories, including explanations of parental actions. Anxieties about parents, or about siblings living with parents, preoccupied them. Even where parents and children remained estranged, children recognized the importance for parents of their status as parents and of information about their separated children. Those interviewed made it clear that they wanted some control over what and how parents were told. Whatever adult judgments had been made about their parents, these people remained their parents.

The perspectives of social workers

As an action research study, a significant aspect of the project was to explore with social workers what impact being a participant had made, on the study cases and on other work, as well as on their views about partnership. The second, semi-structured interview, with 38 social workers, looked specifically at their work to restore partnerships with the parents. A telephone interview with 31 social workers at the end of the project allowed further exploration of the broader impact on their work and positive and negative experiences of having been a participant.

Almost all the social workers were of the view that being involved in the research had made a positive contribution to the work undertaken with the child and the child's family, in terms of knowledge and practice. In particular, they felt that a better understanding of the child's life and history had helped them in direct work. There were problems and frustrations associated with trying to re-establish a working relationship with a parent, but overall workers felt an increased sense of satisfaction with their work.

The training workshops and written materials were appreciated as a means of access to knowledge that was specifically relevant to the work they were involved in and gave opportunities that were not otherwise available. In many instances this led workers to broaden the scope of planned work, but not to change its direction, and to reorder priorities in working with children, their parents and carers. They reappraised the contribution parents could make to their child's development and raised the profile of working with parents relative to other work in a case: 'It has changed my view of how significant this work may be for the child or young person.'

Other workers felt that the project had helped them sustain existing views and commitments to working in partnership within an agency climate which gave little support for this. They took encouragement and gained confidence, when previously they would have given up: 'It gave the impetus for continuous negotiation and to attempt to resolve difficulties as they arise.' The tracing consultancy was particularly valued, since workers felt unskilled in this area. Several workers commented that, without it, parents would simply have remained lost.

However, there were five participants who felt that the project, whilst it had general relevance, had not influenced work in their study case. Only one social worker felt that involvement in the project had made a negative impact and that restoring a working partnership with a mother had contributed to the breakdown of a placement.

At the inception of the project it had been anticipated that the social workers would be enabled to transfer knowledge and skills to other work with children and families, for example in work with children at risk of becoming looked after and their parents, or to maintain tenuous relationships for those currently being looked after. At the end of the project almost all the workers were able to describe ways in which it had made an impact on other work. They referred to a shift in knowledge and understanding leading to changes in how work is conceived from the beginning of social work involvement: 'I have really shocked myself, sometimes. Without the project, I wouldn't really have thought about it any deeper than statutory obligations'; 'It's made an impact across the board and shifted my thinking. It's moved issues from the theoretical to the practice level – it's made it real somehow.'

A strong theme which emerged from the perspectives of social workers was the importance of thinking how direct or indirect contact could make a positive contribution to children and young people's development. In turn, this provided a practice imperative for considering the ways in which working partnerships with parents could be re-established and maintained. This required a response to both parents' and children's needs. Social workers recognized, for example, that women's and children's experiences of domestic violence or sexual abuse could not be ignored. Workers also felt that there were organizational factors which must be confronted if work with parents was to be sustained: 'This involves a general reprioritization which needs to be pushed towards management.'

One worker expressed sentiments which could easily have been made by a parent of young person: 'It made me cynical of the system. I feel angry for these parents. It has made me realize the value of directness.'

A third of social workers referred to the tensions that arise between focusing on short-term objectives and on the longer-term planning. They commented that crisis resolution often displaced longer-term plans. They believed that the project had made them more determined to take a lifetime perspective and view children's development through to adulthood. The vehicle for doing this was a comprehensive plan for the child. There was other evidence from social workers that their involvement in the research had changed their practice. One worker commented, 'I'm acutely aware of the histories in other cases and the way we record things – it has made me record in a way that, hopefully, the case file will be about people and their lives rather than about how their lives are processed.'

Views about partnership

All but one of the social workers viewed partnership as a process, rather than an event. It was an 'essential way of working' and informed by a set of principles, which included openness, respect, good communication, being considerate, honesty, taking trouble over little things, allowing for the validity of different perspectives and valuing cultural diversity. They acknowledged the necessity for working with conflict; partnership was regarded as something to be aimed for which might not always be achieved. In some circumstances partnership may be limited, but it should never be dispensed with, even where there are considerable areas of disagreement: 'It's not all or nothing'; 'Partnership has many levels, the term requires qualification and careful assessment will always be required.'

Various principles were identified as crucial, but these were not regarded as unproblematic; many workers felt that the translation of principles into meaningful practice relied on an analysis of power, powerlessness, disadvantage and discrimination and the impact of these on people's lives.

The social workers located the barriers to partnership in the organizational culture and in the practice of individual social workers. The lack of time generated by high workloads, the dominance of child protection work and gaps in allocation were frequently mentioned as factors which eroded their commitment to and opportunities for practice in partnership. Inequality of power between the agency and parents was believed to pervade both institutional and individual levels of practice. Practitioners were aware that their practice was shaped by their individual beliefs and the demands of their employing authority. Power differentials were difficult to challenge: 'Social services are all-powerful – parents are daunted and intimidated.'

Although there was wide acceptance of this, nearly half of the social workers also viewed parents as a major barrier to working in partnership. At a general level, the concept of partnership was welcomed, but there was a tendency to exclude specific parents from its embrace. Practitioners recognized the inherent conflicts in the social worker's role, particularly where children and young people were implacably opposed to any contact between a worker and a parent. There were conflicts too when children had been sexually abused by a father and realistic fears about further harm necessarily limited partnership. Some workers felt that they lacked confidence or skill in handling such situations. Finally, they all felt the legacy of past practice and how this was experienced by parents was an inheritance that formed a barrier to the working relationships they were trying to restore. For one social worker, the anger of a parent at her past treatment by social services was an insuperable barrier.

Conclusions

An action–research method was consciously adopted with the aim of ensuring that the process as well as the outcomes of the project were achieved from an anti-discriminatory position. Of equal importance was the desire to bridge the gap between research and practice that has undermined the development of social work with children and their families. The focus was on the children included in the study, particularly what could be achieved for them and how this could be done by their social workers. The study necessitated a longitudinal approach, requiring the maintenance of research relations over a three-year period. There were three groups of social workers who participated: those who remained with the project throughout, those who joined initially but could not finish because they no longer had responsibility for the study case, and those who joined the project when a project case was reallocated. Whilst positive research relations were generally achieved with those social workers who remained in post throughout the period, both social services reorganization and, particularly, staff changes had to be accommodated. This highlighted the difficulties of providing consistent care for children who are being looked after and continuous service to their families. A cyclical method allowed for the induction of workers at various stages of the project, although the experience of the late starters could not mirror that of those involved from the outset. Changes in staff also meant that at the end of the project it was not possible to get responses from early leavers who moved to other jobs, taking with them, it is hoped, some gains from their involvement.

When social workers evaluated their involvement in the project two main themes emerged: the value of research with training and consultancy, and the acceptance of potentially intrusive and time-consuming research methods. The social workers were very positive about the support, encouragement and genuine interest in their work from the research team and fellow participants which gave them the energy to take on challenging tasks. As a consequence, with agency consent, they were prepared to accept potentially intrusive scrutiny of their practice and that of their colleagues, and some felt able to facilitate access by the researchers to young people and parents so that their perspectives could be included. With the benefit of hindsight, the involvement of line managers might have strengthened the project by helping to ensure greater support of individual social workers in complex work that they undertook and a management perspective on the issues of caring for children raised through the study.

A limitation of the research was the reliance on the workers' views about how participation in the project had changed their approach to children and parents. Although the action they took on individual cases was recorded as part of the research, it was not possible with the resources available to assess how far workers had been able to carry through these changes for other families. Comparing the different aspects of the research undertaken, disparate and conflicting perceptions as well as commonalities emerge. Social workers' commitments and intentions were challenged by the accounts of young people and parents, albeit a small and non-representative group. Social workers' own accounts also display some internal contradictions between intentions and actions; between the commitment to work in partnership with an awareness of the impact of discrimination, and the tendency to identify parents as a major barrier to working partnerships. The research confirms that conflicting perspectives should not be reduced simply to the views and attitudes of social workers. The chasm between intention and action is created by factors and processes at structural, personal and organizational levels which undermine social workers' and parents' efforts and contribute to the pathologizing of clients.

Attempts to promote partnership require the close scrutiny of the ways organizations work to deliver services to individuals and families. Both young people and parents differentiated between 'the system', which was viewed negatively, and the efforts of individual social workers, which were often appreciated. Even though the direct work involved in re-establishing working relationships required considerable practice skills, it was encouraging that all those involved agreed that core values of honesty, openness and good communication were essential.

Overall, there is much to recommend this form of action research as a method for exploring areas of practice development in social work. At its best it can simultaneously examine in depth the complex factors involved in shaping practice and promote change based on thorough and grounded knowledge. In this way it can both contribute to the understanding of current problems and show how these can be overcome through practice. Even though users, both young people and parents, could not be involved in the development of this study, given that it was about lost relationships, their perspectives were extremely valuable for a full understanding of the impact of practice on people's lives. Their insights about both their experience of loss and the ways it might be improved were essential for the research.

2 Legal issues: partnership with parents and children's rights
Judith Masson

Introduction

Amongst the underlying themes to the partnership with 'lost' parents research was the question, *what can being a parent mean when your child is in long-term care?* Part of the meaning of being a parent relates to the role which a parent can play in the life of a child from whom they are separated. Much of this may depend on practicalities, such as how far the child is living from the parent, whether the parent's or child's health or other circumstances limit opportunities for parental involvement, and on the support available to the parent and child to maintain and develop a relationship which is strained because of separation.

The law is also relevant. This chapter considers the extent to which the law recognizes that parents are different from other (unrelated) adults and seeks to protect parental relationships where parents are not providing physical care for their children. Although children's interests are frequently bound up with those of their parents, the law also recognizes that children may have separate interests. It sets standards and procedures for the balancing of competing interests. The law in the form of statutory provisions and regulations also sets out the obligations, powers and responsibilities of local authorities caring or providing services for children and their parents. Where children are being looked after in the care system, the powers and duties of the local authority, the parent's legal status and the rights of the child or young person all have to be considered. These are crucial to understanding the space the law leaves for parental involvement and children's independence, and the power of the local authority to exert control over parents and children. In the cases in the study, these themes came together when we explored how social workers negotiated their relationship with a child or young person alongside their obligations in the Children Act to consult parents and to safeguard children's welfare.

The focus of this chapter is largely the Children Act 1989, the associated case law, the regulations and the practice guidance issued by the Department of Health. It is also necessary to see this within the wider perspective of the European Convention on Human Rights and the UN Convention on the Rights of the Child. The European Convention helped to shape child care law during the 1980s and the Children Act 1989; its incorporation into the law of the United Kingdom via the Human Rights Act 1998 will increase its potential for influence. No longer will cases have to be taken to the European Court of Human Rights in Strasbourg; the courts in the United Kingdom will be able to apply the Convention, and to identify areas for reform. Amongst the rights guaranteed by the Convention which are particularly relevant to the position of children in care and their parents are the right to respect for private and family life, home and correspondence (art. 8), the right to a fair hearing in the determination of civil rights (art. 6) and the right to receive the rights guaranteed by the Convention without discrimination (art. 14). Where parents' rights and freedoms conflict with those of their children, the Convention allows the state a wide margin of appreciation in the way it sets the balance under its law (Forder, 1995, p.58).

The UN Convention on the Rights of the Child does not provide individuals with remedies. Its importance lies in the international recognition that has been gained for children as people with rights, rather than objects of concern. Also, because of the particular rights which the 191 signatory countries have agreed to recognize that children have (Van Bueren, 1995, p.xx), the Convention is an agreed standard against which law and practice can be measured. It provides that the welfare of the child shall be a primary consideration in decision making by public and private agencies or courts of law (art. 3) and that the rights in the Convention shall be provided without any form of discrimination (art. 2). It requires states to respect the rights and duties of parents to provide appropriate direction and guidance, in a manner consistent with the child's evolving capacities (art. 5), and children's right to express views on all matters which affect them (art. 12), thus emphasizing the importance of the involvement of both parents and children in decision making. Amongst the rights in the Convention which are important in the care of looked-after children are the right to identity (art. 8), the right to maintain personal relations with parents unless this is contrary to the child's best interests (art. 9(3)), and the right to a periodic review for children in public care (art. 25). The United Kingdom ratified the Convention in 1991 and the British government regards the Children Act as meeting wholly or in part many of the obligations in the Convention (DH,

1993, para 1.13). There is, however, a need for further development in many areas (Children's Rights Development Unit, 1994).

Parents' rights and children's rights

The Children Act replaced the terminology of 'parental rights' with 'parental responsibility', with the intention of bringing about a change in the way parents and others viewed parental powers. The Act did not redefine parental power and the exact nature of parental responsibility remains unclear (Utting, 1997, para 6.2); the concept was considered too complex and variable to allow a statutory definition or list (Law Commission, 1988, para. 2.6). Parental responsibility varies according to the circumstances, particularly whether the parent has day-to-day responsibility for the child's care and the child's maturity.

Where both parents have parental responsibility (as is the case for all married or formerly married parents) either may exercise their parental responsibility; the Children Act imposes no requirement for consultation or agreement by the parents. Parenthood is a legal status which the law recognizes regardless of the parent's social relationship with 'their' child. This status is very limited in the case of the unmarried father who has not obtained parental responsibility through a court order or formal agreement with the child's mother. It imposes on him an obligation to maintain the child but only treats him as a parent rather than a stranger to a child by allowing him to make applications to the court without first seeking its permission (ss.2,4,10). A parent who is not looking after his/her child retains parental responsibility but his/her exercise of it may, in practice, be limited. Where a child is looked after by relatives or accommodated by the local authority (s.20) the parents may arrange for the carers or the local authority to exercise some or all of their powers (s.2(9)). Even where parental responsibility is not delegated, anyone caring for the child can only do what 'is reasonable in the circumstances to safeguard and protect the child's welfare' (s.3(5)).

Courts can impose limitations on the exercise of parental responsibility, but the granting of court orders when parents separate is no longer routine. When a care order is made, the local authority acquires parental responsibility and 'the power to determine the extent to which a parent may meet his parental responsibility' (s.33(3)(*b*)), but only if 'they are satisfied that it is necessary to do so in order to safeguard or promote the child's welfare' (s.33(4)). Parents do not lose parental responsibility as they did previously; those with children already in compulsory care regained it when the Children Act was implemented.

The modern explanation of the concept of parental responsibility is clear: parents need powers over and in respect of their children in order to bring them up. The parents' retention of parental responsibility where a care order has been made may appear contradictory, particularly where rehabilitation is unlikely. It reflects the view that parents remain important to their children even where there is a need for the local authority to provide physical care and exercise parental responsibility, and that the responsibility of parenthood is not lost even where children need protection from parents. Where parental responsibility means parental obligations, this may be uncontroversial, but the idea that a parent who has abused his/her position should retain any power in relation to his/her child probably does not accord with the beliefs in the community.

The child's age and stage of development are crucial to their legal position. In law, children are 'children' until they reach the age of 18 years, but many of the rights they, their parents or the local authority have to make decisions about their lives depend, not on their chronological age, but on their maturity. Since the *Gillick* decision (1986) it has been firmly established that children and young people gain the right to make decisions in their lives as they acquire the capacity to do so. Parental power, 'parental responsibility', diminishes with children's maturity unless it is preserved by statute. Generally, at any one time either those with parental responsibility (parents, guardians or the local authority) or children have the right to make decisions, subject only to the power of the court to substitute its own judgment on the basis of the welfare of the child (Children Act 1989, ss.1, 8, 10).

Parents have the right to consent to medical treatment for their child up to the age of 18 years, but not to veto any treatment which children have elected to have (Family Law Reform Act 1969, s.8; Re W., 1993). Where children are able to decide to seek treatment they have the same rights to confidentiality which adult patients have (BMA, GMSC *et al.*, 1995). Parents, but not children, can request the provision of local authority accommodation for their children under the age of 16 years and remove their children from it, but over that age only the young person can decide whether to seek accommodation (s.20). Parents have rights to be consulted in relation to the services provided when their children are looked after by the local authority (s.22(4)(5)). These are not limited by reference to children's age, or the parent's holding of parental responsibility, but consultation in relation to children over the age of 16 must take into account the fact that parents have no duty to provide a home for children of this age, nor any right to prevent the child from being accommodated by the local authority.

Law and partnership

The term 'partnership' does not occur in the Children Act 1989; the notion that social workers and parents should work as partners in the care of children who are being looked after by the local authority is reflected in the local authority's duties to consult parents and to consider their views, and the retention of parental responsibility by parents, including those whose children are subject to care orders. These provisions are reinforced through regulations relating to the arrangements for, and review of, each child's care, and guidance on good practice (Arrangements for Placement of Children (General) Regulations 1991; Review of Children's Cases Regulations 1991; and DH, 1991d). The duties in the Children Act 1989 apply in relation to all children in the care system, including those who entered when there was no obligation on the local authority to inform or involve parents.

* The Children Act 1989 requires the local authority to ascertain the wishes and feelings of children, parents and others about any decision it proposes to make, so far as it is reasonably practicable. It must also give 'due consideration' to these views when making any such decision (s.22(4) and (5)). These duties do not exist in isolation but alongside others to safeguard and promote the child's welfare (s.22(3)) and to endeavour to promote contact between the child and parents, relatives and friends (sched. 2, para. 15). These duties may conflict, for example if parents' views about how their child should be cared for do not accord with what social workers consider to be necessary for the child's welfare.

Chris

Chris, aged 9 years, was accommodated because of major concerns about his welfare at home. He told a teacher that he was being ill-treated; when social workers visited his home to discuss concerns with his mother she readily agreed to his accommodation. Chris's mother wanted there to be no contact between him and the family. She was unwilling for him to continue to see his brothers at school and arranged for them to change school to ensure this. She objected to contact with his grandparents and other relatives. Chris's social worker tried hard to negotiate arrangements which would meet his needs and be acceptable to his mother so that proceedings could be avoided. The social worker considered that loss of all his family links was contrary to his welfare and contacted his relatives to find out whether they were interested in renewing contact with him. They were, but were unwilling to seek a Section 8 contact order by taking proceedings against Chris's mother because they felt this would further strain relationships in the family.

While Chris was only accommodated, the local authority had no parental responsibility; they could only take action on the basis of parental responsibility delegated by Chris's mother or the residual power to do what was reasonable in the circumstances to safeguard and promote his welfare (s.3(5)). Neither power justified arranging contact contrary to the expressed wishes of his mother.

Where there is a conflict between what the parents want and the child's needs, the local authority is expected to seek a solution which does not jeopardize the child's welfare (DH, 1991d, para. 2.10).

If arrangements which are acceptable to the parents and meet the child's needs cannot be agreed by negotiation, the local authority can seek a care order in court proceedings which gives the authority parental responsibility and authorizes restrictions of parental power in the child's interests (s.33(3) and (4)). Court proceedings provide a way of testing the local authority's case that the child's circumstances justify compulsory action and may therefore be seen as safeguarding the parents against coercive threats. In practice, legal proceedings may be very intimidating for parents whose understanding of the system and access to legal advice is likely to be poorer than that of any qualified social worker. There is evidence that some parents who have agreed to their child's accommodation have felt pressured so to do (Hunt and Macleod, 1998). The study included a number of 'lost' parents who had been treated in this way and who commented on their lack of trust of, and respect for, social workers beause of this. The availability of independent advocacy to parents facing the alternatives of accommodation or care proceedings for their child would help to establish a climate for a working relationship between parents and social workers.

In order to obtain a care order the local authority must prove, on the balance of probabilities, that the child's circumstances satisfy the significant harm test (s.31(2)), that a care order is in the child's best interests (s.1(3)) and that an order is necessary (s.1(5)). Where the child was provided with accommodation for his or her protection, the local authority may rely on the incidents which led to this as well as the current circumstances in making their case for an order (*Re M.*, 1994). The court considers the local authority's care plan when deciding whether to make a care order, but all subsequent decisions are left to the discretion of the local authority with a possibility of court review in relation to contact matters and the discharge of the order (ss.34,39).

A care order was obtained in respect of Chris. The local authority used its parental responsibility to make plans for Chris's care and override his mother's objections. Contact was arranged between Chris and his relatives. This contact, together with a good placement, have, according to both Chris and his social worker, made a major contribution to his well-being while in care.

Partnership between social workers and parents should continue even after a care order has been made: 'Where the interests of the child or the non-co-operation of the parents require that initial arrangements are made without agreement, part of the planned work should be to try and establish a working relationship for the future' (DH, 1991d, para. 2.67). A care order does not remove the parents' parental responsibility or the duties to consult them. However, the care order changes the relationship between parents and the social services department. The parents' power is further limited, making it more difficult for them to see themselves and be seen as partners in the care of their children. The process of obtaining a care order may be unconducive to future cooperation between the parent and the social worker and it may be helpful for a new social worker to be allocated, particularly if the parents have requested this.

Chris's social worker continued to try and involve his mother but she changed her telephone number and did not answer letters. When the authority introduced the new *Looking after children* forms, she wrote again seeking the mother's agreement to the arrangements. The mother replied and subsequently contact was renewed. Although this was not maintained, it did enable Chris to gain a better understanding of his mother and brothers.

A further aspect of partnership is the parents' right to make representations or complaints about the way the local authority carries out its powers and duties in looking after their child (s.26). Although this may appear to make the local authority accountable and to redress the balance of power in favour of the parent, in practice the parent remains heavily reliant on the local authority, particularly for information about his or her child. Parents who feel powerless because of their inability to care for their child and the local authority's failure to consult them may be unaware that they have a right to complain, or, if they are, they are unlikely to find it easy to assert themselves. Even if a complaint is upheld there is no legal obligation on the local authority to comply with the recommendation of the complaints board. Failure to do so might justify an application to the High Court for judicial review of the authority's decision, but such applications are difficult; legal aid is only available after the court has given leave for the application.

Thus, although the Children Act 1989 has imposed responsibilities on local authorities to involve parents and to reflect parents' retention of parental responsibility even where their children are in care, it has had little impact on the major imbalance of power between parents and the state. Parents remain dependent on decisions by agencies and their workers; disagreement with these can be referred to a complaints panel, or more rarely and with exceptional difficulty to review by the courts, but these 'avenues of redress' are in most cases both cumbersome and illusory. The impetus the law provides to partnership may thus be through the general re-evaluation the new legislation encouraged, rather than rights it gave to parents, duties it imposed on local authorities or procedures it established.

Access to records

Before the mid-1980s and the legislation allowing access to files, a culture of secrecy operated in social services departments to keep information about social services' clients from clients themselves. Parents of children committed to care or whose parental rights had been removed by resolution under the Child Care Act 1980 or earlier legislation were generally discounted. Their legal status vis-à-vis their children was confused but limited; they had no rights of access to information about their children, they could only enforce claims to be involved in their children's lives through proceedings for the discharge of the care order or the recission of the resolution, and could only challenge complete termination of their access to their child. In practice, parents were often marginalized and ignored once it had become clear that their child would not return home. Information was collected on the basis that it would be kept confidential and this provided the justification for refusing access to it even by those directly concerned (DH, LAC (83) 14, para. 9).

In 1983, Graham Gaskin, a young man who had been brought up in care, applied to the European Commission of Human Rights, arguing that Liverpool City Council's refusal to disclose information about his life in care breached Article 8 of the European Convention on Human Rights. The Commission accepted that there had been a breach and referred the matter to the Court (*Gaskin* v. *U.K.*, 1990). Even before the decision of the court, it was clear that the approach to access to records would not survive scrutiny. Legislation, the Data Protection Act 1984 and the Access to Personal Files Act 1987, and accompanying Statutory Instruments, were introduced which gave clients rights (subject to some wide limitations) of access to personal information about themselves.

Rights to information encompass both *rights of access* to information which the local authority has through the actions of its staff and agents and *rights to the disclosure* of information provided by third parties. Information can be withheld if its disclosure is likely to prejudice the carrying out of social services functions by causing serious harm to the subject or some other person (Access to Personal Files (Social Sevices) Regulations 1989, reg. 9(2)) or if revealing it will disclose the identity of a third party, not professionally employed by the authority, who does not consent to its disclosure (reg. 9(3)).

The Department of Health circulars, LAC (87) 10, LAC (88) 16, LAC (88) 17 and LAC (89) 2, give guidance on the interpretation of the law and the procedures to be followed. No further detailed guidance was issued with the introduction of the Children Act 1989 (DH, 1991b, para 2.86). 'The position of children and that of the rights of parents under the Data Protection Act 1984 are extremely complex' (DH, LAC (87) 10, para. 13). Subsequent guidance has focused on issues of confidentiality: 'All personal information must be treated as confidential' (DH, LAC (88) 17, para. 15) but what this means in relation to parents' rights of access to information is not mentioned. Parents can certify that their children have sufficient understanding to consent to the disclosure of information (to others) and give consent where children lack sufficient understanding to consent (DH, LAC (88) 17, para. 44; DH, LAC (89) 2, para. 42). This would seemingly allow a parent to consent to disclosure to themselves of information provided by the child, but only if the child is not capable of understanding the disclosure issue. The later circular, LAC (89) 2, although stating that it is concerned with rights of access to information rather than its disclosure, largely repeats the approach (para. 45). It precludes parents obtaining information about children who are capable of consenting to access unless they are expressly authorized by their child. Parents can gain access to information if their child lacks the capacity to understand, and authorities are told to accept the validity of the parents' declaration 'unless there is information in their possession that the child has capacity and they have grounds to believe that the child would not consent to access being granted to the parents' (DH, LAC (89) 2, para. 42). However, local authorities are advised that 'a parent should only be granted access to information about a child when the authority is satisfied that the application is made in the child's, not the parent's interest' (DH, LAC (89) 2, para. 43).

The Access to Personal Files Act 1987, the Access to Personal Files (Social Services) Regulations 1989 and the guidance, all of which predate the Children Act and the introduction of the concept of parental responsibility, contain no recognition that parents have rights to information about their children. The parents' role is limited to supplying consent for the child's own access to information. Thus parents can seek disclosure of information only where their child is unable to understand disclosure. In the only reported case on the legislation, *R. v. Derbyshire County Council ex parte K.* (1994) the risk of harm to an accommodated child was held to justify refusing to disclose information about her to her father. There was no discussion in the case whether the father had rights to information, only about the basis on which the authority could decide that disclosure was harmful.

The circulars also exclude disclosure to, or access to information on the application of, parents whose children are in the care of a local authority under a compulsory order. In these circumstances it is the local authority with the order which decides about the child's competence and can consent if the child is unable to do so. Now that parents retain their parental responsibility after the making of a care order, a general refusal to allow them to exercise it appears to conflict with the express provisions of the Children Act which only permit control of parental power where this is necessary to safeguard or promote the child's welfare (s.33(3) and (4)). Had the local authority obtained a care order in respect of the young woman in *R. v. Derbyshire County Council ex parte K.*, it could clearly have justified withholding information on the basis of its parental responsibility. Indeed, considering that she had alleged serious sexual abuse against her father and her behaviour was so disturbed that she required placement in secure acommodation, their failure to do so seems inexplicable.

Parents' rights to information after the Children Act 1989

The general impression from the cases in the 'lost' parents study was of a reluctance on the part of social workers to pass any information about children to their parents. This lack of information had contributed to parents becoming lost to their children and to the sense of loss parents felt at being separated from them.

All the parents who spoke to the researchers had either sought to re-establish a relationship with their children or been contacted by the social worker to obtain information for the child, and all welcomed knowing about their child and spoke movingly about the pain and worry of not knowing whether and how their child was being properly cared for. One mother who had no contact with her daughter for nine years but then saw her at a review meeting said that she felt 'relief ... the whole world [is] off my shoulders.' This mother, who had mental health difficulties and lived in poverty with a violent husband had attempted to keep contact with the social workers but had been given little information. She remarked how dismissively she had been treated and said, 'It's not right that mothers should be treated this way. There should be better ways of treating parents. Social workers need to be put straight.'

The case files indicated that many of the parents continued to ask about their children after their contact with them had ended, also that they were frequently fobbed off.

Lee

Lee, 8 years old and of mixed parentage, had been in care since the age of four months. He had severe physical disabilities and severe learning difficulties as a result of brain damage, probably caused by shaking. The perpetrator was not known but his mother was blamed, despite (or because of) her absence when the incident occurred. Lee's mother went to the social services department area office and spoke to the duty social worker about finding out how her son was faring. She had not seen him for three years because her contact had been terminated. She was told (incorrectly) that termination of her contact meant she had no right to information about Lee. She did not challenge this decision. Subsequently, she contacted the headteacher of Lee's school, who was aware that Lee was in care but nevertheless invited her to visit and provided a photograph, treating her as a parent.

The Children Act introduced a completely different approach to parents based on the value of their continuing involvement in their children's lives. It provides two distinct legal arguments for recognizing that parents have rights to information about their child in care. The first derives from the concept of parental responsibility and the second from the local authority's partnership duty to consult (s.22(4) and (5)).

Access to information about one's child is a central aspect of parental responsibility. A woman's status as a mother has been said to give her 'some strong entitlement to information about her daughter' (*Re C.*, 1996, 808, JOHNSON J). Parents' rights to information are not absolute; children have some rights to confidentiality, and information may sometimes be withheld if this is in the child's best interests. Parents are not free to use information about their children in any way they would like. They are under a duty to keep information about their children's medical and special educational treatment confidential (*Re Z.*, 1996, 209–210, WARD LJ), but it is not clear to what other information this duty of confidentiality applies. Parental use of information about their child is an exercise of parental responsibility; the courts can make a Section 8 prohibited steps order in the child's interests to prevent the misuse of information. Similarly, a local authority with a care order may refuse to provide information where this would safeguard the child's welfare.

Lesley

Lesley's father had terrorized her mother to such an extent that she ran away from him and went into hiding. The circumstances of her escape made it impossible for her to take Lesley, then aged 5 years, who remained in her father's care. Lesley's father obtained custody; her mother was too terrified to oppose this, or even to attend court. Lesley remained with her father and his new partner and was subjected to appalling ill-treatment, including sexual abuse. At the age of 9, Lesley disclosed her abuse to a teacher; she was removed from her father and became the subject of a care order. The father denied the abuse and repeatedly wrote to social services requesting contact with Lesley. An order for no contact was made.

The extreme nature of his violent and abusive behaviour and Lesley's terror of him, together with social workers' real fear for their own personal safety, all contributed to the decision not to disclose any information about Lesley to her father.

However, the Children Act does not limit the local authority's duty to provide information about children who are being looked after only to parents with parental responsibility. The right to be consulted in s.22(4) can have little meaning if it does not include the right to information which relates to the issue under consideration. Department of Health guidance acknowledges this:

> The Children Act 1989 requires that parents (including the unmarried father who may not have parental responsibility) should generally be involved in all planning for the child, and should be kept informed of significant changes and developments in the plan for the child. (DH, 1991d, para. 2.49)

> Once the plan has been decided upon, it should be notified in writing to the parents. ... Good practice requires that the responsible authority's social worker explains personally to the parents and the child what the plan entails and the reasons for reaching the decisions therein. This should be done in addition to any explanations given during the assessment and planning process. (DH, 1991d, para. 2.70)

Information should be provided on the 'need to know basis' within the context of the authority's obligation to consult parents, children and others whose views the authority considers relevant. But the need for information will depend on the nature of the decisions to be taken. For example, a child's proposed placement or schooling might be discussed without identifying the location if giving a parent that information would compromise the child's welfare, as in the case where a parent might try to remove the child.

Where a child or young person is returning to visit or live with a parent after a considerable period of separation, the parent needs information so that he or she can deal with the child sensitively. Parents who were interviewed in the study, most of whom had attempted to re-establish a relationship with their child after a long gap, all said how little they knew about their children. The lack of information made it difficult to relate to their children once contact was renewed: 'We were like perfect strangers ... I had missed out on all his childhood, his growing up.' Such gaps of knowledge and understanding undermined their attempts to relate to their children.

Lack of information for parents is a particular issue where children have experienced mistreatment or abuse in the care system, as many children in the study had. Parents cannot respond sensitively to matters of which they are unaware. The risk of abuse to other children in the family also has to be considered. Carers, including parents, cannot protect young children in their care if they are given inadequate information about a child placed with them. Also it appears that failure to provide information could lead to the local authority being held liable if children in the household are abused by the child returning home. Thus a moral responsibility towards the child's family may also be reflected in a legal duty to other children in the home.[1]

The law gives the local authority considerable discretion over the provision of information to parents. Recognizing that parents retain their parental responsibility and seeking to make them partners in the care of their children suggest that information should only be withheld where this can be justified in terms of either the child's rights to confidentiality or the need to safeguard the child's welfare from misuse of information.

Confidentiality for children

It is not self-evident what is meant by confidentiality, but professionals' relationships with clients or patients may be severely undermined if information is passed beyond what individuals consider to be the proper limits. Professionals may consider that they are respecting confidentiality when they share information with others who have a need to know. Thus a patient's medical confidentiality may allow the whole team, including the consultant, the registrar, junior doctors, nursing staff and the general practitioner to be informed. Similarly, in child protection, 'confidential' information may be shared with a number of social workers and staff from other agencies. Both the need to know and the right to know may justify passing information beyond the boundaries individuals would expect for their 'confidences'. As a matter of good practice, the professionals should discuss their understanding of confidentialty with those for whom they provide services (DH, 1995).

Children and young people growing up in the care system are often acutely aware that information they share with carers or staff is recorded and transmitted to others. This is one reason why they may be unwilling to confide in the adults responsible for their well-being. Nevertheless, like other social services clients, they may expect that, if they are offered the opportunity to speak in confidence, the information they share is truly confidential to the other party. Both professionals and children may be unclear whether parents should be included amongst those with access to the child's confidences.

Legal notions of children's rights to confidentiality are narrow and may not accord with children's expectations or fit with professionals' views about what is good practice, particularly in the area of direct work. Where children and young people are 'Gillick competent' and therefore have rights to seek services, for example medical treatment, they have the same rights to confidentiality as adults. But 'no child, simply by virtue of being a child, is entitled to a right of privacy or confidentiality' (*R. (Mrs) v. Central Independent Television plc*, 1994, 141). This view will need to be reassessed after the incorporation of the European Convention on Human Rights into UK law.

English law recognizes that the relationship between a client, including a mature child client, and his or her doctor (BMA, GMSC *et al.*, 1995) or lawyer (SFLA, 1997, p.11) is confidential and this probably extends to other therapeutic relationships. The obligation to keep confidences exists because of the context of the relationship and does not depend on there being an agreement to do so (Martin, 1989, p.705). Even where confidential relationships are recognized, the need to disclose information is accepted where this is necessary for the protection of others (Hamilton and Hopegood, 1997). The general provision of care or education which are seen at least in part as services to parents (DH, 1991c, para. 3.30; Harris, 1993, p.20) does not create confidential relationships between social workers and children. Confidentiality cannot therefore provide a justification for withholding information from a parent.

Lisa and Jane

Lisa and Jane, aged 16 and 13, lived with their father who was divorced from their mother. Relationships between the parents had always been violent; both parents drank heavily and the children had been neglected when they were young. When the girls were aged 9 and 6, their mother moved hundreds of miles away to live with relatives; she attempted to maintain contact by letters but these were intercepted by the father.

A breakdown in relationship between Lisa and her father led to her moving to live with friends with the assistance of a Section 17 payment. Shortly after, the father became terminally ill and Jane was accommodated by the local authority. Both girls had very negative views of their mother and did not want anything to do with her because of her failure to keep in touch. On hearing of her former husband's death, the mother contacted social services. The social worker expressed a willingness to meet her and awaited her visit with apprehension. She did not seek to make personal contact with the mother either directly or using the local social services department as an agent, nor did she send the mother any information. She explained that Lisa and Jane did not want their mother to know about them and that they had a right to confidentiality.

The decision not to involve the mother in Lisa's care can be justified on the basis of Lisa's rights, her wishes and her welfare. The same cannot be said in relation to her younger sister. After the father's death, the mother was the only person who had parental responsibility for Jane. The father had not named anyone else as Jane's guardian.[2] Jane's mother had both a right to information because of her status as a parent with parental responsibility and a need for information so that she could participate in the planning of her child's care. Although the obligation to consult and consider also applies in respect of children, the objection of a child under 16 to general information about the way in which they are being looked after being passed to their parent does not justify its being withheld. Moreover, the local authority is not able to fulfil its legal obligations, particularly the completion of the agreement in the Arrangements for the Placement of Children (General) Regulations 1991, if it fails to provide a parent with any information about its plans for their child under the age of 16 years.

Jane's mother did not visit the social services department and there was no further contact with her. In the light of the experience with other parents, and parents' own comments about their dealings with social services departments, it is suggested that there should have been a more positive response to the mother's contact.

Where children who are not competent to consent are involved in direct work, a person with parental responsibility must give consent for the child's participation. Where the child is in care, it may not be necessary to seek the parent's consent and information can always be withheld if this is necessary to safeguard the child's welfare. The issue of confidentiality should be discussed when parental consent is sought. Parents can agree that their child should be allowed a confidential relationship with a therapist even where the child lacks the maturity required to enter such a relationship. Both parents and children need to know what the limits of this consensual confidentiality are; parents may find it easier to support their children's confidentiality if they have some idea what the direct work entails. Children may be helped by being told explicitly what their parents are told.

Reviews

Reviews 'form part of the continuing planning process' for all children who are being looked after (DH, 1991d, para. 8.1). The Children Act s.26 and regulations set out the frequency of reviews, the matters which have to be considered and the procedures for recording. In keeping with the principle of partnership, both regulations and guidance emphasize the importance of parental participation (for example, DH, 1991d, paras 8.8, 8.11 and 8.15). Regulations require the local authority 'unless it is not reasonably practicable' to 'seek and take account of the views of' parents and 'so far as is reasonably practicable' to 'notify' parents with 'details of the result of the review' (Review of Children's Cases Regulations 1991, reg. 7(1), (3)). There is no requirement for parents to be invited to a review meeting but, 'so far as this is reasonably practicable', parents should be involved and the authority should consider their attendance (reg. 7(2)). Guidance suggests that parental attendance should be the norm and that separate attendance for parents and children may be arranged where the child's welfare might be prejudiced by attendance together (DH, 1991d, para. 8.15). Arrangements for reviews may be even more complex where parents have been 'lost' and foster carers have become de facto adopters, or if reviews normally take place in the foster carers' home and the carers are unwilling for the parents to visit there.

Where parents have played little part in their child's life and foster carers have shown a long-term commitment to a child, exclusion of the parents from attendance at the review can be justified but is not necessarily conducive to the child's welfare.

Andrea

Andrea came into care at the age of 1 year because of the multiple problems in her family, including her mother's mental health difficulties, relationship problems between her parents and major financial problems. Andrea was placed in foster care; contact with her parents was restricted and then effectively terminated. Andrea had learning difficulties and she attended special school. Her parents, particularly her father, continued to express an interest in her, but the foster carers were resistant to any parental involvement. Following the introduction of the Children Act, and as plans began to be made for Andrea to move towards independence, the social worker re-established contact with the parents. The father expressed concern for his daughter and interest in involvement. The venue for reviews was switched from the foster home to Andrea's school to facilitate this. Nevertheless, the foster carers refused to attend.

The decision to move the review provided the best opportunity for involving all the adults who might be important to Andrea. The refusal of the foster carers to attend meant that further action had to be taken to ensure that their perspective was known. The alternative, to continue reviews excluding the parents, would have undermined the possibility of reinvolving the parents. Not all the social services departments made such efforts to engage parents in the processes of the care system. Even parents who had re-established contact with their children were not automatically invited to reviews, and where they were invited sufficient consideration was not always given to their other responsibilities, such as work and child care when fixing the time of the review.

Contact

Under the Children Act the court's power to regulate contact arrangements for children in care applies not only to face-to-face contact but also to contact by letter (*Re O.*, 1995). Regulation of a child's correspondence by the local authority without a court order could contravene the child's right to freedom of correspondence guaranteed by the European Convention on Human Rights, art. 8. Where contact with a young child is by letter, the courts have required a carer to read the letter to the child, but have also accepted that the carer should have the power to censor inappropriate material (*Re O.*, 1995).

Little attention has been given to developing policies and practices around letter contact in relation to children in care, although its use has grown substantially in adoption, where different agencies take different approaches to their post-adoption 'letterbox' services (SSI, 1995). Whereas some agencies vet the contents of letters, others send them unopened. Where agreements have been made for the exchange of information, some agencies contact parents or adopters to ask for the information they have agreed to provide, whilst others merely forward what has been sent.

These issues are all relevant to children who are being looked after by a local authority, and in this case it is also necessary to take into account the parent's retention of parental responsibility. Parental responsibility gives parents some right to control communication between their child and others, at least so far as they use this in the interests of the child. It does not justify parents, or the local authority, preventing children who are mature enough to choose their own friends, sending and receiving letters as they wish.

Sustaining positive contact by letter involves more that ensuring that letters are passed on (but this is an issue where parents do not have their child's address). Letter writing to one's own child is an unnatural activity for most parents; parents may need help in composing or writing letters and reassurance that letters have been received, preferably in the form of a reply.

Andrea's father was permitted letter contact but failed to write for many months for no known reason. It subsequently turned out that he was illiterate and had relied on work colleagues to help him write. During a long period of absence from work due to ill-health he had been unable to maintain this contact.

Even where parents are used to writing letters, separation from their child quickly leaves them with too little knowledge about their child's daily life to be able to relate to them easily.

There were a number of cases in the study where attempts had been made to maintain or renew contact by letters and presents. Often failure to discuss what was appropriate left the social worker angry at the parent's perceived insensitivity and the parents mistrustful because they were unclear whether letters and gifts had been forwarded. Sometimes it appeared from files that they had not. Carers were also known to intercept gifts. Although social workers and carers were generally acting in good faith, it was not clear that they recognized that both children and parents had rights in relation to their correspondence.

Restoring contact

In many cases where contact has ended the local authority remains under duties to endeavour to promote contact (sched. 2, para. 15) and to allow reasonable contact with parents (s.34(1)). If parents who have lost touch with their children request contact, the local authority has to decide whether or not to work towards restoration of contact. How and when restoration is achieved is a matter of professional judgment, but the social worker needs to make decisions in consultation with both parents and children, and be aware that disputes can be referred to the court. Where negotiated arrangements are possible, litigation can be avoided, although the involvement of the guardian ad litem may ensure that children's interests are properly represented.

If the local authority considers that renewing contact is not in the child's best interests, it must obtain a court order authorizing the refusal of contact. In Millham and colleagues' study of termination of contact before the Children Act 1989, a third of the formal terminations of contact occurred after requests to re-establish contact which had already ended (Millham et al., 1989, p.33). Where contact matters are referred to the courts, a guardian ad litem is appointed to represent the child, to investigate and to provide a report to the court. The court determines disputes about contact with children in care applying the welfare principle and the welfare checklist (s.1). Contact will not be ordered against the wishes of children who are able to express a coherent view (*Re M.*, 1995; *Re F.*, 1995), nor generally where it would undermine the local authority's plan for the child (*Re B.*, 1993). The courts accept that 'contact cannot be pursued to a level which makes a successful placement impossible to find because the child needs a home, and that must be the first priority', but are not willing to sacrifice existing relationships which matter to a child 'for the sake of putative ones which may never be found' (*Berkshire C.C. v. B.*, 1997, 174, HALE J). Where parents have previously lost contact with their child and long-term carers object to renewed contact, the courts may be unwilling to grant contact and put at risk the stability of the current placement.

Where contact has already been formally terminated by an order for no contact or an order giving the local authority discretion to refuse contact, it may be restored without court proceedings. The Contact Regulations 1991 and guidance (DH, 1991d, para. 6.31) empower the local authority to vary a court order by agreement with the person concerned; the agreement of a child 'of sufficient understanding' is also required. The local authority must serve a written notice of the new proposed arrangements on the child and the child's parents, stating the reasons for them and setting out the action they may take if they are dissatisfied. The obligation to serve a notice is additional to the duty to consult which applies to decisions generally.

Parents who fail to re-establish contact through negotiation have a right to apply to the court but face considerable barriers to regaining contact in this way. Legal aid is available subject to a merits test; where the parent's prospects of success are poor, for example because the guardian ad litem has recommended no contact, legal aid will be refused or withdrawn. In contact cases this may mean that a parent is left without representation at the final hearing of their application. This may leave the parent with a sense of injustice because they have not had a proper opportunity to put the issue before a judge, and may make it more difficult for the social worker to continue to try to work with the parent. Although the Children Act provides for repeated applications for contact, except in the rare cases where a restriction on applications has been imposed (s.91(14)), the courts are taking a narrower approach. Only if there has been a material change in circumstances, for example the abandonment of a plan for the child's adoption, do they consider it appropriate to discharge an order authorizing refusal of contact (*Re T.*, 1997).

The court's attitude to renewing contact serves to highlight the weak position of parents even when they appear to have legal rights to redress in the courts, and the substantial power of the social worker and the local authority. If the parent is unsuccessful in persuading the social worker to consider the restoration of contact, he or she is most unlikely to be able to obtain a court order for this.

Conclusion

Partnership with parents necessitates a recognition that parents have a special place in their children's lives, even though they may never look after them. Where possible, there should be discussions with parents about the role they can play and what they can do to meet their parental reponsibility, even where their child is subject to a care order. What information should be provided to parents and the ways this should be done need to be considered. Policies and practices which start from the basis that information cannot be provided to parents run counter to this. They alienate parents from social services and contribute towards the erosion of relationships between parents and children. As children mature they do have increasing rights to make decisions and should be permitted to decide themselves who has information about them, but this cannot be routinely allowed to preclude most parents being provided with any information about their children's general well-being and circumstances. Young people need to learn the value of personal information and the effect on others of withholding it. This does not mean that their views should not be respected, but that they should not necessarily be allowed to take effect without some discussion about the implications. After all, it is young people who face the consequences of passing or not passing on information, particularly the impact on their relationships. Withholding of information should occur only on a reasoned basis that this is necessary to safeguard and promote the child's welfare (s.33(4)), or that it is a matter where the child has the right to make a decision and to have the confidentiality of this respected. Where parents have rights to make or be involved in decisions, they should have the right to the personal information about their child which allows them to attempt to make wise decisions.

Issues of parental involvement, access to information and contact cannot be regarded as fixed but need to be reviewed constantly as the child develops. Parents can be reinvolved in their children's lives for the benefit of their children. The legal framework permits this, but leaving wide discretion to the local authority also permits practices which are less conducive to children's well-being. Both children and parents are dependent on individual social workers and on the social services department for the quality of service they receive; neither the courts nor other complaints mechanisms enable them to obtain better treatment as of right.

Notes

1 In *W.* v. *Essex* C.C. (1998) the Court of Appeal upheld a decision by the High Court refusing to strike out a claim by three children who had been sexually abused by a foster child in their parents' care. Previously the House of Lords has held that local authorities have immunity from liability in negligence for activities relating to the protection of children: *X.* v. *Bedfordshire* C.C. (1995).
2 A guardianship appointment will only take effect during the lifetime of a surviving parent with parental responsibility if the deceased parent had a sole residence order: Children Act 1989, s.5(7)(9).

3 Working in partnership with parents of children being looked after: issues of theory, research and practice

June Thoburn

Introduction: which children and families are we considering?

This book is principally concerned with children who are looked after by local authorities for lengthy periods during which time they lose touch with members of their birth families. This chapter will therefore concentrate on social work practice with the parents of these young people, and less attention will be paid to practice with parents involved in respite or longer-term shared care arrangements.

A review of the backgrounds of young people looked after by local authorities for longer periods immediately shows that in many cases there were originally child protection issues. Rowe *et al.* (1989) note that major changes have occurred over the last 20 years in the backgrounds of children and young people entering the public care system. They tend now to be older at the time they leave their families, and even those who are younger tend to have experienced more adverse circumstances, or are siblings of children who have been maltreated, or have lived within families where multiple disadvantage was a fact of life.

The Children Act 1989 facilitates and encourages the provision of family support services, which include respite and longer-term shared care arrangements based on voluntary arrangements, with the parents retaining full parental responsibility. A series of research studies conducted after the implementation of the Children Act (Thoburn *et al.*, 1997; Brandon *et al.*, 1999; Packman and Hall, 1995) has indicated that those needing longer-term accommodation come predominantly from the most vulnerable families, and that, despite early evidence of lack of investment in family support services, numbers of children looked after for long periods of time have decreased. Very frequently, those who are the subject of care proceedings will have been considered by child protection conferences, and registration will already have been used. Groups of parents who are overrepresented amongst parents of children looked after include those who have a learning disability, those who have a mental illness or are described as having a 'personality disorder', those with problems of alcohol or drug use, and mothers who have been involved in a relationship or relationships with male partners who are known to have maltreated children, and who are thus judged not to be able to protect their children from significant harm at the hands of unstable partners. In parallel with these problems, parents of children who are looked after have often been maltreated themselves as children, or experienced serious marital conflict which may have been accompanied by violence.

It therefore seems appropriate in this chapter to concentrate on partnership-based practice with parents where there is an issue of child maltreatment and the possibility of conflict between parents and social workers. In such cases, issues of unequal power and different agendas cannot be ignored. While other research will be referred to, the chapter is based on two studies of child and family social work practice with families where maltreatment was alleged, or known to have occurred. The first was the study undertaken just as the Children Act was being implemented, on partnership with family members involved in the child protection process (Thoburn et al., 1995). In this study, 27 per cent of the children were looked after by the agencies at some point and 19 per cent of these were looked after for more than a few weeks. The fieldwork for the second study was undertaken between 1994 and 1995 and thus after implementation of the Children Act 1989. This involved the scrutiny of 105 newly identified cases of 'significant harm' or 'likely significant harm' which were followed through for a period of 12 months. Some 65 per cent of these children were looked after at some period and 28 per cent (including six who were placed with relatives) were looked after on a longer-term basis. Reference will also be made to the recent work of Packman and Hall (1995, 1998) who, on revisiting the two areas on which an earlier study of children in voluntary care had been made (Packman, 1986), concluded that 'accommodation' under voluntary arrangements after the implementation of the Children Act was being more extensively used in child protection cases than was the case during the period of the earlier study. The use of 'negotiated', or possibly 'coerced', accommodation and its impact on working in partnership will be discussed later in this chapter.

Research on partnership-based child and family social work practice

Until comparatively recently there have been few studies on partnership-based practice within the child care field, and the major interest has been on working in partnership with adults who have disabilities. Within the field of child and family social work, earlier studies concentrated on family support and day-care services, and on work with the parents of children in care, especially concentrating on the extent to which they were involved in the review and planning processes. Some of these studies specifically set out to look at partnership as an issue in its own right (Brown, 1984; Gardner, 1987; Parsloe et al., 1990), whereas most described practice with children and parents and, as a side issue, touched on the extent to which parents and children were (or more often were not) involved in the reception into care and review processes (Fisher *et al.*, 1986; Packman, 1986; Millham *et al.*, 1986; Owen, 1992). Several of these earlier studies have been summarized in Department of Health overviews of research (DHSS, 1985; DH, 1991a) and influenced emphasis in the Children Act and Guidance on consultation and partnership since they demonstrated how infrequently these were likely to occur.

Research undertaken around the time of the Cleveland Report (Butler-Sloss, 1988) concentrated on the involvement of parents in the formal child protection procedures which, for an important minority of the most vulnerable children, preceded their being either compulsorily or 'voluntarily' looked after by local authorities. These studies, which influenced the rewriting of the child protection guidelines, *Working Together under the Children Act 1989* (DH, 1991e), are summarized by Lewis (1992) and Thoburn *et al.* (1995). Most are small-scale in-house accounts of pilot projects undertaken to increase the involvement of parents in the formal child protection processes, especially child protection conferences. These early studies followed similar formats and involved interviews with parents who were invited to attend the whole or part of child protection conferences, as well as questionnaires given to professional attenders. Some researchers also spoke to parents and professionals about conferences to which family members were not invited, and others looked at the situation before and after the introduction of new policies (Bell, 1996). The earlier studies reached similar conclusions, which can be summarized as follows.

- There was no diminution in the number of child protection conferences called when policies to invite parents were introduced, nor was there any difference in registration rates between conferences where parents attended and those where they did not.

- Parents generally described child protection conferences as stressful, but all studies concluded that they preferred to attend to not being invited.
- Agencies developed protocols for deciding about the circumstances in which family members should not be invited. These 'exclusion clauses' were rarely formally used. However, practice evolved whereby it was mainly the main parent, usually the mother, who was invited. Parents who were the alleged abusers (usually fathers), who were no longer living in the home, were often not specifically invited, even though they were not explicitly excluded.
- As procedures became better worked out and practices evolved to encourage family involvement, the proportion of parents attending increased.
- Although some agencies placed restrictions on the sorts of people parents could bring with them as supporters or advocates, professionals and family members spoke positively of the role of supporters, and practice changed to encourage their attendance. Initially, some agencies precluded the attendance of solicitors, but over time these restrictions were also removed.
- Family members preferred to attend the whole of conferences, although the advantages of participation could be achieved provided they attended for the major part of a conference. If they were to be asked to leave, this should be for the shortest possible time, the reason having been explained to them beforehand. It is preferable for parents to be in at the start of the conference and be asked to leave for a short period, rather than for them to join a conference which has already started.
- Some parents wished to attend conferences in order to 'have their say' and check that the information given at the conference was correct; other parents attended in order to hear what the professionals had to say, so that they could reflect on their own next steps.
- There was little evidence of parents actually influencing the decisions which were taken and, indeed, they were often specifically precluded from taking part in the discussion and decision about whether the child should be registered. Parents did not, however, expect to be fully involved in these decisions, although they would have liked to have been, and a frequently heard comment to researchers was, 'They had made their minds up before the conference even started'.

The studies all indicated that, if parents were to play a more productive role in working together with professionals to secure adequate protection for their children, they must be involved throughout the child protection process and not simply in the conference itself. However, the way in which agencies handled the conference process also determined the other aspects of the work. Those agencies which worked hard to secure family participation in the child protection meetings also began to work hard to secure parental and family involvement in the early stages, particularly by producing appropriate leaflets, providing child care and ensuring that support was made available so that parents could attend meetings and participate as fully as possible.

A Department of Health-funded study of family involvement in seven authorities therefore considered the extent to which parents and young people were involved in the *whole* child protection process, from the very first enquiry, rather than focusing specifically on conferences (Thoburn et al., 1995). Others of the Department of Health commissioned studies which were included in the summary report, *Child Protection: Messages from Research* (Dartington Social Research Unit, 1995) also explored issues of family involvement, especially those by Farmer and Owen (1995), Cleaver and Freeman (1995) and Sharland et al. (1996). These studies all concluded that it was essential to think in terms of different types of families who became involved in the child protection system in order to understand the nature of social worker/family interactions and to consider in which sorts of cases working in partnership with parents was likely to be an achievable goal.

Cleaver and Freeman produced a categorization of types of families which was subsequently used in a study of 105 'significant harm' cases (Thoburn et al., 1997; Brandon et al., 1999). This study found that only 14 per cent of the families referred into the formal child protection system because of concerns about neglect or maltreatment had had no earlier contact with the social services department and around a half were already well known to social workers and other professionals because of multiple and interlocking problems: either being re-referred because of concerns about child maltreatment or being pushed into the formal child protection system by an event or incident not necessarily connected with previous causes for concern. Both Cleaver and Freeman (1995) and Brandon et al. (1999) concluded that a child protection referral was likely to lead to a higher level of services. These two studies and also that of Farmer and Owen (1995) concluded that workers who made a determined attempt to involve the parents and older children, and who had appropriate skills, were likely to engage most of them in the process because family members usually recognized the very great need for help.

However, in some of these cases children were placed in long-term care, often through the courts, and there was a tendency for the work with the parents either to be given second place to work with the children or not to be undertaken at all. In such cases early attempts at involving the parents were likely to 'turn sour' as the parents felt neglected and often betrayed as the help from the social worker they had initially trusted was withdrawn. The requirement to give evidence in court could make it even less likely that family members would work with a social worker because in such cases the sense of betrayal tended to be greater. However, those workers who had attempted to continue to give a service to parents throughout the care proceedings could sometimes overcome the negative impact of the court's adversarial processes.

The second group identified by Cleaver and Freeman, which they described as 'acute distress' families, are those who in better times had been coping adequately, but who were rocked by either one devastating blow or a series of sometimes unconnected events. These families also tended to recognize their needs and to be seeking a service. Skilled workers determined to work closely with them and involve them as much as possible would be likely to succeed in doing so. At least one of the parents in these families had the strengths which would mean that they could be engaged in the provision of long-term help for their children, including the provision of accommodation away from home. Although coercion, either by an application to court or by the use of the formal child protection system, was sometimes necessary in order to persuade parents of the seriousness of the emotional and physical risks to the children, a negotiated approach made by a skilled social worker would often result in a positive and collaborative solution.

The third group was what Cleaver and Freeman described as 'single issue' families, where the family was often not known to have problems until a child protection referral (often an allegation of sexual abuse or harm to the child resulting from some marital conflict) was made. If there was agreement between parents and social workers that abuse had occurred, and about who was responsible for it, it would usually be possible to engage at least one parent in working in partnership, and it was rarely necessary for children to be away from home for any length of time. However, where agreement about culpability or the degree of seriousness proved not to be possible, these were often the families where the worker could not break through the mistrust of family members. Children or young people accommodated from these families, sometimes at their own request, were often separated on a long-term basis and antagonistic relationships prevailed between the young person and the social worker on the one hand, and family members on the other. These studies indicate that parents who are accused of abusing a child but deny any involvement, especially if there is no clear evidence to substantiate the allegation or allocate responsibility, are unlikely to be able to work in partnership with professionals seeking to implement a protection plan. However, Thoburn *et al.* (1995) argue that keeping such parents fully involved, especially if the allegations were made against one parent and not the other, treating them with courtesy and involving them in drawing up a plan which provides for adequate monitoring but is not overly intrusive in family life, can keep doors open for the young person who has left the household. Having recognized that the extent of family member involvement will be determined not only by social work skill and agency policy but also by the obstacles to working in partnership, Thoburn et al. (1995) allocated each case to a 'best', 'middle' and 'worst' scenario group in terms of the extent to which it might be possible to work in partnership with parents. They concluded that the degree of difficulty in some cases made it undesirable in the interests of the child to involve the parents fully, although older children might be more fully involved. However, in other cases a degree of involvement which stopped short of partnership was likely to lead on at a subsequent stage to greater degrees of consultation and even to partnership-based practice.

Arnstein's ladder of citizen participation, adapted for use with individual cases from a community development focus, proved helpful in the construction of a continuum of family involvement along which each case could be plotted (Arnstein, 1969). Successful partnership was identified by 'respect for one another, rights to information, accountability, competence and value accorded to individual input. In short, each partner is seen as having something to contribute, power is shared, decisions are made jointly, roles are not only respected but also backed by legal and moral rights' (Family Rights Group, 1991, p.1). This definition does not suggest that power must be shared equally in order for partnerships to be established, but does imply some sharing of power between social workers and family members. At the other end of the scale were cases where family members were not involved at all, or were placated or manipulated. In the middle of the continuum were cases where family members were kept fully informed and their opinions were sought on some aspects of the case but where they did not become involved in the work or appear to influence the decisions. In some cases this was the choice of the family members themselves since they did not share the professionals' views about the existence or seriousness of problems.

Using this framework for analysis, Thoburn and her colleagues concluded that only 2 per cent of family members were full 'partners' in the protection process, and 14 per cent were rated as participating to a considerable extent. Thus only one in six participated or were partners. This proportion was the same if only the main parent was included. At the other end of the scale, 13 per cent of the total and 7 per cent of the main parents were rated as 'not involved at all', 'placated' or 'manipulated'. It was noted that parents were less likely to be consulted about how the initial enquiries and investigations should be conducted, and about the decisions on whether the child had been maltreated and should be registered, and more likely to be involved in decisions about the ways in which help could be provided.

Since around a third of the cases which reached child protection conferences in this study were considered to come into 'best' scenario groupings, Thoburn and her colleagues concluded that there was much room for improvement in practice and skills. On a less rigorous definition of 'partnership', the authors concluded that 42 per cent of the main parents were 'involved'. The researchers looked especially at the cases in the 'middle' or 'worst' scenario cases where parents did become involved, in order to understand those characteristics of agency policy or social work practice which appeared to be associated with parental and older child involvement. They concluded that in the majority of child protection cases a skilled and determined worker would be able to involve parents and older children, at least to some extent, and move towards working in partnership as the case progressed. The proportion of cases where family members were involved or were partners would have been higher had opportunities not been lost by insensitive or unskilled workers or agency policies which undermined parents who were willing and able to participate in plans to help and protect their children. Thus, whilst failure to work in partnership can sometimes be attributed to aspects of the case itself, including the nature of the abuse or the personalities of the family members, differences between cases where family members were informed, involved and consulted and those where they were not seemed almost always attributable to either the agency policy and procedures or the social work practice, or both together.

The nature of partnership-based practice

The research reports summarised in *Messages from Research* (Dartington Social Research Unit, 1995) have important messages about the nature of practice which can lead to parents becoming more involved in the social work, protection and care process, even in those cases where it is not possible to negotiate a long-term placement and court applications have to be made. More detailed guidance is available in a Department of Health-sponsored training pack (Lewis *et al.*, 1992), and in the Department of Health guidance, *The Challenge of Partnership in Child Protection* (DH, 1995). Research studies suggest that it is necessary both for agency policy and practice, and for social work practice, to aim specifically at involving family members in order for partnership-based practice to lead to the benefits which the research demonstrates can be obtained for the young people, as well as their parents. However, even when agency policy and practice is less helpful than it might be, a skilled and determined social worker is likely to achieve family involvement, whereas agency practice and policy which encourages involvement is unlikely to be successful unless the worker really believes in its value.

Agency policy and practice

The research has indicated that family members are most likely to become involved if practice *throughout the process* from the initial referral to post-placement work is based upon the principles of partnership. However, those agencies which seek to involve family members in the formal child protection processes are most likely also to encourage partnership-based practice in other aspects of the work. Platt and Shemmings (1996) have focused particularly on the early stages of enquiry and investigation, and Shemmings (1996) has considered the particular issue of involving young people.

The key role played by the child protection conference, and other meetings which make decisions either about placement or about allocation of resources, in setting the climate for partnership-based practice arises partly because of the contribution which parents make to the effectiveness of conferences and other meetings, and also because their involvement at these meetings changes the way in which all other aspects of the case are handled. This is especially so if parents attend throughout the meetings, since all professionals know that their practice will be reviewed in the presence of the parents who can thus make public statements if things which have been promised do not happen, or things which do happen leave cause for complaint. One major change has been that professionals tend to discuss with family members the information which they will be bringing to the conference, and seek the consent of the parents, or, if this is not given, discuss with them the reasons why confidentiality cannot be respected, what information might be provided to the meeting and its accuracy. Parents may then decide that they prefer to give this sensitive information themselves, rather than have it given to the conference through the report of the professional. Summarizing the points made by research and guidance, the following aspects of the agency policy and practice encourage family members' participation.

- The provision of clear verbal and written information about the protection process, and the process for providing accommodation when this becomes necessary, or making application to court. This has to be

in appropriate languages and available for those with a communication difficulty or sensory impairment.
- The provision of a list of addresses and other information about where a family might go for additional assistance and support, together with details of the facilities available to help them to attend meetings, including help with the cost of transport, the provision of interpreters, or child-minding services.
- Managers must value partnership-based practice and understand that time taken by social workers in the early stages to establish working partnerships with the parents and young people is likely to be associated with better outcomes as well as being required by social work values and the Children Act guidance.
- Parents should be consulted about the timing and desirability of any change of social worker. If they have views about the ethnic origin or sex of the social worker, they should be listened to and attempts made to accommodate their wishes. If, as a result of the necessity to take court action, the parents have lost confidence in the social worker for the child, it may be appropriate to allocate a different social worker for the parents. Alternatively, the early child protection work may have resulted in a close working relationship between parents and worker, and it would be preferable for that work to continue even though it would be more usual to transfer the case to a long-term team worker. If such a change is considered essential, it should be delayed until a more appropriate time when a careful transfer to the new worker can be made. The more rigid application of 'purchaser/provider split' systems is not conducive to partnership-based practice.
- Chairing decision-making meetings is a highly skilled task which should only be taken on by those who can look at the case with a degree of independence and have had some training in the role and skills of chairing. This applies to those who chair 'looked after' review meetings as well as child protection and family support meetings. There are important differences between these different types of meetings, but chairing skills can be transferred and adapted. It may thus be desirable for agencies to have a team of specialists able to chair child and family decision-making meetings. Coordinators of family group conferences, although fulfilling a slightly different role, might be attached to these teams, and in some cases, with appropriate training, roles may overlap (see Lewis, 1994, for discussion of the role of chairs of child protection conferences, and Lewis et al., 1992, for suggestions about training; Marsh and Crow, 1998, summarize the research on family group conferences).

- Family members should be encouraged to bring a supporter with them when they attend conferences. Voluntary agencies or self-help groups should be encouraged and funded to provide this service for those who wish to use it. In some areas, Citizens' Advice Bureaux, citizen advocacy groups or law centres have trained volunteers available to do this work. Such services should take account of the needs of those whose first language is not English, or who have communication difficulties. Shemmings (1998) has provided training materials for those whose task it is to ensure that young people are enabled to take part in these meetings.
- Receptionists should be trained to understand about the special stress which attendance at such meetings places on family members. Waiting areas and meeting rooms should be appropriate. It will sometimes be necessary to make special arrangements if family members attending different parts of meetings do not wish to see each other. However, separate waiting areas for professional attenders and family members should *not* be provided unless there is a particular reason, such as a fear of violence.
- Both parents should be invited to attend all decision-making meetings for the whole period and rated as full members of the meeting for the unique contributions they can make. There must be clear procedures for decision when this is not appropriate, linked to an appeals system.
- Each agency should have procedures for consulting children and young people about whether they wish to attend meetings, how their wishes will be communicated and how they will be informed about what has happened if they do not attend.
- Most important of all, all members of the department, including elected members and the directors of social services, should create a climate which assures social workers and other front-line workers that when they seek to work in partnership with parents and young people they will have the backing of their managers and of the Area Child Protection Committee.

Social work practice

It has already been noted, and is a continuing theme of this book, that parents of children looked after by local authorities are a far from homogeneous group. When considering the possibility of working in partnership, these differences arise not from characteristics such as ethnicity or gender, or whether there has been parental maltreatment, but rather from features of the case such as whether the parents are seeking help; whether there is agreement about the child's needs, particularly their need to be looked after; whether it has been necessary to use coercion or the use of accommodation; and whether details have been negotiated.⁴ Packman and Hall's work (1995) reminds us that it is just as likely that conflict between worker and parent will arise because parents *request* accommodation for a child and their request is turned down. If, at a later stage, the situation deteriorates and child protection procedures are invoked or a court order is sought, parents can be particularly angry that their earlier requests for help went unheeded, and may be less willing to work cooperatively.⁵

Howe (1992) provides a simple matrix, with one axis comprising the willingness of the family member to participate and the other being the willingness and the ability of the worker to work in partnership. The four typologies of practice emerging from this analysis are as follows:

- worker not willing/not skilled; parent not willing: 'strategic practice' – each tries to outmanoeuvre the other;
- worker not willing/not skilled; parent willing: 'paternalistic practice' – opportunities are missed for creative practice where the energies and ideas of parents and worker are pooled to be of maximum benefit to the child;
- worker willing/skilled; parent not willing and does not want a social work service for self: 'play fair' practice results, in the course of which the worker is honest, keeps the parents informed, consults them and only interferes with parental responsibility and decision making to the extent that this is necessary to safeguard the child's welfare. The worker hopes by behaving in this way (and often succeeds or arranges for a different worker or agencies who may succeed) to negotiate some level of working together;
- worker willing/skilled; parent willing: 'partnership-based' practice.

The Challenge of Partnership in Child Protection (DH, 1995) summarizes the 15 basic principles on which partnership-based practice is founded.

1 *Treat all family members as you would wish to be treated, with dignity and respect.*
2 *Ensure that family members know that the child's safety and welfare must be given first priority,* but that each of them has a right to a courteous, caring and professionally competent service.
3 *Take care not to infringe privacy* any more than is necessary to safeguard the welfare of the child.
4 *Be clear with yourself and with family members about your power to intervene,* and the purpose of your professional involvement at each stage.

5 *Be aware of the effects on family members of the power you have as a professional*, and the impact and implications of what you say and do.
6 *Respect confidentiality* of family members and your observations about them, unless they give permission for information to be passed to others or it is essential to do so to protect the child.
7 *Listen to the concerns of the children and their families*, and take care to learn about their understanding, fears and wishes before arriving at your own explanations and plans.
8 *Learn about and consider children within their family relationships and communities*, including their cultural and religious contexts, and their place within their own families.
9 *Consider the strengths and potential of family members*, as well as their weaknesses, problems and limitations.
10 *Ensure that children, families and other carers know their responsibilities and rights*, including the right to services, and their right to refuse services and any consequences of doing so.
11 *Use plain, jargon-free, language appropriate to the age and culture of each person*. Explain unavoidable technical and professional terms.
12 *Be open and honest about your concerns and responsibilities*, plans and limitations, without being defensive.
13 *Allow children and families time to take in and understand concerns and processes*. A balance needs to be found between appropriate speed and the needs of people who may need extra time in which to communicate.
14 *Take care to distinguish between personal feelings, values, prejudices and beliefs, and professional roles and responsibilities*, and ensure that you have good supervision to check that you are doing so.
15 *If a mistake or misinterpretation has been made, or you are unable to keep to an agreement, provide an explanation*. Always acknowledge the distress experienced by adults and children and do all you can to keep it to a minimum (DH, 1995, 2,20, p.14).

Research studies which seek to identify the nature of *effective social work practice* in complex child and family cases, and the nature of practice which *effectively engages family members in the work*, reach similar conclusions. The essential elements of this practice have been known since researchers first subjected 'effective helping' to critical appraisal, and have more to do with social work values and the characteristics of the workers than with social work methods or techniques. In our study, effective partnership-based practice in the early stages of those cases which resulted in the child being looked after was most likely to be in evidence if a key worker was allocated quickly who combined emotional support with packages of help and therapy.

Efficiency, accurate knowledge clearly communicated, and technical skill were also valued. The social work methods used could vary, and indeed did vary from an advocacy-based approach to therapeutic groupwork. But in the absence of a dependable, honest relationship where there was evidence of sincere concern, none of these methods would succeed in engaging parents in the joint enterprise of helping their children through the traumas of the past, the stresses of loss and the need to make new relationships.

Conclusion

Throughout this chapter I have used interchangeably the words 'parent' and 'family member', and have sometimes referred specifically to the 'child' or 'young person'. In the early stages of the campaign (strenuously engaged in and largely successful) mounted by some members of all the professions involved in child welfare work to find a larger space which parents could occupy when decisions were made about their children's futures, it was not unusual to hear the words: 'Don't get me wrong, I'm totally in favour of what you are suggesting, but what about the children?' The implication was that an increase in parental involvement might lead to a loss for the children. The research has clearly demonstrated that partnership-based practice with parents is likely to be accompanied by greater involvement of the young people, and that parents and young people are equally likely to benefit. Our study of cases of 'significant harm' gave clear evidence that, when there appeared to be a conflict between parents' needs and safeguarding the child's welfare, the principles of partnership-based practice with parents were (often far too quickly) abandoned or 'put on the back-burner' (Brandon *et al.*, 1999).

But in that study we also saw how skilled, confident and principled workers, supported by their managers, continued to attempt to inform, consult, negotiate and share their power with some very angry, or depressed, parents whose children were removed from their care against their wishes. The premise on which they based their highly creative and resourceful practice, and which they discussed with parents, was: 'Yes, the protection and long-term well-being of the child must always be paramount and will be the first consideration if there is any conflict of interest; but the service I will offer to you as a parent will always be a high-quality and caring service. When I am providing you with a service, you are my "prime client" and if I am not able, because you have lost your trust in me, or because there is a conflict of interest with the child who is also my client,

I will ensure that a high-quality service is provided by someone else, and that you have a say in determining who that "someone else" will be.' Sometimes the negotiation about who will be the best 'helper' will be conducted with the assistance of the parent's solicitor. To those who argue that resources are not available for two workers, two reminders should suffice: it is now very common and totally appropriate for foster carers to have their own support worker; and the research points strongly to the fact that, when parents do play a full part in meetings and court proceedings, it is far more likely that sound plans are made, agreements reached and detailed arrangements to secure the child's long-term well-being adhered to.

4 Young people, being in care and identity
Christine Harrison

> Young people: 'Here we have a clearly distinguishable group of people within our society (albeit only in the Western world) who now occupy a firmly established twilight zone of the quasi-child or crypto-adult'. (Jenks, 1996, p.63)

Introduction: the legal context

The 'partnership with "lost" parents' research focused on the re-establishment of working partnerships between parents and social workers and was prompted by the legal reforms embodied in the Children Act 1989. Of equal significance, it was also informed by a broader theoretical understanding and knowledge about why those particular changes were recommended and what they might mean for children and young people who are looked after by local authorities. One of the central threads that bound together the rationale, content, process and outcome of the project was a consideration of the identity needs of young people in public care and the need to re-evaluate the contribution that working in partnership with parents might make to meeting these.

The importance of a secure and positive identity as an aspect of emotional health and well-being is recognized by the United Nations Convention on the Rights of the Child and several of its provisions refer directly to a child's identity; to have an identity, retain an identity and, in certain circumstances, to reclaim an identity:

Article 7 (1)

The child shall be registered immediately after birth and shall have the right from birth to a name, the right to acquire a nationality and, as far as possible, the right to know and be cared for by his or her parents

Article 8 (1)

State parties undertake to respect the right of the child to preserve his or her identity, including nationality, name and family relations, as recognised by law without unlawful interference

Article 8 (2)

Where a child is illegally deprived of some or all of the elements of his or her identity, State parties shall provide appropriate assistance and protection with a view to speedily re-establishing his or her identity

... and where a child is separated form his or her parent(s):

Article 9 (3)

State parties shall respect the right of the child who is separated from one or both parents to maintain personal relations with both parents on a regular basis, except if it is contrary to the child's best interests.

The Children Act 1989 also incorporates provisions that relate closely to or have an influence on a child's identity. There is a presumption in favour of contact when children are looked after (s.34(1)) and a requirement that parents are consulted when planning for children and young people being looked after, whether or not they are likely to return to live with them (s.22(4)). Local authorities must now take into account a child's racial, cultural, religious and linguistic background (s.22(5)(c)).

The guidance accompanying the Act asserts much more explicitly the importance, for young people being looked after, of developing a secure sense of personal identity and underlines the centrality of knowledge about their history and family background to this. 'The integration of what may be puzzling or painful information is likely to be a slow process. Life story books can help, but will only provide a basis for continuing work and can never really take the place of contact with parents, relatives and important people from the child's past' (DH, 1989a, p.10). The importance of considering a child or young person's identity and actively promoting a positive sense of identity is also recognized in the Department of Health *Looking after Children* documentation, in which the Assessment and

Action Records incorporate a section on the child's identity needs (Ward, 1995).

This chapter will explore theoretical perspectives which address the issue of identity development in adolescence. Traditional theories of identity will be contrasted with more recent alternative accounts which examine the 'twilight zone' of adolescence and emphasize the social aspects of identity formation. These latter approaches highlight the impact of disadvantage and oppression on a young person's developing sense of personal identity. They suggest that, for children and young people who are being looked after by local authorities, the development of identity will be influenced by their experiences during and after care, as well as those before care; experiences outside the family as well as inside. Drawing directly on the experiences of young people involved in the research project (see Chapter 1), as well as of other young people, the present chapter proposes that work to promote a positive identity is the right of every child being looked after. It should not be confined to life story work precipitated by impending change or situations where a problem with identity is perceived. Young people being looked after, like young people more generally, do not possess an identity only when a problem is identified.

Research with young people, in and out of care, shows that many of them are involved in day-to-day struggles to establish and maintain a positive sense of identity and self-esteem in the face of considerable disadvantage and discrimination. They have often developed strategies of resistance and survival, either through their own counsel or with the support of peers, with a reluctance to involve adults (Morris and Wheatley, 1994; Butler and Williamson, 1994). The combined experiences of young people being looked after indicates, not only that they confront a hostile climate for their development, but that they are wary of adults, carers and social or residential workers. These adults, as well as their agencies, may well have their own agendas that elevate some considerations and relegate others, sometimes at marked variance with those important to young people themselves (Masson and Winn Oakley, 1999). Work to promote a positive sense of personal identity cannot be severed from these issues, which firmly locates it within an anti-discriminatory, rather than individualistic, model.

Identity: the theoretical context

Identity, it has been argued, is defined by the answer to the question, *Who am I?* (Blasi, 1988). The answer to this question will generate others: *How do I know who I am?* and *How did I get to be who I am?* These deceptively simple questions, which pose what Slugoski and Ginsberg call 'the paradox of personal identity' (Slugoski and Ginsberg, 1989, p.36), have occupied philosophers for many hundreds of years and have more recently preoccupied psychologists and sociologists (Burkitt, 1991; Greenwood, 1994). The concept has been elusive and contested. A review of contemporary theoretical approaches to identity illustrates just how difficult the concept is to delineate. The influence of traditional individual-oriented psychological perspectives has been challenged by a diverse range of alternative accounts whose roots lie in Marxism (Leonard, 1984), feminism (Mitchell, 1974; Foreman, 1977; Gilligan, 1982; Squire, 1989), lesbian feminism (Kitzinger, 1993), cross-cultural studies (Wozniak, 1993; Amit-Talai, 1995), identity politics (Whisman, 1996; Warner, 1994; Steinberg and Epstein, 1997), social constructionism (Richards and Light, 1986; Woodhead et al., 1991) and post-structuralism (Weeden, 1987; Gittens, 1998). These have not only exposed flaws in traditional theoretical perspectives, but have questioned the primacy of the individual subject (Burman, 1994) and the concept of development itself (Morss, 1996; Hill and Tisdall, 1997). They have argued that the normative incorporation of traditional theoretical perspectives in dominant discourses about adolescence has influenced how different professionals claim knowledge about young people and therefore how they work with them (Brannen et al., 1994; Mayall, 1996).

Most accounts of identity describe a complex constellation of interrelated aspects of identity that contributes to knowledge, self-awareness and an overall sense of self (Kroger, 1989; Coleman and Hendry, 1990). Within this, the process of integration and the concepts of continuity and consistency, as both objectives of developmental change and prerequisites for it, are stressed. Alongside this, beliefs, commitments and principles support and to an extent control identity, providing reference points for the experience of emotion. 'Identity is clearly related to self-concept and self-esteem. ... Identity has both cognitive (knowledge) and affective (evaluation) aspects and these two aspects are related to self concept' (Young and Bagley, 1975, p.55). A sense of identity relates to, and pursuit of self-esteem provides the rationale for, involvement in the social world of family, community and social grouping. Identity, what we know and what we feel about ourselves, is an enduring organizing framework that not only holds the past and present together, but also provides some anticipated shape to future life. 'The present tense of the verb to be refers only to the present: but nevertheless with the first person singular in front of it, it absorbs the past which is inseparable from it. "I am" includes all that has made me so. It is more than a statement of fact, it is already biographical' (Berger, 1980, p.370).

Traditional theoretical approaches have tended to privilege the internal, process nature of development within which adolescence is seen as the critical period in the establishment of an adult identity. A period of internal stress is often referred to (Kroger, 1989) with characteristic feelings of anger, counterculture, rebellion and opposition – a furnace of emotional upheaval during which the core of the adult personality is forged. There are unavoidable tasks and separations during this period which, if successfully completed, lead to an integrated sense of identity. Conversely, any difficulties or unfinished tasks frustrate this process and constitute barriers to the realization of a secure sense of identity in adult life. This is epitomized by Erik Erikson's theory of identity formation, which is generally regarded as being the most significant and influential contemporary account (Blasi, 1988; Kroger, 1989; Slugoski and Ginsberg, 1989; Ryburn, 1992).

Firmly located in a Western/North American traditional movement whose roots can be traced back to the philosophers of the Enlightenment, Erikson's framework derives from his commitment to psychoanalytic theory, but also incorporates aspects of social learning theory. The achievement of identity is the fifth stage within an eight-stage schema of psychosocial development which is epigenetic in nature (Erikson, 1977, p.243). Erikson defines identity as a 'subjective sense of sameness' (Erikson, 1968, p.19) with the following characteristics: a sense of psychosocial well-being; a feeling of being at home in one's own body; an inner assuredness of anticipated recognition from those who count (Erikson, 1968).

The experiences of each stage depend on a combination of the physical and intellectual growth of the child and her/his interactions with others. How the conflicts generated by each stage are handled is carried forward and forms part of the future pattern. Although adolescence is viewed as the critical period for the formation of a more or less permanent sense of identity, this is dependent on the reworking of the threads of past experience, and early life events retain significance so that 'identity depends on the past and determines the future' (Kroger, 1989, p.14).

Although necessarily crisis-ridden, a 'moratorium' in adolescence allows young people to try out different roles and life patterns. On the basis of this 'experimentation', choices and decisions can be made which provide the foundations for the establishment of lifelong commitments. The legacy of earlier events, as well as traumatic events within the stage itself, can hinder emotional development. If these unresolved difficulties are serious enough, a young person may experience identity confusion, an indefinitely prolonged failure to develop a firm sense of personal identity.

Identity: the challenge of anti-discriminatory perspectives

Most recent challenges to the predominance of Erikson's theory of identity have questioned the primacy given to the individual as the subject of psychological enquiry in Western thought as well as the universality of its application (Burkitt, 1991; Burman, 1994; Morss, 1996). Although diverse in origin, these alternative accounts acknowledge that the child's identity neither follows a predetermined blueprint nor is impermeable to outside influence; identity therefore cannot be extracted from the broader social and political context within which its development is embedded. In some accounts the social construction of identities lies within the cultural texts available to individuals which 'lay out an array of potentials, while simultaneously establishing a set of constraining boundaries beyond which selves cannot easily be made' (Shotter and Gergen, 1989, p.ix).

Erikson's revisions of psychoanalytic theory did incorporate a social dimension, but it nevertheless remains an individual conceptualization driven by intrapsychic processes (Ingleby, 1986), embodying only a limited idea of the social (Shotter and Gergen, 1989). A sanitized account is presented in which the occupational and ideological role alternatives provided by society are predicated on some notion of choice and decision. It takes for granted both social reality and the social order and assumes a congruence between these and the meeting of individual needs. It takes no account of the way in which institutions which shape and reinforce the social order (of which child care law and social work practice are part) are implicated in the construction of and constraint upon identity. In addition, it provides normative definitions of adolescence against which the behaviour of young people will be measured and judged. If conflict, rebellion and ambivalence are 'normal' aspects of adolescence, indicative of the developmental stage rather than representing real issues in the lives of young people, their views, opinions and concerns can readily be disqualified. Naturally 'rebellious' youth poses much less of a political/social threat than disaffected or oppressed youth. If conflict and rebellion continue indefinitely, or there is other evidence of some supposed failure to secure the firm sense of identity which is the developmental goal of adolescence, this failure is problematized in ways which implicate the individual and her or his parent. The source of deficits may easily be located in the person's earliest experiences of poor, inadequate or abusive parenting.

To place emphasis on adolescence as a distinctive phase of development, during which identity is formed, may be a metaphorical conjuring trick, distracting attention away from the range of social conditions and oppressions which affect young people and which constitute their lived experiences; concentrating on intrapsychic processes and excluding structural inequalities and injustice (Ryburn, 1992; Brannen et al., 1994; Dennehy et al., 1997; Hill and Tisdall, 1997). There are many marginalized or excluded groups of young people, including young people in care, for whom the realities of their lives may mean that 'the envisaging of alternative futures would be a futile and self-delusory exercise' (Slugoski and Ginsberg, 1989, p.37).

As well as emphasizing the structural inequalities such as poverty, feminist writers have scrutinized the significance of gender in developmental accounts. These critiques encompass both limited and extensive revision of orthodox approaches (Chodorow, 1978; Eichenbaum and Orbach, 1982, 1985) and calls for a new epistemological framework (Gilligan, 1982; Squire, 1989). Eichenbaum and Orbach promote a feminist psychotherapy by attempting to combine an analysis of patriarchy with psychoanalytic concepts. For them, woman's search for identity is located within a complex network of gendered relationships and socially defined role expectations. These embody contradictory expectations for young women about their female bodies and emerging sexuality. Adolescence is a painful time; the Eriksonian goals of freedom and independence are in conflict with dominant constructions of adult woman's sexuality. This can lead young women to feel uncomfortable about their bodies, to hide their sexual desires and needs, and to recollect with embarrassment and fear the physical changes of adolescence, together with the proscriptions which accompany them. Developing a sexual identity may be what makes a girl into a woman, and it is identified as a key aspect of adolescent development, but it also has negative connotations and is something to hide and be ashamed of. The development of young women's identity is located in a patriarchal society and contingent upon a 'culturally devalued attribute of femaleness' (Ryan, 1992, p.178).

Carol Gilligan also proceeds from the premise that, because of the way knowledge and theoretical perspectives are constructed to reflect the social structure and a dominant male order, boys' development in terms of identity will always appear more 'normal' than girls': 'The penchant of developmental theorists to project a masculine image, and one that is frightening to women, goes back at least to Freud, who built his theory of psychosocial development on the experience of the male child that culminates in the Oedipus complex' (Gilligan, 1982, p.6).

What is common to the various strands of feminist thought and politics of identity is an attempt to tackle the gender-biased nature of theory and research. This bias not only writes women's identity out of the script, but produces knowledge which reinforces this exclusion. Slugoski and Ginsberg argue that 'not only may Erikson's scheme be inappropriate for marginal and underprivileged groups but there is little place for women's identity within the scheme he proposed' (Slugoski and Ginsberg, 1989, p.38).

This discourse about identity and gender can be extended to consider critically how other forms of oppression affect on identity and to challenge further the normative dimensions of developmental accounts: for example, the development of a positive sexual identity in the context of a dominant discourse of heterosexism and accompanying homophobia which affects powerfully young lesbians and gay men. Whilst heterosexuality is taken as given, not requiring explanation, or in Adrienne Rich's words is 'compulsory', lesbian and gay identity is marginalized and stigmatized (Rich, 1981). In order to maintain a particular social order, sexuality is open to direct regulation (through legislative measures) and indirect control through its social construction as deviant or other (Steinberg and Epstein, 1997). In contrast with Erikson's concepts of rehearsal and choice, a focus is placed on the prescribed, proscribed and attributed aspects of identity. So a powerful condition is attached to the rubric that identity is 'an answer to the question *Who am I?*' (Blasi, 1988, p.226) and identity becomes 'what you can say you are according to what they say you can be' (Kitzinger, 1989, p.82, citing Johnston, 1973).

The concept of ascribed identity is also relevant when considering adoption. Adoption, the only legal process in Britain through which identity can be irrevocably altered and a birth parent replaced by a social parent, effectively extinguishes one identity and substitutes another (Ryburn, 1992). Arguments for this as a preferred route to permanency for children who could not live with their birth parents were supported by developmental accounts which emphasized the need to completely sever the birth relationship in order to promote the substitute relationship (Goldstein *et al.*, 1973). The complete nature of this process has, more recently, been mitigated by rights of access to birth records in adulthood. The development of more open models of adoption (Mullender, 1991) with limited continuing contact with a birth family is based on different views about the nature of attachment (Schaffer, 1990) and acknowledges that there are different routes to permanency (Thoburn *et al.*, 1986). Whilst adoption can for many children provide the consistency, continuity and personal and familial knowledge on which identity is founded, a lack of information or the shock of discovery can undermine a young person's ability to confidently answer the question, *Who am I?* Some adopted people will have no answer, experiencing not only a loss of identity but a painful realization that knowledge and possibly relationships may have been, albeit well-meaningly, withheld from them. Even when a child knows from an early stage that they are adopted, they may not have received sufficient information to integrate their knowledge of past and present, leading to a degree of uncertainty or confusion about identity (Haimes and Timms, 1985; Triseliotis, 1973).

In relation to black identity, black perspectives have challenged the Eurocentricity of dominant paradigms in psychological theory (Robinson, 1998). They have sought to demonstrate how children of African–Caribbean and Asian parentage living in a predominantly white society may experience low self-esteem due to their experience of racism and discrimination, rather than through an individual failure of adjustment (Maxime, 1986; Banks, 1992). Although many black children do have a positive self-image and identity, derived from their families' and communities' strengths and survival skills, this is not true for all black children. While it should be stressed that black children are 'are not doomed to be the victims of an oppressive, racist society' (Chambers et al., 1996, p.xii), the impact of insidious and pervasive racism must be considered. Where a 'sense of racial worth is not publicly and positively encouraged by the media, literature and various systems in society such as education and the law' (Maxime, 1986, p.114), a sense of identity confusion may be the result; this may be the experience of some black children in institutional care or placed transracially.

What is distinctive about these diverse theories is their attempt to establish the significance of social and political context in the process of identity formation. They also undermine the individual/society dichotomy which has characterized developmental psychology (Burkitt, 1991). Instead of putting the individual under the microscope, they compel us to examine complex social structures, processes and their institutional forms, and to look at how these are implicated in the formation of identity. In trying to expose the myths of development, they create space for different voices and narratives to be heard (Martin, 1998).

Before, during and beyond care

In working with children and young people who are being looked after by the local authority, these alternative perspectives, which are inextricably linked to an analysis of oppressions, can provide a conceptual and practice framework. They help those who work with or care for young people to understand how the intertwining of history, circumstance and experience in a social world influences the fragile development of personal identity. They suggest that, to promote a positive sense of identity, it would be inadequate only to register those experiences before entry to care, or to limit attention to harm caused within the parent–child relationship. A much more complex nexus of considerations is required. This would incorporate an evaluation of the impact of the material, economic and social context of early life and parenting experiences, and of social conditions such as poverty, sexism, racism and homophobia. If identity is an inner landscape then these conditions constitute the prevailing climate which gives definition to the landscape.

A young person's experiences within the care system must also be considered, including an awareness that being looked after or in care may itself constitute a stigmatizing experience, even when a high quality of personal care is given. If identity is grounded in the sum total of experiences, historical, personal and social, then every aspect of a child's or young person's life must be included and viewed from a lifetime, rather than a childhood, perspective. While it may be imperative that, for example, a child who has been the subject of emotional abuse has the right kind of therapeutic help, the child is not solely the abuse she or he has experienced. They may also have experienced many losses, of school friends, siblings, cultural and class-based aspects of their life, as well as other forms of oppression like racist bullying. In the long run, these losses and other negative experiences, which may be compounded by experiences of disruption while in care, may have as much impact on identity as the concerns that precipitated their entry to the care system.

No claims are made that the accounts explored here are representative, either of the general population of children and young people being looked after or of those who have been in the public care on a long-term basis, and this is not the point of their inclusion. There is an assumption, however, that, in the tradition of ethnographic research, they are stories that deserve to be told and that, not only are the experiences validated in being told, but something important can be learned for children and young people who become looked after. It is assumed that a story told can have political as well as individual dimensions.

Evidence continues to accrue about the impact of disadvantage and oppression in relation to gender, class, 'race', disability and sexuality in the lives of those in receipt of welfare services generally, and families whose children become looked after particularly. There is also evidence that welfare and social services have failed to take sufficient account of this and have, albeit inadvertently, compounded discrimination in their interventions with children and their families (Bebbington and Miles, 1989; Ahmad, 1990; Hooper, 1992; Langan, 1992; Barn, 1993; Milner, 1993; Booth and Booth, 1994; Morris, 1995). Young people's accounts add an experiential dimension and underline the admissibility of children's accounts.

'Hey! This is my life'

Like the social workers and parents who participated in the research study, the young people we interviewed were generous with their time and serious and considered in their responses. Participation in the research, although it may have validated their experiences, was unlikely to be of any other immediate benefit to them. Nearly all of the young people said that they agreed to participate because they wanted their views to be conveyed to an audience, be it of social workers, carers, managers or students, so that things might be different for other children; they hoped that their contribution would make a difference.

Although their lives reflected considerable diversity, significant themes emerged from their narratives. Their views about personal identity, the significance of family history, and parental involvement were inextricably linked, and impossible to abstract from their broader life and care experiences. Reading through the transcripts of conversations with them, what is striking is their active attempts to reach some understanding of their lives, to deal with conflicting feelings and knowledge, to accommodate the most painful personal experiences of rejection and abuse overlaid with fears and anxieties generated by a social world which deals them poverty, isolation, racism and little solidity or, in their eyes, trustworthiness. They were not passive victims, but were constructing their identities in difficult circumstances with strengths they were able to acknowledge as well as weaknesses. Although emerging key themes and issues which the young people have in common are described, the social origins of which have already been acknowledged, it is also important neither to deny nor to dilute the individual ways in which these have been lived experiences.

Living in and beyond care

All the young people interviewed, whether currently in or out of care, had spent the larger part of their lives in the care system. The majority had experienced disrupted lives while in care, and many described painful and damaging experiences both before and after admission. For some, entry into the care system had provided an initial relief, for example from sexual abuse.

> It was a relief really, that I had got out of that environment.

> I was like a spaghetti ball when I first came into care, that had dried out. It was all stuck together. Well then, you know, you just begin to pull bits out, to unravel it.

> I loved it. At first it was like a great holiday because suddenly there was meals which I wasn't used to ... So for the first year, I must say, it was a bit like being on holiday.

Where the initial feelings were of relief or pleasure, these were often subsequently replaced by more negative or ambivalent feelings. This was particularly the case when children began to be aware of differences between the way they were treated compared with birth children or when they began to evaluate the various dimensions of being in care. Over time, the significance of relationships, rather than material benefits, came to the fore. The result seemed to exacerbate the feelings of loss they had already experienced, and to compound children's feelings of worthlessness and sense of confusion.

> It was like I was going through a Cinderella syndrome ... I would do all the housework for my pocket money and [carer's daughter] would automatically get hers ... see what I mean?

> After the first year it wore off slightly ... because ... I don't know ... the material things didn't matter so much any more ... although they are a substitute family they're not your family ... they are supposed to treat you as their own, but in some ways they can make it more obvious that you're not theirs.

> Her [foster carer's] daughter was perfect and I was ... just like ... the rotten child.

Most of the young people had spent some time in foster care and this, particularly, had generated feelings, not just of being treated differently from birth children, but of not being treated properly, not having privacy and not having anyone to trust; these conspired to emphasize children's feelings of separateness, difference and not belonging. They gave graphic accounts, not just of material differences between the way they and birth children were treated, but of how their concerns were responded to differently, how they were less likely to be listened to or, alternatively, how their concerns would become the property of the household. 'I knew my stuff had been gone through and that my mail had been opened.'

Characteristically, they did not feel that they could tell anyone about their most painful experiences, finding it difficult to talk to their social worker and anticipating that other adults, foster carers or residential workers would be believed in preference to them. One young woman, who had been raped while living in foster care, had told her foster mother and had not been believed. 'I was raped and because I didn't want to go to court, I was called a liar ... by my own foster mum, because I didn't ... I wouldn't go to court.' She had left care and recently become a mother. She had reconsidered this experience in the light of being a mother herself, drawing the following conclusion: 'At the end of the day the [foster] family means nothing. Because they're not your own family. And I know from looking back because I have a son of my own so I know. Whatever, you would believe your child over anyone else.'

Some of the young people described more than a lack of understanding of their circumstances and experiences, and described bad treatment, discrimination and abuse, in both residential and foster care.

> When you were naughty [in the foster home] you had to put your hand up or your leg up. And you weren't allowed to put your leg down and you weren't allowed to put your hands down till they said. And if you put your hand down they used to hit you. But they didn't do that to their children, though.

> It's the way they ran the place [residential unit] ... it was fear ... we were all petrified ... it felt like prison.

> They didn't write down that they used to smack us, you know.

For most of the young people, their experiences of foster care had resulted in profound cynicism about the primacy given to substitute family care. They felt that the supposed 'normality' of foster care was a sham. For some young people, the perceived gap between the promise and the reality had calcified into a distrust, not just of this kind of care, but of the ideology of the family itself. Additionally, some children resented what they felt to be attempts to displace or replace their birth parents.

> Well I felt like an intruder while I was living there.

> That's the thing that really used to get me going ... you're supposed to be in a normal family environment ... and you can't even go to kip at your best mate's ... you can't have a normal life in care, you just can't ... you can't do the things a normal child would do.

> When I was 12 and expecting love and expecting that that was what I was going to get because this is what all the social workers promised, I was going to get a family that loved me ... then because of what happened I hardened myself to think, 'well you're not' because they're not my family.

> The ideal nuclear family you know ... little boy, little girl, mum and dad ... that only happens in TV soaps. ... My idea of a family is that they're a waste of space. People who only want to know you when they want something.

Some young people were explicit that these feelings of difference, discrimination and powerlessness, and a fear of being disbelieved, led to them behaving badly to effect their removal from particular foster placements: 'I began to seriously regress to acts of bad behaviour.'

Comparing residential and foster care

Overall, there were more extensive criticisms of foster care than of residential care and most of the young people who had experienced both expressed a preference for the latter. In part, this may reflect the traumatic and negative things which had happened to them in both birth and substitute families. For some of the young people, quite simply worse things had happened to them in families than in residential care, where they had comparatively better experiences. They described feeling under less pressure to fit in and, because there were several members of staff, that they had more control about who they confided in. Some conveyed the sense that they felt there was greater fairness and more accountability in residential care.

> Children's homes are probably one of the best places to live. You can get quite a lot of responsibility ... I don't like foster homes that much. ... Like when we get told off we get sanctions. Like you can't go to football. ... But they [residential staff] wouldn't make us sit at bottom of the stairs like the [foster carers] used to ... What about that one night, Michael, when we had to stand outside our bedrooms? ... Five hours we were out there.

> They [residential staff] ask your opinion and you can give your opinion and they write it down.

> It [residential care] was much better. You know, not just because there were lots of kids there and they were supportive or whatever ... it was because of the fact that I didn't have to be a part of a family, you know?

One young man, who was living in a small residential unit but who saw the couple who ran it as more like foster carers, gave his account of what they had given him as follows.

> We have our ups and downs and we have a laugh ... That's expected of every family ... we don't get smacked or really badly told off ... It's a loving family. I'm loved ... I didn't love anybody when I came here. ... I rejected everybody and everything ... I used to hate ... if they don't love you, you're not going to love anybody because you're not going to know what love is, are you?

School, friends and everyday life

The young people spoke in detail about the ways in which being in care is stigmatizing in itself and they were painfully aware of the (usually mistaken) assumptions that other people would make about them. This had an impact on every aspect of life, often making them feel compromised and ashamed. In everyday terms, this meant children and young people had to make calculated decisions about who and what to tell, once again making them feel at best different and at worst discriminated against.

> It's really embarrassing going to school ... you know it's like your parents must be really bad.
>
> I had a few people thinking it was my fault that I was in care ... that I was a trouble maker ... friends' parents like.
>
> You're just a kid in care ... you're just trouble ... The whole thing of being in care is you get a bloody image for yourself.

A brother and sister placed together in residential care had different views about how to deal with the school situation. The young woman said she would tell school friends that she was in residential care. If they had a problem with that, it was their problem. Her younger brother would not tell anyone as he was too embarrassed. Another young man in a small residential placement said he would not talk openly at school, since he felt that this might give something away about other residents and he felt he should protect their right to privacy.

As well as this leading to social exclusion in its own right, being in care for some young people powerfully combined with other forms of oppression, such as racism:

> School was a nightmare as well 'cause ... like everyone was white and I was the only black girl in the school ... and it was in a dead posh area. So I used to get hassled by the other kids ... they called me racist names ... and when I started to fight back it was like in the teacher's eyes I was the trouble maker because I was in care.

Overall, young people felt not just different but unequal and unfairly treated.

The care system, files, reviews and so on

All the experiences already referred to were seen by the young people as almost inevitable and part and parcel of a 'system' of care which is dehumanizing, not just for them but sometimes for workers as well. They were able to recognize individual workers or carers whom they trusted, but they were still inside the system. Although the care system may try to provide an ordinary family life, time and again the children and young people pointed up the contradiction between this aim and their experiences. They repeatedly drew attention to things that made them feel different, intruded upon, unable to have a say in or control over their lives, and which reinforced the cynicism already referred to.

> The thing about care is you're so low that you have got no control over your life whatsoever.

> What I hated most was telling people and strangers my life story.

> When I was fairly small and you'd walk in the room ... it used to scare me when I was little ... that they're all sat looking at you, asking you questions. ... And I didn't like the way they read something to do with you ... it was too formal ... it's not natural, you don't do that with your own kids ... not with strangers.

For nearly all this, admittedly small, group of children and young people who had experienced a high degree of change and disruption in their lives before and during care, their case file, and the range of documents it contained, was the most significant, if not the only, source of knowledge and information about themselves and their history. Files, written primarily to meet specific organizational demands and priorities, may embody dominant policy and practice considerations, the ideological perspectives of the time at which they were compiled. Where young people have been in care over a long period, files too frequently become crisis-driven, more likely to catalogue difficulties than achievements. Young people, however, desperate to know more about themselves and their familial history, may eagerly seize upon any records, with a profound impact on their sense of self. One young woman who had seen the content of her file drew attention to the way the file as a source of life history not only describes but constructs a young person in particular, often negative, ways.

> In your files, right, it's all the bad things, what they write in your files. And they don't put the whole truth in it. Like ... not once in the file does it say ... it might say that I was fighting with someone ... or I'd done this or I'd done that. And even to the point where they word it. It's like ... I could have been upset about

something or whatever and they wouldn't put that down. They'll put 'she was very aggressive'.

Contact with family, siblings and parents

All the children and young people interviewed had siblings, although only one pair of siblings was interviewed. Some of the young people had several siblings, not just full siblings but half-siblings and step-siblings. The significance of these sibling relationships was evident from their discussions. Most of the young people expressed concerns for and worries about siblings, whether or not they currently had contact with them. They confirm the view that 'siblingness' tends to be underrated and some of the young people were very explicit that a sibling relationship was more important to them than contact, direct or indirect, with a parent. The significance to a young person of a sibling does not necessarily relate to the amount of their life they have lived together, nor were the young people more interested in, for example, a full sibling than in a half-sibling.

Two young people who had experienced abuse before their entry into the care system were very concerned about younger children still in the family. They felt a continuing sense of responsibility, and that they had in some ways 'left them behind' to have similar experiences.

> I've definitely lost my mum and I've definitely lost John. By rights he's my half-brother. ... Contact will never be there, basically. ... And I do worry about him a hell of a lot ... because he's nearly the age that I was [when the abuse started] ... I haven't any pictures of him or anything.

> After I came into care I didn't see my brothers. So I asked to see my brothers and I saw them. And I wished they had gone into care as well, the way they were being treated. I've worried about them a lot, you know. I would have liked to see them under better conditions, but unfortunately it wasn't in my power to do anything.

Other young people were unhappy about either the level of contact they had with a sibling, or the arrangements they had to comply with in order to have contact. Organizational structures failed to take into account the importance or normality of the relationship: 'I've been told by a social worker that I have to give four weeks' notice for contact. That's a bloody month's notice. That's [to see] my own sister.'

One young woman had pictures of her brothers and sisters and one of her whole sibling group around her sitting room. The sibling group had come into care together in particularly traumatic circumstances in which she had tried to take care of her younger siblings. The group was split up when in care and she had lost contact with some of them. She showed the interviewer these pictures, expressing feelings both of missing them and of hope for a reunion as adults.

> That one [picture of sibling group] was a few years ago ... My brother Matthew, he's living in [nearby district], he's adopted there. Not five minutes away over the fields and we don't know where. ... I think I bumped into him once. Well, it looked just like him. I don't know whether it was or not. ... It might be hard, finding each other like ... I've got two sisters in [county some distance away] ... well, they were in children's homes down there. ... I don't know why they took them all the way down there.

One young woman, who had a younger sister in another foster placement and whose youngest sister had been placed for adoption, expressed feelings akin to those mothers of who have lost children through adoption. She herself recognized that the relationship was more like that of a parent and child, even though she was herself very young when she began taking responsibility for her sibling.

> I think ... just basically it's important because they're my sisters ... with Samantha, when we was living with our parents I looked after her most of the time ... so there was more of a bond there ... I have always looked after her like a daughter because when she was born I was six ... even though they're my sisters I feel more of a mother to them ... because I have been a mother to them.

A brother and sister who had come into and stayed together in the care system had wanted to be interviewed together; throughout the interview they checked with each other how they were describing what had happened to them, making sure that different as well as similar experiences were captured.

> I would say never split up the children who come into care. I think they get on more in life if they have each other ... as long as they have each other. ... And I told him [her brother], as soon as anyone does anything horrible to him, always come and tell me.

Where children and young people had maintained or renewed contact with brothers, sisters or other family members, this had given them an important sense of belonging and made a positive contribution to their sense of personal identity. They were positive and enthusiastic, like this young man trying to explain why contact with his nan and granddad was important to him:

> It's been going for about a year now [contact] and it's important because ... I didn't have, I didn't have any other relatives, you know? And then one day they just wrote me a letter, saying that they were sorry that they couldn't do anything about what my mum did and what my step-dad did ... and they apologized and they started visiting and then I started going at week-ends. And it was worrying at first and I was really nervous. And after that I just sat in my normal place. I was their grandson and that was it. And I've got lots of cousins and half-cousins and I got all the photos of them downstairs.

For black children and young people who experienced racism, contact with family members reflected the vital significance for them of having access to their cultural roots, in terms not merely of information but of validating their identity and having something to be proud of. For one young black woman who did not have contact with her birth family this sense of pride had come from a black residential worker: 'I'm black. I used to say I'm not black, I'm half caste ... she [residential worker] brought me to an understanding of what my colour is. Something to be proud of.'

Where direct contact with parents was concerned, young people often expressed more ambivalent or conflicting feelings, seemingly related to understanding the place of their parents in their personal histories, and the part a parent had played in what had happened to them. Few of the young people interviewed seemed to hold idealized views either of parents or of renewed contact leading to them living together again. Where young people were angry this tended not just to be focused on parents but to span their lives before, during and, sometimes, after care; more disquieting, perhaps, several of the young people interviewed appeared to be resigned to abusive and harmful experiences, before and during care. While they did not explicitly blame themselves, they did give the sense that this was all they could expect from life.

Their preoccupations were more with mothers than with fathers. Despite this, however, most of them felt that social workers should be in contact with and working with parents. They felt that there should be some exchange of information, even when young people did not want to have contact, or where contact was not possible for other reasons.

> Parents should still have information about their children, 'cos it's nice to know that they still want you and care for you even though you're not with them ... maybe a photo now and then, or a letter, even if social services have written it ... I shouldn't be on my own to sort it out now.

> I think it's always important for parents to have information even if it's not possible under no circumstances to have contact ... some parents don't necessarily care, some don't, some ain't in a mental state to know ... but there are those

who are, who do care and, although they've done wrong, they still care. I think it would solve a lot of problems in a lot of ways if there was more information and stuff.

After care

Many of the young people we spoke to were now living independently or were preparing for independence. Making this transition was not always easy, however much it had been longed for, and mixed experiences were accompanied by mixed feelings. There were concerns about unemployment, poverty and housing.

> I just wanted to finish school, get out of care and get on with my life.

> I left care and moved in with a friend and it didn't work out ... then I was homeless. I hated the hostel. It was all smackheads and prostitutes in there. You couldn't trust anyone. I was there for about three months in the hostel. Then I got this flat.

> I've had some bad periods – no money, no food.

It is not that young people leaving care necessarily live in worse conditions than other young people leaving home, although many of them do, but they are likely to be younger and less likely to have access to consistent and continuing emotional and material support. On occasions, leaving care has meant a shift from a very high level of supervision and control to negligible involvement, which has been experienced as an abandonment, the more poignant since it is unlikely to be the first.

> I was literally ditched and I never seen them [foster carers] again.

> I do get lonely sometimes, but I haven't got a choice. It's just the way it is.

Most of those who had left care mentioned not only poverty and poor housing, but also fears and concerns about other dimensions of their lives. Young women talked about the unsafe environments in which they had to live and their lack of control over this. Whether justified or not, they feared they would be the subject of crimes such as rape and murder. Several of the young women had experienced domestic violence as young adults.

I don't know anybody round here. I like the flat, but the people look dodgy. And it worries me because there's a lot of muggings and rapes. ... And like, to get on the bus, you've got to go through this big underpass.

It's not a very nice place ... lots of unemployment, drugs and everything you see around here is unbelievable.

Young black people, who had already talked about their experiences of racism within the care system, referred to the continuing impact this had on their lives. It is not suprising that, on leaving care, so many young people try to re-establish some contact with their immediate or extended family, however unsatisfactory relationships have been in the past, or to gravitate to the geographical area in which their family has lived (see Chapter 7 of the present volume).

Impact on relationships

The young people who had already left care talked about the impact they felt this had on the relationships which were significant to them and, in particular, who they felt they could trust. Most expressed a view that they had to rely on themselves and that in a crisis this is exactly what they would do.

I just try to sort things out myself.

I wouldn't want to talk to anybody about it. I have always relied on myself.

Where young people had a partner or were involved in a close relationship, they were aware that sometimes they were suspicious of this closeness and that they questioned their partner's motivation.

My boyfriend, when we were first going out being very affectionate and all that ... I was looking out to see if it was false or not ... looking for the let down, you know what I mean?

I'm not a very trusting person at all ... I find it difficult to trust anybody.

As when they were in care, young adults who had left care were faced with dilemmas about who to tell and what. Where young people had shared some of their experiences, often preceded by a degree of anguish, there had sometimes been negative consequences.

I don't like talking to strangers about my life story, cos it's none of their business. It doesn't matter how much I try to hide it, it'll always come up.

My ex couldn't understand about my past ... that affected him quite badly ... I don't understand why ... They [my current partner's family] are very strange ... it's like they want me to be part of a family and I can't be that ... I don't want to be that ... I'm basically very much of a loner.

You write this down, then. Love and trust, what do they mean? I don't know the meaning of those words.

Where young people had continued support from a social worker, this was valued; the point they made was that this could not compensate for the absence of other support systems. It could not compare with contact with and support from 'proper' family, friends or siblings.

Social workers and social working

Although most of the children and young people had negative views about the care system and expressed a desire to get away from being in care and the stigma associated with it, they were often remarkably positive about individual social workers:

It's fine ... I like Sarah. ... I have to admit ... I've liked most of my social workers.

They're all good in their own way ... she [current social worker] is fantastic. She understands me a lot and she listens to me, you know, she doesn't try to avoid me ... like some kids who haven't seen their social worker in years.

They wanted their social worker to stay in touch and to visit them, even if only occasionally, finding solace in talking to someone who knows something about their history. They particularly valued having had a worker for a period of time who had been through some ups and downs with them, and could be honest with them.

When she's here ... usually I sit down and just blurt and tell her everything.

I've never had a social worker for that long. I've always had a different one ... There was one ... where ... I had her for about two years and we started to bond a relationship.

My social workers have always been up front with me ... I need someone to be straight with me. Someone who is honest, you know? But not everyone is honest with you. They'll be nice to your face and then say all kind of things behind your back, and if someone is honest with you and you trust them, then that's OK.

It was important that the relationship had some elements of equality. Young people know that workers are workers, but they value the courtesies of friendship, including having some elements of choice and control in the relationship. If they have had a worker for a period of time they need recognition, as in a parent/child relationship, that they are older and that the nature of the relationship has correspondingly shifted: 'And the social worker comes round and that, but now it's more of an adult relationship.'

Loss, knowledge and identity

The children and young people we talked to had endured many separations and associated losses, not just of parents, but of the many other people significant to them, including siblings and other family members. When an individual becomes lost then so may knowledge, family, cultural, ethnic, linguistic and personal history. This can have a profound impact on personal development and cause considerable pain and worry for young people. They may be left with many unanswered questions and 'holes' in individual histories, with consequent implications for identity. Many of the children and young people talked about information that had been useful to them or information that they did not have which they felt they needed in order to make sense of their lives.

> You can't just leave them with a blank space. You've got to fill in the gaps so they understand ... So you've got to listen to what the child wants and do it and if you can't do it you've got to tell them why, explain to them so they can understand. Otherwise they get confused and then it gets worse for them as they grow up. ... You know, whether it's good or bad news, you've got to tell them. ... There may not be a good outcome, in my case there isn't, but I know why. ... And that's good enough, you know.

Discussion revealed that the need for and pursuit of information are closely linked to each child or young person's personal history, the emotional impact of this history and their individual identity. In this sense, there are no facts, information is not value-free, nor can it by sanitized. Any information given will be imbued with relevance and meaning by the young person, as it is viewed through the prism of their experiences, and may have far-reaching consequences for them. The meaning to the young person may be quite different from that accorded by others and this may change as the child moves through different developmental stages, not just in childhood but through adulthood also. What may seem to be of marginal significance to a worker dealing with the day-to-day demands of a heavy caseload may be of great value to a child – even a scrap of a handwriting or a blurred snapshot can mean the world to a child in care. It was sometimes disconcerting for the researchers to come across, say, a letter from a parent to a child, stuck in a file with holes punched in it and scribblings on the envelope; or to find through case recording that a mother had repeatedly approached a duty worker bringing information for her child and asking how she was getting on, to read that she had been 'fobbed off' and that it had not been made clear to her that the cards and small gifts she brought would never find their way to the intended recipient.

What became clear through the young people's accounts was that they wanted not just information but knowledge and understanding. They wanted to truly know, not just to know about. This struggle to translate information into knowledge and understanding, to resolve uncertainty and confusion, was evident. For example, many of the young people seemed unsure why they had entered care and had ambivalence or confusion which they thought a parent might have the answer to.

> I know all my life ... but sometimes it's difficult to understand why. You know, I can understand it, but ... I would love to ask my mother why she put me in care. ... I think I know why I came into care, it would have had something to do with her not being able to control me very much because I wasn't a very good behaved lad.

This young man talked about other aspects of his life in care, but kept coming back to what he described as a puzzle he needed to solve:

> I'll never forget her face ... Not since the time she put me in care. She never cried, she never cried ... I hope I find out off of her in future ... But if she did want to see me ... I think I would deny her existence because that's what she's done to me. And even though it's like paying someone back and I know you shouldn't, you know I've learnt not to do that. ... Well I think I will, I think I'll teach her what she's done to me.

A young woman described ambivalent feelings towards her mother, feeling that her mother may have lied to her or not told the truth, but also feeling that her mother might have had mental health problems.

> I see my mum, but I don't know my mum. I don't know nothing of my mum's background. I know my mother's ill but I don't know exactly what's wrong with her and nobody can tell me ... I needed to know if I had anything in common with my mum, I needed to know ... I couldn't really remember certain things ... I wanted to know how much of my mum I really take after. I do feel like she's lied a lot, but I don't know ... She's mentally not there, but I don't quite know why.

There were indications from the young people, as well as from file recordings and interviews with social workers, that life story work had been undertaken; some of the young people referred explicitly to their 'life story books'. In most cases this work had only partly met the expressed needs of the young people themselves. There may be several reasons for this. Information that young people wanted may not have been available to a worker not involved at the time when the young person came into care. Where information was available it was biased and incomplete. Whatever information was uncovered there remained the difficulty of interpreting and integrating it.

If an essential part of the forming of personal identity lies in the telling and retelling of the story with significant and known adults then it can be inferred that undertaking bursts of life story work related to major changes (either preceding or following them) may be of limited benefit. A much more concerted and sustained approach will need to be undertaken, where assessing and trying to meet a child's identity needs is a continuous part of work with them. For social workers, the responsibility for finding the answers with a young person may seem onerous, particularly if this may involve approaching parents or others who have become 'lost' and trying to re-establish a working relaionship with them. The reality is that (see Chapter 7 in the present volume), either before or after they leave care, young people are likely to try to make these contacts and find the answers themselves. Where contact occurs, both young people and their parents may be left to deal with the most painful and difficult emotions, and to rebuild relationships without the benefit of mediation or support.

Conclusions and implications for practice

> I don't expect no-one to hand me anything on a plate. I know whatever I get I have had to work for it and I have had to struggle for it.

The accounts of children and young people make evident the complex individual, familial, social and political influences which shape identity and which may have engendered for them painful experiences before, during and after care. In contending with these difficult circumstances, young people have often tried to use what power was available to them to resist the impact of this discrimination, abuse, rejection and oppression, having to make difficult calculations about who to trust and who to tell what. They have strengths and attributes which can be acknowledged, even while the experiences through which they acquired them are deplored. Like the young people interviewed by Butler and Williamson (1994) they 'often conveyed a tremendous resilience, almost against the odds, given the situations they were facing' (p.105).

For the worker faced with the task of building up a relationship with a child or young person, they must confront not just the understandable lack of trust and even hostility that such difficult experiences generate, but an organizational context which is often antithetical to this. Doing so requires not only theoretical knowledge, but imagination, ingenuity and considerable practice skill. It is daunting, but the critical hope that such an enterprise requires is also provided by the accounts of the young people. With perhaps surprising grace and no little generosity, they were able to separate workers' efforts from the system, to identify and appreciate the better qualities they have been on the receiving end of and to give to others the benefit of their experiences.

Through the accounts of their lives, the young people demonstrate how every aspect of their lived experience is an intrinsic part of the development of personal identity, with lifetime, and not just childhood, implications. Identity must, therefore, be a constant preoccupation, and not only considered at times of change or where a problem is perceived.

The organizational context of social work with children and families remains, and is likely to remain, difficult. In such circumstances longer-term considerations can be easily displaced by more immediate concerns. This occurs where child protection dominates both team and individual workloads. Even within an individual social worker's caseload this can happen, when work is reactive, rather than proactive, and where assumed placement stability can lead to a marginalization of the needs of children being looked after on a long-term basis.

There are messages within the 'lost' parents research, and other chapters in the present volume, about the need to keep parents involved in more than tokenistic ways from the point at which a child becomes looked after. Maintaining and promoting relationships with significant people may have important benefits for them after, as well as during, care. The complexities involved should not, of course, be underestimated, nor should the potential conflicts in working in partnership with children, young people and their carers at the same time as maintaining relationships with parents. However, the alternative is that young people and parents may be just left on their own to rebuild tenuous or damaged relationships, without the benefit of support, advice or mediation.

5 Partnership with parents of children in foster care or residential care
David Berridge

Social work could certainly do with some good 'spin doctors' and, if it had them, it is unlikely that they could come up with a better phrase than 'partnership with parents'. The term has political appeal, its radical edge suggesting the enhancement of the rights of the powerless and disadvantaged. It also has an attraction to professionals, who strongly endorse the notion of 'partnership', notwithstanding their frequent inability to deliver it. 'Partnership with parents' lends itself, too, to the treasurer or accountant, for whom 'offloading' may be a rather more attractive principle than the more benign 'sharing' or 'delegation'. There is also some alliteration thrown in to enhance its appeal.

It is no wonder, then, that 'partnership with parents' became a cornerstone of the Children Act 1989 and managed to convince audiences as wide-ranging as Prime Minister Margaret Thatcher, politicians on the Left and Right, researchers and the social work profession. There is something in it for everyone, which is a significant civil service achievement (Parton, 1991). Indeed, the public at large probably perceived that the 1989 Act was specifically brought forward as a response to the unsatisfactory situation in Cleveland in 1987, in which, over a six-month period, some 125 children were diagnosed as having been sexually abused by their parents, the majority of whom were removed from their homes (Butler-Sloss, 1988). While this crisis was an important element, the legislation's scope and objectives were much wider (Packman and Jordan, 1991).

This chapter, therefore, looks at partnership with birth parents of children looked after by local authorities and living in foster and residential homes. We consider the general consensus of professional opinion and recent research evidence. This is important because attitudes towards parental involvement have altered considerably over time. Until relatively recently, separation from parents was rigidly enforced and the family was felt to be a contaminating influence. In its most extreme form, many thousands of children brought up under the Poor Law in the 19th century were dispatched by the voluntary agencies to the outer reaches of the British Empire, especially Canada and Australia, a practice which continued after the introduction of the welfare state, ceasing only in 1967. While ostensibly concerned with children's welfare, it also conveniently remedied the desire for cheap labour in rapidly growing but sparsely populated countries.

More recent social policy, based on research evidence discussed below, instead emphasizes the benefits of continuity for separated children. Thus, under the Children Act 1989, birth parents share parental responsibility even where a care order is in force. The local authority generally now has to encourage contact between children and birth parents. Attempts should be made to enable children to live locally, in order to facilitate visiting as well as to maintain school arrangements. Attention should be paid to racial origin, culture, language and religion. Furthermore, parents should be involved in planning and decision-making processes. These are laudable goals, more easily articulated than enforced.

In discussing this area, we should not overlook the fact that partnership with parents covers a range of issues. It includes parents attending planning and review meetings. They should be given a say in decision making. Parents may visit children in foster and residential placements and children often spend time at home. Contact may also be indirect, such as by telephone and letter and by exchanging cards and gifts at important times of the year. In addition, children can benefit from having information about parents and themselves even in the absence of any other contacts (Masson et al., 1997). And though the particular focus here is on parents, other relatives such as siblings, grandparents, aunts and uncles can also be important figures, especially where parenting has been inconsistent or ineffective. Moreover, while they may be at the root of the family's problems, absent fathers often receive scant attention and can have some future potential for care or concern.

Different perspectives on partnership

At a general theoretical level, several authors have considered fundamentally the nature of relationships between parents, social workers and the state. For example, Tunnard (1991), in an often quoted passage, has emphasized the inherent power imbalance, but attempting to work in a spirit of genuine partnership can go some way to rectify this:

the essence of partnership is sharing. It is marked by respect for one another, role divisions, rights to information, accountability, competence and value accorded to individual input. In short, each partner is seen as having something to contribute, power is shared, decisions are made jointly, and roles are not only respected but are also backed by legal and moral rights. (Tunnard, 1991, p.27)

The idea of a 'ladder of participation' has also been developed, ranging from parents holding 'high power', such as by helping to design a service or being seen as partners, down to 'low power', where they are manipulated or merely placated. The full 'ladder' is as follows:

High power
    Helps design service
        Partner
            Participant
                Involved
                    Consulted
                        Informed
                            Placated
                                Manipulated
                                  Low power
(Thoburn *et al.*, 1995; Sinclair and Grimshaw, 1997, after Arnstein, 1971).

Another way of approaching partnership with parents is reflected in Fox Harding's (1991) useful contribution to different conceptual approaches to the problems of families of children in need. She identifies four broad lines of thinking. First, there is what she terms *laissez-faire and patriarchy*. In this, it is felt that the state should play as small a role as possible in family life and the authority of parents should not be undermined. It implies acceptance of the status quo and the traditional subservience of women and children to men. The approach demonstrates a mistrust of professionals.

Second, there is *state paternalism and child protection*. Here, in contrast, there is a much more interventionist approach towards children's welfare, and children rather than parents become more the focus of attention. Confidence exists in the state and professionals' ability to act in children's best interests. Alternative family placements, especially adoption, are highly valued and their problems minimized.

The third conceptual approach is defined as *defence of birth family and parents' rights*. This is much more sympathetic to the situation and needs of birth families and maintains that the biological link within families is extremely important and should be maintained wherever possible. A feature of this perspective is the reference to structural problems such as poverty, unemployment, class and racial inequalities. Thus: 'adequate support services should be provided and it is a contravention of civil liberties for children to be removed from poor families where the major factor determining the quality of care offered is a lack of resources' (Berridge, 1995, p.40).

The final perspective outlined by Fox Harding is *children's rights and child liberation*. This advocates a high degree of self-determination, with the state not intervening in children's lives purely on the basis of age. As childhood is a socially constructed concept, it is argued, children should be able to express their own preferences and not depend on adults to articulate these for them. In its purest form, at present, this perspective is unlikely to be reflected in law and social policy; however, it is now more commonly acknowledged, for example in the Children Act 1989 and (at the time of writing) in proposed changes to adoption law where young people aged 12 or over would have the right of veto, as they do under the Adoption (Scotland) Act 1978.

On the basis of Fox Harding's work, Jolly (1994) distinguished between four paradigms of parental contact which help us to clarify what is its purpose. First is the *rehabilitation* model in which the purpose of contact is primarily as a means to return. Second, there is the *continuity* model, in which the general emotional benefits of contact are valued irrespective of any specific objectives. Third, a *disruption* approach takes a less positive view and sees the dangers of contact for the maintenance of placements. Finally, there is the *deterrence* model, in which continuing contact is seen as discouraging to alternative substitute carers.

Clearly, Fox Harding's different perspectives have important implications for partnerships with parents. Parents would be 'highest up the ladder', using the idea outlined earlier, in the third perspective, the defence of birth family and parents' rights. It is important to appreciate that these are essentially philosophical or 'ideal type' positions rather than individually and separately determining policy. Indeed, various strands are likely to work in combination. However, it is interesting to observe that notions of partnership with parents are likely to be prominent in only one of the four positions. If partnership is absent, therefore – though we may personally object – an explanation is that it is inconsistent with the thinking and cultures that professionals, teams and agencies have developed. Seen in this way, its presence may be more exceptional than its absence.

Nonetheless, it is significant that the Children Act 1989 has been felt to be closest to the defence of birth families and parents' rights perspective, though there are also elements of children's rights (Fox Harding, 1991). The Act

> extends preventive powers; stipulates responsibility towards a wider group of 'children in need'; makes it a legal obligation for different agencies to collaborate

with social services; strengthens the legal rights of parents in conflict with social services; rationalises the court structure and tries to reduce delay; and enforces complaints procedures within local authorities. (Berridge, 1995, p.46)

Though others have reached a different conclusion (Parton, 1991), it is felt here that the Children Act 1989 was quite unlike any other major social policy legislation of the 1980s (Packman and Jordan, 1991; see also Dean, 1995, ch.9). It was child- and family-centred and did not set out to transfer major responsibility to parents and away from the state. Hence the concept of partnership with parents emerges as significant and the purpose of this book is to contribute to its development and implementation.

Professional and research approaches to partnership with parents of looked-after children

The idea of partnership has been emphasized in professional and research literature both since and prior to the 1989 legislation. Probably the best text to combine practice and theory in foster care dedicates a chapter to this topic (Triseliotis *et al.*, 1995). The importance of working with families becomes particularly important when working towards reunification, which will usually be the eventual goal in foster care. It is emphasized that partnership needs to be demonstrated *before* the child enters accommodation: collaborative working is more likely to happen if it is encouraged from the early stages, for example by carefully planning entry to foster care and involving parents and children in the selection of the placement and preparatory visits. Consultation with parents is important and misconceptions or feelings of guilt can be addressed.

Partnership with parents of children in residential care is equally important and a parallel text aimed at those working with the 150 000 children at any one time living away from home in groups – boarding schools, children's homes, hospitals and so on – also stressed this dimension (Kahan, 1994). Contact with family provides an important form of continuity and stability in children's lives although, as with foster care, its suitability, location and regularity should be carefully scrutinized by staff, especially where abuse has been a feature of the relationship. However, it is stressed that children should have a right not to see parents if they so wish. The organization of activities and physical space within residential homes is likely to influence parents' perceptions and habits.

Much of the evidence and enthusiasm for partnership with parents stemmed from the Department of Health research programme of the early

1980s. Four of the studies included in the overview report were designed to be complementary and focused on different aspects of decision making for children in need. The results were not encouraging. It was revealed that decisions were often made rapidly and in crisis; consequently, when it occurred, entry to foster and residential care was not well planned. There was too much arbitrariness about who entered public care and who did not. Compulsory powers, particularly emergency measures, were used too often and were often counterproductive. Family support services were underdeveloped. In addition, once children entered foster or residential care there was a tendency for social work attention to fade. Placement change was frequent. Discharge or remaining in care was usually not the result of social work planning, while reviews and case conferences were not central to the decision-making process. Perhaps most alarmingly, social workers lacked time and skills for direct work with children.

One of the studies, by the Dartington Social Research Unit, concentrated specifically on the family contact of children looked after by local authorities (Millham et al., 1986). Though the findings are now becoming rather dated, they are still felt to be very relevant and there is no evidence that the major problems identified have all been overcome. The study concluded that partnership with parents should remain a key element of the care process. There was no conflict between nurturing links with birth parents and the need for 'psychological parenting' with, say, adoptive or foster parents because, as the authors put it: 'Most who linger long in care are adolescents with well-forged family links; these they wish and ought to maintain, because it is to the family or its neighbourhood that young people will return' (DHSS, 1985, p.26). Continuity in family relationships was also important as placement changes were frequent and stability in care situations was therefore difficult to achieve.

A major problem identified by the Dartington study was that social workers attached insufficient importance to maintaining links between parents and child. Contacts were left to 'emerge' and were usually a *consequence* of other decisions rather than being a main priority themselves. As a result, three-quarters of the sample of 450 children experienced significant difficulties in keeping in contact with their parents. It was especially disconcerting as this was not what social workers intended. The researchers distinguished between, on the one hand, *specific* restrictions, where formal constraints on access were imposed, and *non-specific* restrictions caused by barriers in placements, such as distance or unwelcoming carers. Twice as many children were affected by the latter as by the former. It was also disquieting to note that social workers' visits to children, parents and carers declined over time and restrictions on contact were inadequately reviewed.

These poor practices have serious implications, since the researchers concluded that:

- if a child remains in local authority care for longer than five weeks, he or she has a very strong chance (two out of three cases) of still being in care two years later;
- the maintenance of close contact with their families is the best indicator that a child will leave local authority care rapidly;
- children and adolescents, even if their chances of returning home are slim, function better psychologically, socially and educationally if they remain in regular contact with their families (DHSS, 1985, p.26).

Recent evidence suggests that the Children Act 1989 has led to more effective involvement of parents in the planning process (Grimshaw and Sinclair, 1997a). Compared with the previous situation, parents were more likely to be consulted and asked their views prior to planning meetings; more parents attended reviews; and more received written copies of minutes; parental involvement in the meetings themselves was also more effective. Yet there remains much room for improvement. For example, parents were ill-informed both about how social services departments operate and about their rights when children are looked after. Participation of fathers was low.

Other important developments to enhance partnership with parents are occurring regarding family group conferences (Marsh and Crow, 1998), a forum which is convened by an independent coordinator, who arranges a meeting between extended family and professionals to consider the welfare of the child and agree suitable future plans. Family group conferences are popular in other countries, such as New Zealand and Canada, and are being developed more extensively in the United Kingdom. They typically follow four stages: preparation, information giving and private family time, followed by plan and agreement. If no consensus is reached then other approaches are pursued. Important elements of family group conferences are felt to be a clear, jargon-free style; a wide and inclusive concept of family; an independent coordinator; respect and support for family views wherever possible; focusing on family strengths and the negotiation of services; and maximum flexibility in operation within the basic model.

An evaluation of family group conferences in four social services departments, referred to above, produced very positive results. It was concluded that they succeeded in involving the extended family. Generally good outcomes were achieved and high levels of satisfaction were reported among participants. Indeed, of the 80 conferences studied in detail, 74 produced results that were felt by professionals and families alike as being in the best interests of children. Placements with extended family members seemed more likely to occur than in alternative approaches and professionals considered that adequate protection for children was provided.

Pleas to form stronger partnerships with parents of looked-after children need to take full account of the complexities of the situation. For example, a recent, albeit quite modest, study in one local authority suggested that a surprisingly high level of family support had been attempted prior to the young person's entry to accommodation (Berridge et al., forthcoming). This was contrary to expectations and not what other literature indicates (SSI, 1997). One of three sets of circumstances tended to apply where family support services were *not* forthcoming. First, a small number of complex cases were characterized by unsatisfactory liaison between education and social services departments. These typically involved school carers in special education. Second, there were cases in which offers of services had in fact been made but these were declined by parents: such families were often described as uncooperative, refused to accept responsibility for children's difficulties and sometimes had been aggressive towards professionals in the past. No doubt parents would say that social workers themselves were not always beyond reproach, although presumably they were not violent (Cleaver and Freeman, 1995). The final category where family support services were not delivered overlapped with the second and concerned cases in which abuse, usually sexual, had been alleged: young people had made claims which they refused to retract despite parental denials. Either parents had insisted they leave home or the young people refused to stay. Clearly, circumstances such as these contribute significant complications to forming partnerships with parents.

Another factor which introduces greater complexity to forming working relationships with parents stems from the changing nature of family life. Indeed, the families of looked-after children are often highly turbulent, with new members joining while others depart. Social workers, therefore, are not always relating to a stable entity and the numerous demands on their services may mean that they are not fully acquainted with the up-to-date composition of households. The Dartington study discussed earlier found that, within six months of entry to care, as many as almost half of their sample had experienced a major change in family structure (Millham et al., 1986).

Others have emphasized that it is not just the membership of families that influences partnerships but also their structure (Fisher et al., 1986). In particular, it is seldom acknowledged that a significant minority of children entering accommodation – which has been estimated at a quarter – in fact originates from *step-families*. Moreover, many of the lone-parent families include some degree of step-parenting, possibly on a part-time basis

(Loughran and Riches, 1996). The important point this raises is that there is a tendency in social work to explain problems that children in need experience exclusively in terms of individual pathology or dysfunctional families, rather than as sometimes an extension of stresses that *all* step-families experience. Issues relevant for social workers identified by researchers and practitioners in this area include prejudice and discrimination against step-families, the legal rights of step-parents, understanding the life cycle of families and step-families, differences in relationships within step-families, and transition points. The debate about protecting step-children is also complex and there is a need to be cautious about stereotypical images, for example of the step-father (Brodie and Berridge, 1996). The particular circumstances of step-families clearly have important implications for forming partnerships with parents. Almost all children entering care from step-families have another living parent whose relationship with them is tenuous at most.

Partnership and placements

Foster care

The social work research literature has highlighted specific partnership issues affecting the two main forms of placements of children looked after by local authorities – foster care and children's homes. We start with the former, which predominates numerically: the latest figures available at the time of writing indicate that, on any one day, there are some 33 200 children in England living with foster carers, compared with the rapidly decreasing number in children's homes – 4000 (DH, 1997). Naturally, many others join and leave over the course of a year.

Having been neglected over a long period, by policy makers, social workers and professionals alike, there are signs at long last that foster care is now getting the attention it both needs and deserves. The Department of Health has inspected local authorities' fostering services and the Association of Directors of Social Services (1997) and National Foster Care Association (1997) have produced important reports.

New research on foster care has also been commissioned. Two reviews of results from previous investigations help take stock of the existing state of knowledge (Berridge, 1997; Sellick and Thoburn, 1996), although the first of these concluded that there have been barely 13 research studies over the past 20 years with foster care as the main focus. Despite this, some useful messages emerge. For example, it is a relatively recent development that birth parents of children living in foster care should generally continue to fulfil a significant role. Indeed, a previous research review 20 years ago did not even include a section on parents (Prosser, 1978). The updated version (Berridge, 1997) remedies this deficiency and summarizes current awareness of parents' situation.

It is shown that parents tend to be highly disadvantaged both economically and socially, and this needs to be taken into account in forming relationships and expectations. Thus instability in relationships, violence, poverty and lack of social support are common. Higher than average levels of physical and psychiatric illness have been reported and mothers are frequently without partners. As a result of these experiences, parents are often angry, sad, guilty and ashamed, and these factors are insufficiently acknowledged by social workers (Palmer, 1992). Unless these experiences are addressed, parents' future propensity to care or keep in contact will be affected.

Evidence about the extent to which parents have been involved with their separated children makes depressing reading. We await research evidence about whether the Children Act 1989 has changed matters but, previously, parents frequently had little control over the selection of foster placements and were allowed or perhaps even encouraged to lose touch. One 1980s study of statutory reviews for children found that half of all the meetings for those in the sample living in foster care lasted less than 10 minutes and parents or foster carers were seldom present (Sinclair, 1984)!

Past foster care research has generally revealed low levels of contact between children and absent parents. Visiting foster (and residential) placements is stressful for parents and requires sophisticated social skills. Children can be understandably distressed on seeing parents and this can be misinterpreted as contact being harmful in the longer term. It has been suggested that this general absence of parental participation and partnership stems as much from social workers' attitudes and their desire to protect placements as from any animosity from foster carers themselves (Berridge and Cleaver, 1987). Parents often receive very little social work attention compared to foster households.

Despite these past practices, it is more commonly argued now that 'inclusive permanence' is often appropriate, with birth parents continuing to be involved (Thoburn *et al.*, 1986). The main factors affecting parental visiting have been said to be social worker encouragement, carers' attitude, parents' circumstances and perception of their importance in the child's life (Triseliotis, 1989). Young people's attitude and response can be added to this list.

Though beyond the scope of this chapter, it is interesting to observe that studies have generally concluded that fostering with relatives tends to be very successful (Sellick and Thoburn, 1996, section three). In view of this it is puzzling that it is infrequently used, although in the past children could have lived with relatives through different administrative arrangements.

In evaluating the outcomes of foster care, parental contact has emerged as the key variable which independently influences return home for children in *temporary, task-focused foster placements*. Since in any case some 90 per cent of all children looked after eventually return home, maintaining contact makes sense for the majority (Bullock et al., 1993b). It has been stressed that getting children safely back home works best where partnership develops before separation occurs: where there is a close working relationship between the child's social worker, parents, carers' link worker, carers and older children, and where contracts or agreements are in place (Sellick and Thoburn, 1996, section three).

The consensus of opinion is that maintaining contact with parents benefits also children living in *long-term placements*, including their emotional and social development (Millham et al., 1986, 1989). Some studies have found specifically that such links help avoid placement breakdowns, whereas others have concluded that it appears to make no difference. Research has not found that parental involvement jeopardizes placements. Obviously, contact should be carefully structured to ensure that it is part of a care plan and children's needs are being met.

Residential care

Many of the above points would apply also to residential care and, indeed, some of the major findings have been deduced from recent studies of children accommodated in a range of settings (DHSS, 1985). Yet it is interesting that, hitherto, studies of residential care specifically have had little to say about children's family relationships and this has been a significant gap in our knowledge (Bullock et al., 1993b). Researchers have too often accepted at face value residential establishments as closed social systems – which of course for much of history they have been – and not incorporated a wider perspective. Paradoxically, therefore, though there has been a fraction of the research in foster care that has taken place in residential settings, we actually know a great deal more about parental circumstances and barriers in the former than the latter.

However, this is in the process of changing and there are currently some 12 studies of residential care coming to fruition, two of which will be mentioned here. First, the present author and a colleague revisited a group of 12 residential institutions used by three local authorities that were first researched a decade previously (Berridge and Brodie, 1998). The backgrounds of residents revealed the high level of dislocation suggested earlier. However, an interesting finding was that the level of parental contact was surprisingly high. Excluding the group of disabled children living in homes for short breaks ('respite care'), half of residents were in regular contact with their parents on a weekly basis and another quarter saw them monthly. Fewer than one in 10 had no contact. This level of interaction is higher than in the initial study. Interestingly, levels of contact were also high in two of the 12 homes for younger children, the task of which was to prepare them for future permanent alternative family placements. The research concluded that this provided some evidence that the partnership philosophy of the Children Act 1989 was gaining acceptance.

Participant observation in the 12 homes revealed that staff were noticeably more positive about parents and family contact than their equivalents in the 1980s. Staff were generally well informed about the parental situation. Children and parents regularly spoke on the telephone and staff followed up calls with general inquiries about any news or worries. Yet, as in 1985, visits to the children's own homes were very rare, which contributed to the sense of *social disconnectedness* that was identified. Several factors could account for this. Most young people lived relatively close to home and could visit at short notice, sometimes on a daily basis. Child care responsibilities of lone parents looking after younger siblings also complicated matters. It is also not uncommon for adolescents in the company of peers to be sensitive to, or even embarrassed by, the presence of their parents. No doubt the experiences of conflict, abuse, rejection, family crisis and feelings of inadequacy also had a bearing on decisions to stay away.

A second, important, study from the current round of research investigated a wider group of 44 children's homes (Sinclair and Gibbs, 1998). Significantly, this makes the point that the previous literature is by no means unequivocal about the merits of parental involvement: adoption studies show considerable benefits; high-risk groups may be vulnerable; the advantages of parental contact may be questionable for groups of adolescent girls and delinquent boys; and for contact to occur between parent and offspring, it should be a joint decision. Masson and Harrison return to this discussion in the next chapter.

Young people interviewed in this study brought out the important distinction that, once they left 'care', they wanted continuing contact with parents but often did not want to return home to live. Interestingly, there was no pattern that those who had been away longer had fewer links. Contacts with siblings were especially missed: half of the interviewees would have liked to see more of at least one brother or sister. Other relatives and friends were also commonly missed. Encouragingly, the majority of respondents felt that social services had been helpful over contact. Families clearly emerge as important for these young people, a finding which is consistent with the other residential study discussed.

Conclusion

This chapter has covered a broad territory and we now pull together some final thoughts. We have seen that the topic of partnership with parents of looked-after children has recently generated much interest. This follows a long period in which such parents were seen as an undesirable and contaminating influence, so that children would be best served by having a fresh start. Professional attitudes, informed by research, are altering and the benefits of partnership and contact are more widely acknowledged.

Yet the actual evidence to date about the extent of parental involvement has been discouraging, in both foster and residential care. Most worrying, perhaps, is the finding that parents have been generally excluded even when social workers stated that this was not their intention. Social work and placement processes erected insurmountable barriers. Most children eventually return home, or adolescents negotiate acceptable relationships, and these enforced divisions are illogical. However, this does not mean of course that contact should not be planned and structured, and the safety of the young remains paramount.

But there are some encouraging signs that attitudes to birth parents in recent years may have become more welcoming, encouraged by legislation and other policy initiatives. This is a key issue and we should be confident about the reliability of evidence on which policy and practice are based. Quinton *et al.* (1997) issued a timely reminder that more robust research is needed on this topic before we can be certain about the benefits of different forms of contact for specific groups of children in particular circumstances. Not all practitioners are convinced by the scientific method. We should also not dismiss more qualitative approaches in which participants' own views and experiences are central. Moreover, researchers do not have a monopoly of expertise and an 'evidence-based' approach relies also on the practice wisdom of experienced social workers who have dealt previously with many similar situations (Schšn, 1983).

The plea from researchers for more research is predictable and it would be a brave, and unpopular, academic who argued for fewer studies and reduced research funding. However, on this occasion, the concern for better evidence is justified and we need to be more reliably informed. Social science can confront few more important topics than the care and protection of deprived and separated children and the optimal roles of parents and the state.

6 Rebuilding partnerships with parents of looked-after children

Judith Masson and Christine Harrison

The purpose of this chapter is to examine issues relating to the loss of links between children, their parents and the social services department that is looking after them. The rationales for, and benefits to children and young people of, working in partnership with parents is explored throughout this volume. They apply equally where there is currently no working relationship between a child's social worker and his or her parents, where parents are 'lost'. Trying to establish or re-establish working partnerships between parents and social workers, the focus of the 'lost' parents research (Masson et al., 1997), raises dilemmas and poses challenges which operate as barriers to social workers and their managers taking on this work. The findings of the study provide a basis for understanding these barriers to partnership and how they may be overcome. This leads to a reflection on the nature and meaning of outcomes in child care work. The complexity of this work cannot be underestimated; re-establishing relationships necessarily affects all aspects of a child's life and care arrangements. Forethought is essential so that social worker, carer and child can plan and prepare for the possibilities which may emerge.

Losing parents

Although losing parents is a recurrent theme in literature, it has not been regarded as a major issue in child care in the United Kingdom. Parental loss is often portrayed as transient, as when parents and children become separated in a crowd, or associated with the death of parents before their children reach adulthood, an event which has become mercifully rare in the Western world in the 20th century. The loss in death is complete; nothing can be done: a view which, if followed in other cases of parental loss, legitimates inaction. Relationship breakdown now means losing parents for up to half the children who experience it (Richards, 1996) but the importance of this as a life event remains contested (Rodgers and Pryor, 1998). Both parents with care and absent parents can reassure themselves that their child maintains important family bonds. However, in countries ravaged by war and blighted by natural catastrophes and famine, parental loss still occurs; parents and children lose each other in the course of the mass migration of refugees. In such circumstances, separation can become parental loss which deprives a child of his or her identity. Too young to know or remember names and changing rapidly as they develop, become sick or recover from illness, children may rapidly lose the ability to recognize their parents. Similarly, parents cannot recognize their children. Even if children can be located, care by strangers may mean they learn to communicate only in a language unknown to their parents. Consequently, it is considered essential for work to identify the families of separated refugee children to be undertaken without delay (United Nations High Commissioner for Refugees, 1994).

Where children are in public care there is a broad spectrum of parental loss, much resembling the fundamental form of loss occurring at times of disaster but happening slowly, insidiously and individually, rather than during the turmoil of mass flight. Although parents are lost, it is perhaps more accurate to regard them as displaced, misplaced or marginalized. Parents are lost to children simply through the fact that there is no contact between them. Lack of contact may result from or be confirmed by formal termination of contact which was estimated in the 1980s to have occurred to 18 000 children in the care system at any one time (Millham *et al.*, 1989, p.4). Since the implementation of the Children Act 1989, orders for refusal of contact have been made for about 1000 children each year, but far more children lose contact because of a plethora of non-specific barriers such as those Millham and colleagues identified. Where parents are not in contact with their children they are also unlikely to be in touch with their children's social worker (Bilson and Barker, 1995). Work with parents diminishes rapidly where rehabilitation is not part of the plan (Millham *et al.*, 1986); plans relating to contact are frequently not implemented (Grimshaw and Sinclair, 1997a). The current focus on task-centred work with children serves to remove attention further from parents. Although emphasis is placed on involving parents in reviews, the necessary positive support to facilitate and encourage parental involvement is not always given (Grimshaw and Sinclair, 1997a).

Frequent changes of personnel in social services departments mean that parents not in regular contact with their children are often unknown to the child's social worker. Although the parent's whereabouts may be well known, the parent as a person is lost both to the social worker and to the child. This was the case for two-thirds of the fathers and a quarter of the mothers in the 'lost' parents study. Where he or she has not met the parents, the social worker only has the picture of them presented in the case file, often created at the time when the child entered the care system and reflecting the needs of the system to establish the parents' inability to care. In the study, social workers' views of parents were more likely to be more positive after they had met them.

More lost still are the parents whose whereabouts are unknown to social services. However, many of these parents can be located (see Chapter 10 in the present volume) and others may reappear unexpectedly. In the study, a third of the 'lost' mothers and a sixth of the 'lost' fathers took the initiative by contacting social services after a period of absence. Case files also recorded similar calls or visits in the past by many of the 'lost' parents. Parents may be unaware that social services is interested in their whereabouts, or is unaware of their address. Where parents are in frequent contact with the state through the benefits system, the NHS, housing authorities and Council Tax collection, the idea that they are 'lost' can seem inconceivable.

In addition there are fathers whose identity is not known to social services; this was the case for seven of the 54 fathers in the study. There were three main reasons for this. A transitory relationship between the mother and the father might leave the mother without a clear idea about the father's identity, and also leave the man unaware that he had become a father. Even where a woman knows the father, she cannot have his name entered on the child's birth certificate without his agreement or a court order. Consequently, there is no official record of the father's name. Some of these fathers also deny paternity. Women may also keep the child's father's identity a secret because of threats or fear of violence; domestic violence is a common feature in the lives of women whose children enter public care (Hunt and Macleod, 1998; Mullender, 1996). It also appeared that when the children in the study came to public care from their lone mothers, social workers had been less concerned to record details about their fathers, sometimes believing that his identity was unknown (with all that that suggested about the mother's character) even though it was recorded on the birth certificate.

Where parents are lost, children have frequently lost contact with other family members, including brothers and sisters who may remain at home with the parents, be placed separately in foster care or live with relatives (Who Cares? Trust, 1993). Black children may also lose contact with their black communities (Rowe *et al.*, 1989; Barn, 1993). In some cases the loss of links with siblings was more keenly felt than those with parents. Quite young children expressed concern about younger siblings, now placed for adoption, whom they had cared for, and for those still living at home whom they felt to be in danger. Young children were powerless themselves to maintain the links that kept kinship ties alive, although some were fortunate to have older siblings or other relatives who tried to do this.

Becoming lost

Just over half of the children and young people in the study had lost contact with a parent, most commonly with their father, *before* they entered public care. Loss of contact while children were *in care* affected more mothers and in consequence most of the children in the study had no contact with either of their parents.

Becoming lost does not occur in a vacuum, and there are many contributory factors to this process. Although often consigned to the history of the case, they are likely to be of central significance for social workers trying to restore working relationships, as they constitute considerable barriers which current social workers will need to take into account and attempt to overcome. Amongst the most powerful are those which constitute dominant ideas, beliefs and values which have shaped policy and practice in child care.

Perspectives on parenting

Although there has been increased recognition of the diversity in family forms, dominant legal and social constructions of parenthood in this society tend to construe it as an exclusive set of responsibilities, in comparison with other societies where the tasks, roles and responsibilities associated with caring for children are more broadly distributed and undertaken (Wozniak, 1993; Crosskill, 1994). As Ryburn (1994) has argued, 'a family can suffer few more public judgements of social failure than to have a child compulsorily removed from its care' (p.159). It is likely that for some parents and families a voluntary arrangement or the retention of a child in accommodation or care is little less stigmatizing or personally wounding. The consequences of having failed to discharge parental responsibilities are costly and, certainly in the past, loss of custody meant playing no further part in a child's life and development. Both mothers and fathers may have found themselves in this position, although the consequences of having failed as a parent have adhesive qualities more likely to stick to women than to men. Negative judgments about having failed as a parent combine with the absence of a recognized role for parents who may care about, but who are not caring for, their child. This is particularly the case if the child is in state care.

> Our long-standing traditions of child rescue have meant that first Children's Departments and then Social Services Departments have tended to marginalize parents even when acting benevolently towards them. Strong emphasis on the welfare of the child often pushed parents' needs and wishes into the background and departments have assumed full control of children admitted to their care and assumed they knew best. (DH, 1991a, p.45)

Or, in one parent's words: 'It makes me think, what can you do if you do not see them? When they are having all their needs met by other people and by a large organization which has plenty of money. I am not sure what else you can do for them apart from letters and presents.'

The file histories of children in the study indicated that social services departments had employed harsh measures against specific sections of the population. Parents' own accounts of their actions were largely absent, having been either omitted from social work records or displaced in favour of competing explanations that have been elevated to the level of expertise (Coombe and Little, 1986). These 'expert' opinions have frequently been employed as the yardstick with which to measure and test parental commitment. The influence of the tradition of child rescue was clearly documented. There was little evidence, for example, of mothers being helped to improve their circumstances so that children could return; rather, their commitment to their children was judged in terms of their perceived ability to rebuild homes and relationships unaided. Interviews with current social workers demonstrated their awareness that a substantial number of the children's parents became lost in a period when social work practice was informed by a very different value base. These workers often felt there was evidence of poor or even discriminatory practice, and that, given a different kind of intervention, a child would not have entered the care system or stayed in care. Even where workers considered that there had been no alternative to a child or young person being looked after, they were aware, from the case records, that parents, particularly mothers, had been treated in oppressive ways.

Mothers and fathers

The Children Act 1989 uses the term 'parent' and makes no distinction between mothers and fathers with parental responsibility. In reality, parental roles are largely based on a gendered division of labour, and when the elements of parental responsibility are disaggregated into rights, duties, powers and responsibilities it becomes clear that 'parents' are also different and unequal. Women, as primary carers, are expected to ensure that children are cared for and protected in terms of their developmental needs, social, emotional and physical. These expectations, combined with assumptions about a mother's sexuality and marital status, are applied whatever the woman's circumstances. The labour of caring for children often consists of daily routines, in an isolated environment and within a set of social relations, which frequently render women powerless. This has particular implications for black mothers, lesbian mothers, and lone mothers. Intrahousehold poverty (Pahl, 1989), racism, domestic violence (Dobash and Dobash, 1992; Mullender and Morley, 1994; Mullender, 1996) and poor physical and emotional health (Bernard 1973; Graham, 1994) are prominent features in the lives of many women and children.

The early records of cases in the study were primarily about women, and demonstrated how the individualized nature of social work intervention has tended to dislocate motherhood, in particular, from its operational moorings. Neglect is divorced from women's poverty, failure to protect from their powerlessness, and taking more of the responsibility has meant taking more of the blame. Both at the time of the initial intervention and at later stages, case records indicated that parental actions were heavily interpreted according to dominant and Eurocentric familial ideologies. Case examples demonstrated the contradictions between what is expected of parents and the realities of women's lives which were crucial in terms of care for children. The processes of intervention not only failed to resolve these contradictions but often compounded them, as researchers in other fields of child care have found (Hooper, 1992; Milner, 1993; Booth and Booth, 1994; Farmer and Owen, 1995; Mullender, 1996; Mullins, 1997).

At the time when their child came into care, half of the mothers in the study were known to have been in poor health, over two-thirds were facing problems of poverty, poor housing or social isolation, and a quarter were the subject of domestic violence. Where women had male partners, many were undermined rather than supported, through denial of resources or male violence. This was a major factor in eroding mothers' capacity to care and separating them from their children. Where women had experienced mental health problems, this may not only have been the reason for a child's removal but also used to justify the termination of contact.

Andrea

Andrea's mother, Mrs Earle, was subjected to domestic violence and, in an attempt to protect herself and Andrea, she applied for an injunction to exclude her partner from her home. In court, Andrea's mother found that, rather than being seen as protecting her child, she was viewed as having failed to protect Andrea, who was committed to the care of the local authority. Although the care order was overturned on appeal, Andrea did not return home; her mother's confidence and ability to care for her had been undermined by her experiences at the hands of both her partner and the agencies to which she turned for help.

Because of this preoccupation with women, men were largely written out of social work scripts; there was information about less than half of the fathers involved. This routine omission of fathers continues (Sinclair and Grimshaw, 1997). The responsibilities of fathers were constructed in strikingly different ways from those of mothers, which effectively prevented a full appraisal of the father's potential for involvement in a child's life. Where information was available, it indicated that a third were homeless and a quarter in poor health, while a third had been accused or convicted of offences which had implications for their care of children (Schedule 1 offences). The active or passive exclusion of fathers from files may have quite divergent consequences. On the one hand, it obscured their responsibility for abuse, either of the child's mother or of the child. On the other, it meant that, for children and young people who wanted information about or contact with their father, this was precluded.

Substitute family care

The familial ideology against which birth parents, particularly mothers, are measured influences the provision of substitute family care. Judgments about the culpability or inadequacy of parents sit alongside assumptions that foster carers are by definition more adequate parents. The concept of the sharing of parental responsibility (whether through involving, consulting or informing) has to develop within a set of fundamentally unequal relationships – not just between workers and parents, but between carers and parents. The guilt and depression associated with 'filial deprivation' (Jenkins and Norman, 1972) generates considerable difficulties for parents in maintaining contact. It becomes even more difficult for parents to maintain contact where their involvement is viewed negatively or as a destabilizing influence. Nevertheless, it was apparent from the case files that some of the 'lost' parents had continued to enquire about their children for a considerable period of time after they ceased to have the care of their children. These enquiries demonstrated that they continued to care about their children. Where these overtures were not viewed positively, parents were discouraged and eventually stopped coming forward.

The histories of children in the study indicated that a key factor in the losing of parents lay in social workers' overriding belief, or perhaps more accurately fear, that parental involvement would threaten placement stability. Precedence was readily given to the views of carers who, whether they were aware of it or not, had considerable power in relation to social workers, children and parents. There were many examples in the study of support being provided for carers which had not been made available to parents, and of strenuous efforts to maintain foster placements even where the social worker explicitly acknowledged their inadequacy. Symptoms of instability in placements also provided the rationale for the formal termination of contact or for informal discouragement of parental involvement. As well as evidence in files that some parents had tried against the odds to keep in touch, there was evidence that, where parents had given up, this was viewed with relief by carers and social workers.

The influence of law

The law has also played a part in the loss of the parents of children in the public care. Parents are required under the Arrangements for Placement of Children Regulations 1991 to keep the social services department informed of their address. Prior to the introduction of the Children Act 1989, failure to do so was a criminal offence and was grounds, statutory abandonment, for the local authority to pass a resolution removing parental rights. Thus the law has expressly placed the responsibility to remain in touch on parents. Where entry to the care system was through court proceedings, the use of emergency procedures without prior notification contributed to parents becoming lost. The trauma of the event and its effect on self-image and self-esteem was very difficult for parents to overcome. Moreover, the exclusion of parents from full participation in care proceedings which occurred before 1988 encouraged parents to give up at this point. The state appeared to take no responsibility for involving parents. For example, in one case in the study the mother had apparently vanished shortly after her children had been removed because of neglect. It later transpired that she had been in a serious road accident and had been in hospital throughout the proceedings. The current practice of detailed investigations by a guardian ad litem and representation in proceedings should minimize the risk of parents becoming lost through exclusion from proceedings. Nevertheless, it remains true that there is frequently little consultation and active involvement of parents in planning their child's care during the proceedings (Freeman and Hunt, 1998). Also relationships between parents and the social worker may be so damaged by the court process, particularly the presentation of evidence against the parents, that a new worker is required if a working relationship is to be established with the parents (Farmer and Owen, 1995). The position of parents may be no better where social services arrange the child's admission to accommodation rather than take care proceedings. The parent may have no access to support or advocacy, and experience the relationship with social services as manipulative or disempowering. There were examples of this in the study; the Bristol researchers also found that parents felt pressured into agreeing to accommodation in some cases where proceedings were subsequently brought (Freeman and Hunt, 1998; Hunt and Macleod, 1998).

Termination of contact is a very obvious way in which legal measures may lead to a parent losing touch with their child. Safeguards in the form of clear processes and review by the courts were introduced in 1984, but the prior consent of the courts only became a requirement for the termination of contact in 1991, with the implementation of the Children Act. In practice, legal measures appear to have provided little protection for relationships with parents. Courts have viewed contact as important primarily in cases where it may lead to rehabilitation, and otherwise see it as a barrier to permanent placement (Masson, 1990; Jolly, 1994). They have tended to defer to the views of the local authority (Masson, 1997) and, along with the Legal Aid Board, limited parents' opportunities to have decisions about contact reconsidered in the face of opposition by the local authority. The duty in the Children Act to promote contact is always subject to interpretation from the ideological perspectives outlined above. Thus it becomes only too easy to say that it is not 'reasonably practicable or consistent with the child's welfare' to promote contact at a particular stage of a child's life.

Erosion of contact continues to occur through non-specific barriers such as placing children in foster homes where parents do not have easy access or are not welcome. Parents find it exceptionally difficult to visit their children in the care of other parents, an event which clearly serves to reinforce their own feelings of inadequacy. Difficulties are exacerbated where parents have not been introduced to carers (Family Rights Group, 1986, p.56). The shortage of foster homes compounds these problems and may strengthen the position of foster carers who are unwilling to allow contact to take place at their home. This too was a factor in the loss of contact for some parents in the study and, in relation to these and other carers, made re-establishing parental contact more difficult subsequently. Recently, guidance has been given to the courts that orders should not be made for contact to take place in the foster carer's home unless the court is satisfied that these carers have given 'informed consent to the specific order sought'

(Children Act Advisory Committee, 1997, p.31). This weights the balance further against parental contact.

Organizational factors

Parents can become lost relatively quickly if the impression is given that they have little contribution to make towards their children's well-being and if positive steps are not taken to encourage them to remain involved. Parents may need the help of social workers in finding a meaningful role for themselves. The organization and management of social work can undermine parents' and social workers' attempts to retain a working relationship (see Chapter 9 in the present volume). Staff changes, particularly when the departure of the social worker responsible for a child is followed by a period when the case is unallocated, end relationships which parents may have found helpful. While cases are unallocated there is no one for the parent to contact, or at least no one for the duty worker to pass requests to and get action from. Where new social workers were unknown to parents, it was more difficult for parents to contact them, particularly if they did not even know their name. The new social workers faced the task of getting to grips with a whole caseload and sometimes a considerable backlog of work, often without adequate records of past work. Faced with such difficulties, without a clear idea about what to do, with little encouragement in agencies for proactive work in such circumstances, and particularly where parents were not readily located, it was not surprising that social workers did not take steps to try and introduce themselves to the parents of children in care. With the passage of time and each successive change of social worker, the parent became more distanced from the agency and consequently from their child.

Gaps in files were a major feature in the cases in the study, arising from periods of non-allocation, social work strikes and sometimes allocation to workers who, without adequate supervision, failed to undertake or to record work with a child or family. That these failings are not simply a matter of history is clear from the reports of the Social Services Inspectorate (Laming, 1998; Select Committee on Health, 1998). Poor file recording left later workers unaware of issues in the parents' background, of action that had been taken and the circumstances through which children entered or remained in the care system. It also made it more difficult for the current worker to know whether and how to respond to current issues. It deprived children and workers of information, such as a father's full name or a parent's or grandparent's address which would be vital in the search for parents. Again there were examples of this in the study, with house numbers wrongly noted (one parent's address had to be correctly identified by the researcher using the electoral roll) and the telephone number of a found parent being mislaid (fortunately, she rang again).

The prioritization of child protection within social work with children has been recognized as drawing attention and resources away from family support (Dartington Social Research Unit, 1995; Stevenson, 1992; DH, 1991a). Similarly, child protection eclipses longer-term work with children who are looked after and with their families, particularly where there is no ready solution to the issues and difficulties raised. There has been insufficient attention paid to the health and educational well-being of children in long-term care (Audit Commission, 1994; Select Committee on Health, 1998; Fletcher-Campbell, 1997; Sinclair, 1998). Similarly, issues relating to identity and individual and family history have been left on the back burner. Workers' focus has turned to these issues only when they have been a problem. Work with children in placements thought to be stable has largely been displaced by the demands of crises.

Managers share the responsibility with social workers for the losing of parents in these ways. The culture of the department is the responsibility of managers, and of elected members who have the ultimate responsibility for policy and to ensure the quality and effectiveness of services. Lack of systems and of supervision are important, but so is the allocation of resources in ways which deny workers the time to undertake the complex work necessary to find and involve parents before they become too lost.

The impact of loss

In addition to the impact on identity discussed by Harrison in Chapter 4 of this volume, the fact that parents are lost, to whatever degree, makes work to establish partnerships more difficult. There were multiple and interlinked consequences for the children and parents of their loss of each other. Their lives developed in separate directions, leaving behind points of reference. Parents found it difficult to relate to the different person their child had become. Getting older, living in a different area and within a different milieu, particularly for black children placed transracially, served to distance children from their parents. Parents' lack of knowledge and understanding sometimes became obvious through the letters and presents they sent in an attempt to remain in touch with their children or as a prelude to renewing contact. For example, the dress one mother sent for her daughter was far too small, another sent pretty underwear for a daughter who had little interest in such things. Gifts and letters were always open to scrutiny and interpretation; parents might easily be criticized for writing too much or too little, or for spending too much or not enough. Failed gifts, like those above, served to underline, for parents and for social workers, the parents' presumed inadequacy in their role. Children too found it hard to accommodate their parents' current lives with their memories, experiences and understanding of their past life together. Where parents were coping well with other children, their own apparent rejection was magnified, but parents in difficulty were a source of worry rather than of comfort.

These deficits are not just gaps in knowledge, but have an impact on both parents' and children's sense of self. Young people felt puzzled and incomplete because of the missing links with family, friends and culture. Parents were anxious about what had become of their children, and concerned about children being left without an understanding of their histories. Our research leads us to believe that the restlessness which those brought up in care experience relates to family loss as well as the quality of substitute care. The experiences of those who have been adopted (Triseliotis, 1973; Haimes and Timms, 1985) and of parents who lost a child to adoption (Howe et al., 1992; Mullender and Kearn, 1997) tend to confirm these views.

Barriers to partnership

All the circumstances and beliefs outlined above constitute barriers to rebuilding partnerships; others related to the dominance of the status quo, the philosophy of rescue, the emphasis on rehabilitation in work linked to contact or partnership, and the particular interpretation applied to children's rights. Barriers were constituted of things which had to be done before contact with parents could be attempted, such as tracing their whereabouts, attitudes that challenged the legitimacy or appropriateness of such work, and the difficulty of undertaking some of the work which would be required. For example, the possibility of communication with parents could place the social worker in the unenviable position of having to disclose that their child, who had been removed because of the quality of parental care or even for less compelling reasons, had been abused while in care. If parents were contacted, this information had to be conveyed to them; failure to do so would jeopardize whatever relationship had been established in ignorance of this. Although barriers operated individually and together to deter social workers from taking the steps necessary to work towards partnerships with parents, none were insuperable. No direct relationship was observed in the study between the existence of barriers, or any particular barriers, and the lack of any attempts to create links to parents.

Maintaining the status quo

The status quo, the prevailing situation, has been identified as the key factor in determining the outcome of court decisions about children's residence in disputes within families (Cretney and Masson, 1997, p.728). In these cases, where the basis for the decision is the paramountcy of the child's welfare, maintaining the current situation is seen to be synonymous with what is best for the child. What is known and can be seen to be working has the attraction of some certainty where alternatives can only be based on predictions of what might be. The reality of any untried alternative may not live up to expectations; consequently, this has to appear far better if it is to be chosen in preference to the status quo. The emphasis on the status quo develops from and is reinforced by the wide acceptance of particular theories in child development. These stress the child's need for security and continuity, identifying change, particularly interruption of relationships between children and those caring for them, as especially damaging (Goldstein et al., 1973). Where children's lives have already been disrupted by repeated changes, continuity is seen as more important and thus changes as even riskier.

From a social work management perspective, the status quo has further attractions where carers receive little support when they appear to be coping and social work resources are applied chiefly to new cases, or to crises in existing ones. Anything which might destabilize the arrangements may be unwelcome because it is likely to increase demands on the service. In such a case, resources may be deployed for maintaining a placement, known to be unsatisfactory, where alternatives will be exceptionally difficult to find. Similarly, a long-term carer's objection to work with a child's family has particular weight if there are suggestions that a change of placement might result from involving parents. Within this context, a social worker who wishes to search for and attempt to contact family members for a child being looked after long-term may not receive support or encouragement for this.

For foster carers the possibility of parental involvement is sometimes an unexpected and unwelcome intrusion. Lack of support from social services has often left foster carers to cope with many difficulties, some relating to the child's anxiety from lack of understanding of their situation and knowledge of their family. Without social services' involvement foster carers can lose touch with their role as carers on behalf of the state, denying the importance that parents and birth families have for those in their care. These experiences and attitudes make foster carers barriers to partnership with parents. In the study, this occurred in its most extreme form for two children who had been led by their foster carers to believe that they were their own children. Even without such deception, where the placement has been long-standing and alternatives are not readily available, the emphasis on the status quo makes the foster carers' wishes paramount, shaping both the decision to try to involve parents and the form of involvement they are offered. For example, when Andrea Earle's social worker involved her parents after a long period during which their existence had been ignored, reviews had to be moved from the foster home because the carers would not agree to Mr and Mrs Earle entering their house. The review took place at Andrea's school, but the foster carers refused to attend because the parents were present.

The philosophy of care

The advantages of the current arrangements may be magnified by the belief that the parents' way of caring for the child has been damaging. The idea that social services, and before them charitable bodies, are engaged in rescuing children from inadequate homes has been a dominant perspective in child welfare thinking for over a century (Hendrick, 1994, p.79; Fox Harding, 1991; Packman, 1975). Until recently, little attention has been given to the quality of care provided by the state in place of parents, suggesting that any comparisons were simply not relevant: state care was obviously better. In this context, the care of foster carers who have been selected and approved by the social services department appears necessarily superior to that of parents who have been unable to care for the child. The parents' failings may be emphasized by the fact that the child's admission was the result of court proceedings approving the local authority's views, and by the instrumental nature of recordings at entry.

Failure in the past to recognize the existence of, or accord significance to, difficulties in parenting of factors such as domestic violence and mental ill-health reflects the view that there was no alternative to the child's removal. But a re-evaluation does not necessarily provide an impetus for involving parents. Indeed, the feeling that they have been poorly served by the agency may itself present a further barrier to their being reinvolved by the worker. It may also make parents reluctant to respond to any overtures.

The twin notions that parents were bad and that state care is better together create a powerful barrier to seeking out 'lost' parents and trying to work with them. Taking account of parents' views may be seen as diluting or undermining the approach of professionals; where parents' own experience as carers is regarded negatively, their claim to have a valid opinion appears weaker still.

Partnership, contact and rehabilitation

The conflating of partnership and contact was a further barrier which had to be overcome if efforts were to be made to find parents. If partnership could only exist where parents were in contact with their children then attempts to create it appeared pointless where contact seemed inappropriate. There were some children and young people for whom, at least initially, contact with their family was ruled out. Concerns here related to previous parental failure to remain in touch or to other negative perceptions of the family, to carers' anxiety about or rejection of family involvement, to young people's expressed preferences, and to emotional or developmental conditions that indicated that children might have difficulty in understanding that they had another family. Moreover, if contact was to result from attempts to work with parents it could present a long-term commitment of social services resources to maintaining relationships, work which has not, at least in the recent past, been highly valued.

Research in the 1980s identified the importance of contact between children in the public care and their families to the children's return home (Millham et al., 1986; Bullock et al., 1993a; Berridge, Chapter 5 of the present volume). Contact became identified with rehabilitation and little attention was given to promoting contact where the plan was for the child to remain in care permanently, or to be placed for adoption (Masson, 1990, 1997). Indeed, such plans became a major justification for formal termination of contact (Millham et al., 1989, p.91).

Where the issue is reinvolvement of the parents of a child looked after long-term, the linking of contact with rehabilitation also presents an obstacle to any approach to the parent. Both the length of time the children and young people in the study had spent in state care and their experiences there strongly suggested that rehabilitation to a parent was an extremely unlikely prospect (Farmer and Parker, 1991) and thus a major rationale for contact did not apply. Contact might destabilize the current arrangements but would not necessarily provide a better placement. The link between contact and rehabilitation could also impinge on parents, affecting their approach to the social worker, and ultimately the social worker's response. Where contact seemed to work smoothly, some parents wanted it to progress to rehabilitation; others were concerned that social services wanted them to provide a home for their child and that successful contact might lead to pressure on them to take on a role, full-time carer to their child, that they felt was beyond them. The fears of both parents and social workers about contact leading to rehabilitation obstructed good communication between them. Social workers were anxious if parents offered too much; parents were concerned about whether or not to offer more. In addition, the checks required by the regulations (Placement with Parents etc Regulations 1991) delayed progress from meetings to longer stays, were further work for social workers, and were experienced as intrusive and demeaning by parents and relatives. Refusal to cooperate with them, for example to consent to a police records check, was a very real barrier to the development of contact because it precluded the child from staying for any period in excess of 24 hours.

Children's rights

Children's rights could be either a barrier or an impetus to trying to contact parents; depending on the views they expressed and the social worker's response to them. Some young people were very clear about wanting to see, or not to see, their parents; amongst these were those who maintained a consistent view during the project's involvement and others who were ambivalent. However, all the young people who were able to express their views were consistent in wanting knowledge and information which was probably only obtainable through parents. And those who were interviewed also wanted some control over the process of finding out. Although identity may be seen as a right following the UN Convention on the Rights of the Child, in the areas of family contact and public care there is a clear tension between the rights of children and young people and their welfare. Rights are frequently seen as secondary to welfare, so that if a young person wants something that is believed by adults to be contrary to his or her best interests it can be denied. On this view, a young person's interest in knowing their parents, if it does not coincide with professional thinking about their welfare, may be regarded as a (current) preference rather than an attempt to assert the right to identity. In contrast, children's rights may be taken to eclipse parental rights, so that a young person's objection to the social worker's involvement with their parents can justify precluding such work. Thus the notion of children's rights is used differentially and, as a consequence, may not encourage work with parents.

Overcoming the barriers

The social workers who participated in the project demonstrated their willingness to try to overcome the barriers to working in partnership with parents in the most difficult circumstances. Even those who had more limited success on behalf of the child included in the project felt that they had benefited from their participation and the attempts they had made. They found a broader relevance in the study for working in partnership with parents in child protection and maintaining partnership at all stages of a child's stay in the care system.

There are always likely to be difficulties for social workers re-establishing working relationships with parents where earlier attempts have not been made, or have failed. As time passes, each successive change of social worker, and in parents and children's lives, takes them further from each other. Attempting to find parents and to get a response from them can seem like a very risky activity. There is never a good time to do it, but the passage of time is likely to make it more difficult rather than easier, as further experiences add to the issues that have to be explained by the social worker and accommodated by the parent. Whether the barriers were overcome depended on the three key people involved, the social workers, the parents and the young people. The young person's circumstances, including their care arrangements, at the time when the issue was raised were also crucial.

The study included disproportionately few children under the age of 10; the reasons for this were not clear. It could be that there were comparatively few such children without contact with their parents, because of changes in social work practice or the relatively short period during which they had been in public care. Another possible explanation is the importance of young people's interest in finding their family as a major motivator for social workers. Issues of identity are experienced intensely during adolescence (see Chapter 4 in this volume); older children are more likely to attend reviews and to be able to express their views. Indeed, there were 10 instances in the study where the child's expressed interest in their parents had galvanized the social worker into action. In addition, two children found a parent through their own efforts. Reliance on the young person's expression of interest as a trigger may also mean that action is not taken at an earlier stage, before the child has spoken out, and when the passage of time would not have created such a gulf between parent and child.

Barriers were also overcome through the persistence of parents in approaching social services for news of their child. From the study it was clear that mothers whose contact had been terminated continued to think and worry about their children. Children's and young people's files recorded sporadic contact with the social worker by mothers wanting to know how their children were faring, requests which, prior to the research, appeared to be regarded as intrusions. The opportunity to re-engage with the child's family was generally not taken; mothers were swiftly dismissed, sometimes with a photograph. After repeated rebuffs, parents generally gave up; some of these parents did not respond to letters from social workers requesting contact with them. Interviews with some of the mothers who later renewed contact with the social services department confirmed the recorded accounts and elicited the mother's feelings about such treatment. They had been 'fobbed off' and felt devalued. It was as if social services thought it was better for their child to have no parents than to have them as a parent.

Parents who approached social services during the study were usually accorded a more positive response, but this did not automatically overcome all the barriers to establishing a working relationship. Parents and social workers initially appeared to have quite different agendas and time scales. Some common understanding about the action which would best serve the child's needs and wishes was necessary before progress could be made. A meeting between the social worker and parent generally made this easier; social workers tended to regard parents less negatively once they had met them. Parents were grateful and relieved at receiving a more positive response than they had had earlier. The lack of knowledge about how or whether their child was being properly cared for had been a constant anxiety for them; nevertheless, social workers often had to work very hard to overcome parents' negative views and experiences of the social services department.

The re-evaluation of the role of the child or young person's family had to be even greater where the social worker was not responding to the young person's request or the parent's approach but seeking to make contact on their own initiative. Even though the social workers had joined a project where this work was clearly contemplated from the start, at least by the research team, it did not necessarily follow naturally after the identification of a parent's whereabouts.

Social workers remained very concerned that their actions might produce more problems for the young person than they solved. Of particular concern was the fear of destabilizing placements or upsetting carers. There was also the fear of the unknown. With so little knowledge about the family's current circumstances, the social worker often could not know what she would find. The discovery that the parent was successfully caring for other children, or that she was continuing to experience extreme difficulties in her life, could be thought of as having potentially a negative impact on the young person. In this context, a belief that there would be no response at all or, alternatively, that the young person's circumstances could not be any worse, appeared to encourage social workers to try to contact parents. But neither of these expectations provided a strong basis for positive and sensitive attitudes towards parents. In addition, re-establishing contact with a parent after the breakdown of a long-term placement could raise the significance of the event to heights which could never realistically be realized and could set up the parent to fail.

A more positive approach necessitated a re-evaluation of the significance of parents to their children. This could be generated in a number of ways.

The changing knowledge base in social work when combined with detailed knowledge about the early involvement of social services in the child's family gave social workers a greater awareness of the impact of discrimination on parents. Detailed reading of the child's case file could provide this understanding so long as the social worker took account of the partial nature of the recordings. But reading the case file might reinforce negative views of the family and act as a further barrier. Without good knowledge of the child's and family's history, the social worker might easily miss clues to the parent's whereabouts or cues in later contact with the parent.

Whether or not parents' circumstances or capacities had actually changed, a belief that they had was important for spurring the social worker into attempts to contact them or to work with them. If parents were coping with other children, this was a positive sign that they had changed, although it might also mean that removal of the child, or their retention in care, had not been an appropriate response to earlier difficulties. It was more difficult to view positively parents who continued to experience major problems in their lives, even though this might seem an essential factor for children's continued presence in care. But even these parents could be seen to have changed enough if they were appropriately responsive to the social worker's proposals and were cooperative.

Martin and Max

The re-evaluation of the parents' role was sometimes more instrumental; this too failed to provide a positive foundation for building a working partnership. For example, contact was renewed with Martin's mother when the local authority was having difficulty in containing Martin, now deeply involved in delinquent behaviour. His long-term foster placement had broken down, but his sister continued to live with these foster carers, and his residential home appeared unable to handle him. Martin's social worker arranged for him to stay for weekends with his mother, with whom he had had no contact for a number of years. This arrangement soon broke down. Martin's mother, facing numerous other difficulties in her life, commented in interview that she felt the social services had only turned to her because they could not cope with Martin.

Similarly, Max's first visit to his mother for two years was a two-week stay which coincided with the annual holiday of his carers. Max was taken to her home, in a different part of the country where he had not previously lived; the distance and lack of a telephone meant that no support was available for either mother or son during this crucial period. Although contact continued, there appeared to be no attempt on the part of social services to establish a working relationship with the mother.

Where contact between the social worker and parent continued, it allowed the parent's role to be re-evaluated, but these opportunities were not always recognized or built on. Even where contact between parent and child was restarted, parents were not always invited to reviews or actively involved in other ways in the process of planning their child's care. Some social workers seemed to be unsure how to work with these refound parents and did not accord significance to their status as parents. Others were prepared to go the extra mile and take steps which they would not routinely take, for example collecting parents personally to take them to any meetings which they wanted them to attend and regularly meeting them after contact visits to ask about them, not just about their relationship with their child. Parents too could be uneasy in their dealings with social workers; some sought to maintain relationships with their children without having anything to do with the social worker, a strategy which could allow them to unite with their child against social work intrusion but could also leave them without help in handling the emotional maelstrom which reunion caused.

Conclusions

Over recent years the concept of outcomes has been in the ascendant in professional debates, particularly in the field of child care (DH, 1991a; Parker *et al.*, 1991; Ward, 1995). Although this debate and associated attempts to shift attention to assessing outcomes in practice are timely, particularly alongside discussion about empowerment and users' perspectives (Cheetham and Kazi, 1998), they are not in themselves sufficient. In child care there are inherent difficulties in defining what constitutes a good outcome, and in knowing that such an outcome has been achieved, particularly in the light of changing philosophies and practices. The local authority, like other 'parents', must deal with the knowledge that what happens in childhood will have consequences for the whole of adulthood.

Most studies, this one included, provide only a snapshot of individuals' lives: the perspective on outcome they give is specific to the time when the picture is taken. Each child and young person involved in this study will repeatedly reflect on the changes achieved for them through attempts to reinvolve their parents. As their lives develop, their interpretation of events may change. For example, Chris (see Chapter 2 in this volume) who re-established a contact with his mother and brothers which subsequently broke down, found through this a new understanding of his earlier rejection, and of himself. He was able to view his family from a different vantage point and see that the difficulties in relationships were not his responsibility. Assessing the outcome of this short-lived contact without Chris's perspective could indicate, erroneously, that it was not successful. The subjective view reveals that it enabled him to move forward in a positive way.

There is evidence that working relationships with parents can be established and nearly always bring some positive gains to both parents and their children, or open the door to future possibilities. Recognizing and countering discrimination, past and present, is essential in work to restore and maintain parental involvement.

There is a need to centralize children's identity and view this from a lifetime rather than childhood perspective. Carers and other significant people need encouragement and support to accommodate this alongside other developments in their role. Re-establishing working relationships with parents may proceed with less anxiety and better planning if it is incorporated within a long-term approach. This requires a recognition of the role that parents can play, even where rehabilitation is unlikely or contact limited. It directly connects to children's need to understand themselves and their histories. Working in partnership does not obviate the need to consider carefully continuing protection concerns for both women and children. Where, for example, men have been responsible for domestic violence or sexual abuse, this will necessarily qualify the role they have. Parents' needs (including their concerns to know about their children's lives) must also be recognized and responded to. Despite the many barriers, it is possible to reinvolve parents who have lost contact with their children in care. But rebuilding relationships between parents and social workers, and between parents and their children, takes skill, time and effort. Nevertheless, where parents experience respect and understanding for the past, they can, with support, develop and maintain a role that is satisfying to them and to their children.

7 Partnership and leaving care
Nina Biehal

In recent years partnership with parents has emerged as a key component of effective and ethical work in child care, its principles enshrined in the Children Act 1989 and the accompanying Guidance. Local authorities are expected to work actively with parents as partners, including consulting them when decisions are made and giving due consideration to their wishes and feelings. This growing emphasis on partnership in social work must be seen in the context of wider changes in welfare in recent years. Changes in the production and consumption of welfare since the early 1980s have involved a shift from 'mass, universal needs met by monolithic, bureaucratic/professional-led provision to the diversity of individual needs met by welfare pluralism, quasi-markets, reorganized welfare work and consumer sovereignty' (Williams, 1994, p.49). With this has come a greater emphasis on consumer choice, consumer involvement and consumer rights, and it is within this framework that the principle of partnership with parents has gained increasing prominence.

This emphasis on partnership with parents is also linked to political concerns, evident in a number of areas of social policy from the mid-1980s, that the state should encourage greater parental responsibility. From a different perspective, a series of research findings emerged during the 1980s which identified the damaging consequences of failing to support and maintain contact between parents and looked-after children, and of failing to recognize the value of cooperative working relationships between professionals and parents (Berridge and Cleaver, 1987; Fanshel and Shinn, 1978; Fisher et al., 1986; Millham et al., 1986). Partnership between parents and professionals, it was argued, could lead to better planning, better decisions and better parental cooperation (Aldgate, 1989; De'Ath and Pugh, 1985-6). These findings, which indicated that the encouragement of both family contact and parental involvement in decision making could contribute to ensuring the welfare of children, both influenced professional practice and fed into managerial concerns with the quality and effectiveness of services, which had themselves developed in the shift to public sector consumerism.

In the Children Act 1989 and its associated Guidance, these professional and managerial perpectives were articulated with broader political concerns about the undermining of parental responsibility by welfare professionals. Clearly, one means of promoting both parental involvement and parental responsibility is through working in partnership with parents. In addition, pressure from user and voluntary organizations for greater parents' rights and a shift in power relations between users and professionals added impetus to the developing interest in partnership with parents during the 1980s. Partnership and participation in decisions about a range of public services have been proposed as a means of ensuring the rights of service users as citizens (Beresford and Croft, 1986; Coote, 1992; Family Rights Group, 1986; Lister, 1990). There has therefore been a broad political and professional consensus as to the desirability of partnership, so that the concept has been embraced by those concerned with promoting individual responsibility and consumer choice as well as by those committed to empowerment.

In view of the varied discourses which have contributed to the contemporary interest in partnership, it is perhaps not surprising that this concept may contain a plurality of values and intentions rather than a single coherent approach. In developing partnership with parents, it is important to make explicit the ideological foundations of different approaches to partnership, since these implicit values will influence decisions about the ends and means of partnership practice. In addition, in order to discuss the potential for partnership with parents of care leavers, it is important to examine the nature of contact between care leavers and their families. The first part of this chapter therefore examines the family context of leaving care, drawing on the findings of a four-year study of young people leaving care at the age of 16 and over in three local authorities. The study involved a survey of patterns of leaving care for 183 care leavers and a follow-up study in which up to three interviews were carried out with 74 care leavers, their social workers and leaving care workers during the first two years after they left care (see Biehal *et al.*, 1995). The second part of the chapter will discuss the issues involved in translating principles of partnership into practice with parents of care leavers, and will consider ways in which partnership might be promoted in this context.

Leaving care, returning home

Care leavers are often expected to live independently at a much earlier age than other young people and are likely to receive less family support than young people who have not experienced family separation. Young people generally leave care earlier than most other young people leave home. Around two-thirds leave their final care placements at the age of only 16 or 17, with a quarter leaving at 16 (Biehal *et al.*, 1992a, 1995). This is very different from the pattern for most other young people, where the median age of leaving home is 20–22 years (Jones, 1987). In the general population, two-thirds of young people are still living at home at the age of 19, many of them still receiving the day-to-day practical, financial and emotional support that families can offer (Banks *et al.*, 1992). Once they do leave home, many young people continue to turn to their families for support and often return to live at home for a while if they experience difficulties with accommodation or employment. However, for care leavers, a particularly vulnerable group of young people, separation from their families means that family support is less likely to be available at this stage in their lives.

Very few young people leaving care at the age of 16–18 return to live with their families. In our survey, only 10 per cent of those leaving foster or residential placements moved to live with parents or other relatives when they left care. We found a similar pattern in our follow-up study, where only a tiny minority of the young people (8 per cent) returned to live with a parent when they first left care and only one young person was living with a parent by the end of the study. In fact, during the first two years after leaving care, only 12 per cent of the young people returned to live with one of their parents for three or more months at any stage.

Around half of the young people did stay briefly with a relative during their first two years after leaving care, but in many instances this was only for a matter of days or weeks. In some cases, relationships with parents had virtually broken down, but they were able to return home for just a few nights during a crisis, when they had nowhere else to go. Many of these stays were only very brief and, in a substantial minority of these cases, the situation broke down rapidly.

Earlier research on children and young people who are in substitute care has shown that the majority eventually return home, with over half returning to relatives within six months and 82 per cent reunited with their families after five years (Bullock *et al.*, 1993a). However, our research indicates that there is a relationship between age and patterns of returning home. Our findings suggest that the majority of young people who remain in substitute care until the ages of 16–18 are those for whom a return home has not been negotiable. The question remains, however, as to whether a reconciliation with parents might indeed have been possible for at least some of these young people if serious attempts had been made at an earlier stage in their lives to broker a return home, in cases where this was both desirable and acceptable to the young people.

Patterns of family contact

Although very few were reunited with their families, both our survey and our follow-up study showed that the majority did have some contact with at least one family member in the early months after leaving care and two-thirds saw relatives at least weekly at this stage. However, frequency of contact alone can tell us little about the *quality* of these family relationships, how *supportive* they were to the young people, the *diversity* of family members with whom young people maintained contact and the *significance* of these relationships for the young people.

In our follow-up study, less than a third of the young people could be said to have reasonably positive, supportive relationships with one or both parents during their transition from care.[1] However, within two years of leaving care there was a rapprochement between a number of the young people and their parents and, by the end of this period, one half could be said to have reasonably positive relationships. While most parents did not offer the young people a home (or the young people did not wish to return), a number of the care leavers felt that the quality of their relationships with their parents had improved. Those with positive relationships with parents valued having somewhere they considered to be their home base, even if they did not actually live in the family home. They needed to know there was somewhere they could go if they felt lonely, or during a crisis. As one young man said: ' 'Cos like he never saw a lot of me when I was in care ... it's like he wants to see me now. 'Cos he knows he made a mistake then, so I don't really mind sleeping on the settee. It's a base, innit?'

For some, the initial period after leaving care was a time when they attempted to renegotiate relationships. Most young people involved in this process of renegotiation did not actually move back to the parental home, but leaving care was a time when they re-evaluated their relationships with parents or made attempts to renew contact. For a few young people there were reconciliations. These young people had felt hurt and angry about their past experiences, but the loneliness, stresses and crises they experienced on leaving care prompted them, or their parents, to renew contact. Some of these young people showed a poignant need for reconciliation and cautiously responded to parental overtures despite having experienced years of rejection. Crises such as homelessness, a death in the family or mental health problems sometimes led young people and parents to begin the difficult process of rebuilding their relationships, as one young woman describes: 'It used to be, I don't know, like visiting a distant relative you didn't know, just sitting there making polite conversation. But now it's totally different. You know, I sit down and talk to her about most things and it's getting a much stronger bond, I think.'

Most of those who were well supported by their parents also had links with members of their extended family and these links were very important to them. But for some of the young people, their extended family was their *primary* source of support: aunts, uncles, siblings, grandparents or step-parents all had an important role to play. Siblings were a particularly important source of emotional support and for some of the young people their closest and most supportive relationships were with brothers and sisters. For a few young women, their relationship with older sisters had a parental quality and they would rely on them for support, advice and guidance. Some young people had been cared for by members of their extended family and had developed close bonds with them, seeing them as additional or surrogate parental figures. A few had lived with grandparents at some stage in their lives and maintained a positive relationship with them, which they found very helpful. For others, contact with siblings, grandparents, aunts, uncles and cousins did not offer clear practical support but it fulfilled an important symbolic role for young people who sought contact with extended family members to meet their need for a sense of belonging and identification with their families. However, for young people who had suffered severe parental rejection, this identification with the wider family could not fully meet their needs.

Sadly, over a quarter of the young people in the follow-up study either had no contact at all with family members or had poor relationships with both their parents and their extended families. Relationships were characterized by conflict, a lack of interest by family members or only infrequent contact. Some young people saw their parents regularly but did not experience this contact as supportive; parents were either reluctant to see them or were uninterested in them; or conflicts regularly occurred during visits. They were deeply disappointed by their family's lack of commitment to them: 'I expected me family to mean more, think more of me and try to support me more. ... You see, it's the people that aren't related that seem to care more for us, which seems funny.'

Patterns of rejection established before they were separated from parents continued once the young people had left care and remained a source of considerable distress to them. Almost a third of the young people interviewed had experienced rejection by one or both parents. Some of these young people attempted to renew contact with parents after many years, only to have their advances met yet again with outright rejection, with parents making it clear that they wanted no contact. These episodes left the young people feeling still more hurt. Rejection from an early age remained a source of considerable inner conflict and distress which these young people were still struggling to resolve at the point of leaving care. One young man poignantly described how painful this early rejection still was for him at the age of 18: 'It were just a family I saw in the park once. Christmas Day. So I went out for a ride on me bike, sat on a park bench watching these kids play. They were flying a kite so I went up to them and says, "What's it like having Christmas with your family?"'

Some of the young people with poor family relationships developed strategies to help them deal with their distress. Some were so distressed, angry and resentful about abandonment, rejection or past abuse that they sought to distance themselves from their families. Some said that they chose not to see their parents at all. Not surprisingly, these young people's feelings about their families were complex, full of conflicts and ambivalence, and even those who said they 'chose' estrangement from their families were clearly deeply distressed by this and remained angry and hurt: 'If anybody mentions me family I just say I haven't got none. I don't want to know them.'

Other young people who had been consistently rejected by parents for many years had built up idealized pictures of them, constructing explanatory narratives of their lives which sought to exonerate parents or rationalize their behaviour, sometimes by blaming themselves or by blaming social workers. They tried to reconstruct their parents' actions in positive ways, or tried to construct narratives which would explain why parents had given them up or failed to maintain contact without tarnishing their image of the parent. These conflicts led some to blame themselves for the abuse or rejection they had suffered and left them confused about relationships in general. Others cherished fantasies of rebuilding relationships with rejecting parents and became angry if any suggestion of blame was attributed to a parent, even after suffering serious physical or sexual abuse at their hands: 'I just wish I had a family from when I was young. Things wouldn't be so complicated. … I want to see them regularly. Yeah, be involved with them, do things with them, like a family.'

For many of the young people who continued to be looked after until their late teens and had had poor relationships with their families before they were separated from them, these had not improved while they were being looked after. Even where relationships had been less problematic, separation sometimes created additional strains, leaving young people feeling they did not really know their families any more. In such cases, the prognosis for support from their families once they ceased to be looked after was poor.

It is clear that, given the complex and often difficult relationships that many care leavers have with their families and the ambivalence that some feel towards them, working in partnership with parents cannot be an essentially technical exercise, a matter of simply inviting parents to planning meetings as the date of leaving care approaches. Partnership with parents in the context of leaving care raises a number of issues, some relating to the particular nature of family relationships in care leavers' lives, some to the plurality of values inherent in the concept of partnership, and some to questions of power and rights.

Consumer choice, effectiveness or rights?

We have seen how the concept of partnership with parents has its origins in the shift towards public sector consumerism, in professional and managerial concerns, and in pressure for greater participation in public services in order to enhance users' rights. The term 'partnership' may therefore, at any one time, contain a plurality of perspectives and may mean different things depending on who is using it. For example, a social services inspectorate discussion of principles of partnership in child protection employs both managerial and rights-based perspectives in its justification of a partnership approach, arguing that the reasons for working in partnership with parents are 'effectiveness, families as a source of information, citizens' rights [and] empowering parents' (Social Services Inspectorate (SSI), 1995, p.9). Yet, while there may be a general consensus as to the desirability of partnership, the different values and interests underpinning this concept mean that some consideration of the connection between perspectives, ends and means is needed if we wish to translate the principle of partnership into practice in any given context – in this instance, the context of leaving care.

The shift from direct local authority provision of most services to a greater diversity of service providers means that care leavers have increased access to services provided by the voluntary sector. This may include leaving care schemes and supported accommodation projects as well as semi-independence units or independent flats directly provided by social services or housing departments. In this respect, they can perhaps be seen as the 'consumers', conceptualized by market-driven models of welfare consumerism, who are able to choose between services on offer. In these terms, partnership can be seen as consultation with both parents and young people as to the best choice of services for each individually tailored leaving care plan. However, the status of most of the care leavers in our study as 'consumers' of services was limited by the fact that they were either unemployed or in insecure, casual employment interspersed with periods of training or unemployment. Over half had left school with no qualifications and the majority failed to establish themselves in further education, work or training upon leaving school. Their marginal position in the labour market and dependence upon benefits and income top-ups from social services meant that for many their 'choices' were necessarily limited to those which could be funded either by social services or by benefits. The widening of choice through expanding the range of services on offer is of course a positive development and provides a context in which professionals can work in partnership with families, drawing on their knowledge and understanding of their children, to help care leavers make the most appropriate choices according to their particular needs and abilities. However, it is important to recognize that the choices available may be constrained both by the marginalization of care leavers in the labour market and by the socially disadvantaged circumstances of many of their families.

The development of more fragmented service provision by private or voluntary sector agencies alongside social services has brought with it a greater emphasis on management skills to coordinate services. It has been argued that, in this 'mixed economy of welfare', managerial concerns with effectiveness, quality and outcomes have supplanted professional forms of knowledge and that social workers are increasingly expected to act as coordinators of care packages rather than drawing on therapeutic skills (Clarke, 1996; Parton, 1996). Working in partnership with parents may, according to this schema, make services more responsive to consumer demand and make them more effective through involving parents as partners in making the best decisions for their children. Yet, in those agencies where social workers are expected to function primarily as coordinators of services, there may be fewer opportunities for them to intervene directly to address the complex feelings that planning for the future may bring to the fore in both parents and young people. However, evaluating the outcomes of leaving care services may in itself be a valuable exercise, but only if both parents and care leavers are involved in drawing up the frames of reference whereby quality and effectiveness are defined. Partnership with families in monitoring outcomes can help to ensure that leaving care services are needs-led.

Partnership with users of social services inevitably involves differences in power and status. Social workers may feel powerless within their own agencies but, as providers of information relevant to making choices and as gatekeepers of resources, they are more powerful than both young people and parents. Parents may feel they have little power to change the course of their own lives, or in relation to social workers, but they have the power to offer or withhold support to young people. Young people leaving care also have little power, although they may refuse to take the advice of professionals and parents and simply leave their placements to do as they wish. But in the context of limited access to social security benefits, employment and affordable housing they have few positive options and are relatively powerless at this point in their lives. While partnership in this context is not a matter of equal power, recognition of these differences in power can lead to the development of strategies which seek to take account of these imbalances to genuinely involve young people and parents in decision making. Rights-based models of intervention see users of social services as citizens whose rights to participate fully in decisions must be guaranteed.

However, the ambiguous legal and social status of young people aged 16–18 makes the nature of their citizenship problematic. Both the Children Act and the social security regulations contain the expectation that parental responsibility continues until the age of 18, yet young people are able to live independently once they are 16 and parents are not required to support them. Young people may marry at 16 but may not vote until they are 18. The transition to adult status and adult citizenship rights therefore extends over a number of years and the status ambiguity this entails can serve to place young people in a position where they have little power (Coleman, 1992).

The ambiguous nature of citizenship for young people age 16–18 raises difficult questions for a rights-based approach to partnership in the context of leaving care. Whose rights are to be ensured? Parents' rights to be involved in decisions about their young adult children or young people's rights to make their own choices? The *Gillick* ruling (1986) indicated that parental right may yield to the child's right to make their own decisions 'when he reaches a sufficient understanding and intelligence to be capable of making up his own mind on the matter requiring decision' (Lord Scarman). The *Gillick* case was concerned with decisions about medical confidentiality for young people under 16. In the case of care leavers, who are in any case 16 or over, this would suggest that the views of young people should take precedence and in practice this is likely to be the case (see Chapter 2 of the present volume).

Ideally, both young people and parents should be involved as partners in the decision-making process wherever possible. Although conflicts of interest may exist, there may also be compatible needs and wishes shared by parents and young people which can form a basis for negotiation. Yet we have already seen how complex, difficult and fraught with conflict the relationships between some care leavers and their families can be, and in situations such as these negotiation may be difficult. Indeed, for the minority of care leavers whose families have shown little interest in them over the years, it may be appropriate to recognize that not all parents have their children's best interests at heart. In situations such as these, young people may not wish their parents to be given information about them and may not wish to have their parents involved in decisions about them. Where earlier work to reconcile young people and parents has been unsuccessful or undesirable, social workers will need to respect the rights of care leavers to confidentiality, and to give their agreement about the involvement of parents.

Clearly, as research has shown, in most cases the young people's needs and rights are best met by involving parents from the time they start to be looked after, so that the foundations for a three-way partnership between young people, parents and professionals have already been laid. However, given the age of the young people and the complex family issues involved, a children's rights perspective on partnership with care leavers and families is most likely to safeguard the interests of young people. This approach, while ensuring parents' rights to participate as partners in decision making wherever possible, recognizes the impact of power relations and possible conflicts of interests, and prioritizes the rights, needs and wishes of young people. There may be a resulting tension between a commitment to children's rights and a commitment to partnership with parents and those operating within a children's rights frame of reference may feel that in these circumstances partnership with parents should be of a more limited nature than partnership with young people.

Promoting partnership

In setting the legal framework for partnership, the Children Act 1989 requires local authorities to give due consideration to the wishes and feelings of both children and parents and to consult parents when making decisions. There is an expectation that authorities will work actively with parents and, where children are accommodated, make written agreements with them. However, the Act makes it clear that the welfare of the child should be the paramount consideration in all decisions. So, while the wishes of parents must be taken into account, in effect the Act's primary concern with safeguarding the welfare of children means that partnership is primarily a question of consultation and information sharing, with limits potentially set to the degree of participation by the paramountcy principle. In practice, however, while limits to partnership with parents may be set in this way, it is difficult for social workers to impose decisions they consider to be in care leavers' best interests, as these young people may simply ignore their advice.

Arnstein's well-known ladder of citizen participation suggests eight levels of participation (Arnstein, 1969; see also Chapter 5 of the present volume). According to this schema, partnership involves a higher level of participation than simply sharing information and consultation, which are defined as tokenism. Developmental research on partnership practice in the late 1980s suggested that partnership requires the sharing of information, choice, accountability and participation in decision making, with decisions based on negotiated agreement (see Biehal and Sainsbury, 1991; Biehal et al., 1992b; Marsh and Fisher, 1992). The Family Rights Group argued that partnership exists where 'each partner is seen as having something to contribute, power is shared, decisions are made jointly, roles are not only respected but also backed by legal and moral rights', while a recent study of partnership in child protection defined partnership as information sharing, consultation and participation (Family Rights Group, 1991; Thoburn et al., 1995). Those writing from a children's rights perspective have focused on participation rather than partnership, arguing that participation by children (and young people) should be seen as a right, with recognized procedures for ensuring its implementation, in order to redress the imbalance of power between adults and children (Cloke and Davies, 1995; Lansdown, 1995).

In the context of leaving care, partnership must be based on earlier work to maintain contact with families or on work to promote reconciliation between young people and parents, where desirable. Partnership at the point of leaving care can then be based on the sharing of information and participation in decision making.

Maintaining family contact

Research on leaving care has shown that continuity of family relationships through maintaining links between parents and children looked after is crucial. In our study, continuity of contact between parents and children being 'looked after' was a good indicator of the level of support the young people could expect from them after leaving care (Biehal et al., 1995). Of the 21 young people who had positive relationships with their parents when they first left care, all but one had maintained regular contact during most of the time they were looked after. Contact had been welcomed and encouraged by social workers and carers. Even though regular contact did not necessarily lead to reunification with parents, in these cases it at least allowed the child and family to keep in touch. It enabled them to maintain, and in a few cases improve, their relationship.

For those young people for whom regular family contact was not maintained, the majority had poor relationships with parents on leaving care. Even for those young people for whom a return home was out of the question, some contact with parents or with members of their extended family had important implications for their sense of identity, and could lay the foundations for at least some degree of family support once they left care.

Our study also showed the importance of links with members of the extended family when young people leave care, especially where relationships with parents are poor or non-existent, and siblings in particular were an important source of emotional and practical support once young people left care. So in those cases where it is not possible for strong links with parents to be maintained, it is particularly important for links between children looked after and members of their extended families to be maintained. In these situations, it may then be helpful to work in partnership with key members of care leavers' extended families, drawing on their knowledge of the young people and exploring what kinds of support they might feel able to offer.

Building on and maintaining family contact while young people are looked after is of vital importance to care leavers, since professional support tends to fall away rapidly once young people leave care. Our study found that within two years of leaving care only two-fifths of our follow-up sample were still in contact with social workers, and the nature and frequency of that contact varied considerably. In contrast, support from families, where it is available, is more likely to continue long-term.

Supporting reconciliation

We have already seen how, for some of the young people with poor family relationships, leaving care was a time when they tried to renew or repair these relationships and in some cases there was a rapprochement between young people and their parents. Several young people spoke of the strain that separation had placed on relationships and of the gradual process of re-establishing a *modus vivendum*. The renewal of relationships with parents sometimes proved to be a disappointment as past difficulties surfaced or new problems emerged, and these disappointments sometimes brought back to the surface old grievances about what they saw as parental failures leading to their initial entry to substitute care. Yet, despite the young people's continuing distress about their relationships with their parents, the majority of their social workers did not see work on family issues as a priority in their work with care leavers and only a few were mediating between young people and parents, although many of the young people themselves felt considerable distress about the quality of their relationships with their families.

Fewer than a third of the social workers in our study were working on family issues, although in some cases the young people were unwilling to discuss their families. Of those who did address family issues, some were involved in counselling young people, assisting them in dealing with conflicts or in managing family relationships. In several instances social workers played a mediating role, helping young people repair links with parents or other relatives, or brokering a return home. In some cases the work focused on maintaining links with siblings still in care or on key members of their extended families. In others, where certain family relationships were perceived as destructive, social workers were trying to encourage young people to assert themselves or to distance themselves from their families. Some social workers seemed to feel that, however negative family relationships appeared to be, most young people would nevertheless benefit from maintaining some contact, however poor the quality of that contact.

Where care leavers wish to work towards some kind of reconciliation with parents, social workers have an important role to play in promoting and supporting this reconciliation. If they are successful in assisting young people and parents in arriving at a reconciliation, however fragile, they may be able to engage parents in working with them as partners with the shared goal of helping to support the young person living independently. And if they have worked in partnership with parents throughout the time a young person is looked after, this can provide a sound basis for mediation work at this stage in the young person's life, if this has not been possible earlier. Working in partnership with parents throughout the time a child is in substitute care *and after* could be a productive way of involving parents more closely in the lives of their children when they leave care and ensuring that they receive some support from their families at this stage in their lives.

Sharing information

Sharing information is an important element of working in partnership. If young people and parents do not have clear, accessible information available to them about options and services, they are obliged to accept professionals' judgments as to which services they need to know about. Working in partnership implies that decisions are openly negotiated and are based on equal access to information about services.

The question of access to information about the young person is more complex, as already indicated. There may be situations where parents have had little involvement with their child and the young person does not want certain information shared with them. This raises difficult issues about the potentially conflicting rights of young people and parents (which are discussed in Chapter 2 of this volume).

Partnership in planning for leaving care

Planning for leaving care should begin well before young people leave their final placements, and this planning process should include an assessment of the extent and quality of support young people can expect to receive from their families once they leave care.

Partnership is not merely a question of consulting parents and young people in meetings. Work needs to be done with parents and young people outside planning meetings to discuss what support young people would like and what parents are prepared to offer: is it possible to work towards the young person returning home, or are parents prepared to offer at least a temporary refuge in times of crisis? If planning for leaving care directly involves parents in this way, leaving care plans can ensure that family support is encouraged and facilitated. For example, a number of the young people we spoke to were anxious to find accommodation near their families. Living nearby made it easier for them to maintain or renew family links of some kind, enabling them to drop in regularly. In some cases relationships improved after a young person moved to the same neighbourhood as a parent.

Working in partnership with parents to plan strategies for avoiding the isolation and loneliness that many care leavers experience can be helpful to young people in two ways. First, it can help to encourage parents to give young people leaving care some much needed practical and emotional support, helping them realize that they still have an important role to play. Second, involving parents as partners in the *process* of planning for young people leaving care can constitute one element of more wide-ranging work to mediate between young people and parents, clarifying each one's expectations of the other and helping to establish clear goals negotiated between them that social workers can help them to work towards.

This can be a complex area of work, particularly where relationships between young people and their parents are poor. Our study found that planning for leaving care required great sensitivity on the part of professionals as it brought to the fore questions about young people's relationships with parents that had not been resolved, and made rejection – or simply a lack of long-term commitment – by parents more explicit. For some young people, planning for leaving care could make them painfully aware of how little support their families were prepared to offer them. So working in partnership with parents when planning for leaving care has to build on earlier work with young people and their parents, both in maintaining family links and in working on family relationships.

Participation

Working in partnership implies genuine participation in decision making. However, professionals may consult young people and parents without allowing them the opportunity to participate fully in decision making. Earlier research on partnership has found that professionals sometimes assume that a combination of honourable intentions and a focus on the mechanisms of participation, for example drawing up written agreements and asking service users along to meetings, will ensure that partnership takes place (Biehal, 1993). They may feel that they 'do all this already'. It is therefore useful to examine the practice of partnership a little more closely, breaking it down into two overlapping processes: defining needs and making decisions. The question of who defines the needs of service users is fundamental to debates about partnership, since decisions about the nature of people's problems determine the solutions that are offered to them. Care leavers, parents and social workers may all have different views about a young person's needs and it is important that neither the young person's nor the parents' views of problems and needs are marginalized or reframed by professionals. Similarly, decisions should arise from a process of open negotiation between young people, parents and professionals, based on a clear agreement as to aims and objectives.

However, both young people and parents may lack the confidence to influence decisions. They may have had little experience of exercising any degree of control over decisions taken by professionals. In this respect, young people's and parents' low expectations and lack of power may act as a barrier to partnership. Proponents of children's rights have pointed to the danger of confusing participation with empowerment, arguing that children may need to be empowered in order to participate effectively (Katz,

1995). Working in partnership cannot simply be a question of allowing young people and parents to take part in existing organizational structures, but requires imaginative ways of encouraging young people, in particular, to express their wishes and feelings and develop the confidence to participate fully. In leaving care, this may involve encouraging young people and parents to express their views in a more informal setting outside meetings, setting the agenda for planning meetings and deciding who should attend jointly with young people, as well as involving young people in informal decision making in all aspects of their lives throughout the time they are looked after.

Also, as we have seen, for many care leavers their relationships with their parents are complex and may be shot through with ambivalence and conflict. From this it is clear that working in partnership with parents of care leavers cannot simply be a matter of carrying out simple procedures such as inviting parents to planning meetings. Skilled work may be needed both within and outside these meetings in order to explore the views and aspirations of both young people and parents as a basis for encouraging real participation in decision making.

Conclusion

In view of the fact that care leavers are young adults, and in order to safeguard their rights, partnership practice in the context of leaving care should involve young people as well as parents. Partnership at this stage in young people's care careers needs to be founded on earlier work engaging parents as partners throughout the time a child is looked after, and ensuring that contacts between parents and children are maintained and promoted wherever possible. Where relationships are poor, it is important for social workers to mediate between young people and their families both while they are looked after *and* once they have left care, to help these young people maintain links with key members of their extended family. Working in partnership with parents can not only benefit young people during the time they are looked after but also, by encouraging parental involvement, promote increased family support once they leave care, to help them avoid the isolation that so many care leavers face. Working in partnership with young people can help them effect greater control over their own lives through full involvement in decision making.

Note

1 Defining the quality of relationships for a sample of this size is difficult, since each family relationship is a unique web of shared histories and experiences. We therefore based our assessment of the quality of relationships on the perceptions of the young people themselves, taking account of the views of professionals who knew them well. In the following discussion, positive relationships are defined as those which the young people saw as positive and supportive, in the broadest sense, and where this view was confirmed by their social workers or leaving care workers.

8 The experience of making contact with birth parents in adoption
Alan Burnell

Introduction

There are striking similarities between the experiences of children and young people who have been in state care for a long period of time, in either residential or foster care, and those who have been placed in adoptive families. The lives of these children before they were placed for adoption were marked by trauma which matched that of those who remained in care. General deprivation, neglect and sometimes abuse occurred in their birth families (Triseliotis *et al.*, 1997). Admission to the care system, often on a number of occasions, was followed by a series of temporary placements; even after adoption plans were made there was a considerable delay before a placement was found (SSI, 1996).

For social workers, multiple placements mean repeated pressure to find suitable care for the child, with all the work that entails. For children, they mean repeated separations and introductions, sudden moves, uncertainty, anxiety and the difficulties of integrating into new families and remaining where you are no longer welcome. Moves in, out and within the care system, especially for children who are quite young and when they occur with little warning, leave children with incomplete histories of their lives. The adults caring for them are not part of their history and do not hold memories about their earlier lives. Consequently, they are unable to rekindle and reinforce children's knowledge about previous experiences. Good communication between parents, social workers and carers can go some way to ensuring that children are aware of their histories, but substitute carers are unlikely to know the little details which can be so significant to children or to be able to draw widely on children's previous experiences in helping them to integrate current ones. The gaps in children's histories increase as their own memories become confused or fade. For example, one 10-year-old boy in the study arrived at his current placement with a series of family photographs, but was unable to identify the other people in the groups or whether they were previous foster carers or members of his family. He also associated photographs with moving on; on a number of occasions, carers had taken his photograph shortly before the placement ended.

Being in care and being adopted are both experienced by children as aspects of their lives which make them different from other young people. These are not experiences which they share with most of their peers; consequently, they can interfere with their peer relationships. Acknowledgment of difference has been identified as a positive factor for adoptive parents (Kirk, 1964) and acknowledgment of origins is now considered to be important to adoptees for the resolution of identity issues (Triseliotis et al., 1997), but the difference associated with being in state care is also stigmatizing and leads to discrimination in children's school and social life (Who Cares? Trust, 1993). Despite the wide media coverage of social services activity in child protection, care remains associated with delinquency. Those in care are thus seen negatively and become ready targets for blame.

Both adoption and care generate feelings of divided loyalty and unresolved grief. Some adoptees feel inhibited from attempting to find out more about their birth family while their adopters are alive, or while they are living at home (Triseliotis, 1973). Young people who have long-lasting placements have similar feelings. Reluctance to seek or contact parents may reflect their understanding of their obligations or fears of further rejection by carers or parents. Grief is a recognition that being brought up outside one's family amounts to a loss, whatever gains this brings (Triseliotis and Russell, 1984).

In contrast to care, adoption is seen to provide clear advantages to very many of the children who are adopted. Evidence of children's ability to form positive relationships with carers even after damaging early experiences has been a major factor in promoting the use of adoptive placements for older children (Triseliotis et al., 1997) although not all the evidence has shown adoptive parents to be better than foster carers in securing children's well-being (Gibbons et al., 1995). When account is taken of age at placement, adoptive placements are not more enduring than permanent foster placements (Fratter et al., 1991), but the number of adoption breakdowns is far fewer than of foster placements which end prematurely. Thus children and young people who have been adopted are less likely than those who are fostered to go on to experience repeated changes of placement. For most adopted children, adoption provides a family for life in substitution for their birth family. This may occur in fostering where carers foster in the hope of achieving adoption, but such motives can lead to confusion, distortion of roles and eventual disappointment (Triseliotis *et al.*, 1997). However, the majority of children brought up in care experience the attenuation of birth relationships without the compensation of making enduring relationships with a single set of carers.

The experiences of the Post-Adoption Centre in London provided vital insights for the 'Lost' parents research. Both Alan Burnell and his colleague, Diana Reich, shared their work with the social workers who took part in the study at workshops organized for the project. Many of the issues raised in post-adoption work apply equally where children have not been adopted. The parallels are strongest in long-term placements which may feel to parents, carers and children rather like adoption, and also exist for parents and children who have had the more typical fragmented care careers.

The Post-Adoption Centre was established in 1986 to develop services for anyone involved in adoption. One of the primary groups the Centre was concerned to support was adoptive parents. Between 1986 and 1991, the Centre had contact with an average 1500 people per year by letter, telephone and in person. These contacts were from adults adopted as babies, birth parents and other birth relatives. Also there were adoptive parents who had adopted babies or young children and who made up around 20 per cent of the total contacts.

Initial evaluation of the Centre's work with families showed that adoptive parents were experiencing concerns about difficult behaviour during the teenage years of their adopted children, insecurity about the adoption in middle childhood and anxieties about how to explain or 'tell' their child about the adoption. A common theme across the three main referral groups (adults adopted as children, birth parents and adoptive parents) was the issue of information about the birth parents and family. The information parents had was 'fossilized', usually simplified, and gathered around the time of the adoption. In all the adoptions the Centre dealt with at that time, any kind of contact between the adoptive parents and birth families had ceased, if indeed there had been any at all. There was usually no updating of information.

The child's need for information and contact

One of the important findings at the Centre in the 1980s was that a child's understanding of adoption changed with his or her stages of cognitive development. An American psychologist, David Brodzinski, had linked Piaget's cognitive development theories with his research interviews with children about what they understood by adoption, not just as an event but as a process and a way of forming a family. What he concluded, and the Centre's experience confirmed, was that, in essence, up to the age of six (approximately) children had little understanding of adoption issues. Between six and 10 years of age they were able, because of their cognitive development, to understand the differences between biological and adoptive family formation, albeit in very concrete ways. As a consequence of this, middle childhood for adopted children was characterized by a period of what Brodzinski called 'adaptive grieving'. During this time children could understand that being adopted included losses – loss of the birth mother, siblings and so on – and as a consequence they needed to grieve for these losses. This grieving was adaptive, in that it was an appropriate response to their growing awareness that separation meant loss, and their understandable feeling that such separations and losses might be repeated in the adoptive family. During this period children would often either become withdrawn, at home or school, act out angry feelings, or appear insecure about the permanency of the adoptive family and be questioning about the subsequent fate of birth family members. As a result of these behaviours adoptive parents would contact the Centre for help and advice. They would be concerned that their child, who in early childhood had appeared happy and well adjusted, had become difficult or insecure.

The 'adaptive' element of this grieving was that, if the mourning process in the child was appropriately managed by the adoptive parents, it prepared the ground for adolescence, where issues of identity came to the forefront for the child. Central to the managing of these two major developmental crises by the parents, and resolution of them by the child, was the need to have full, balanced and up-to-date information about the birth family, past and present, together with information not only in the form of written reports but also photos and other life story material.

Therefore, in order for the Centre's counselling staff to help parents manage and address the adoption dimension of their child's development at these stages, it was recognized that more information, and in some cases reopening contact with birth family members, was essential. It was often not sufficient to go back to the adoption file and gain a fuller picture, as that information was 'old' and also not gathered for the purpose of life story work, but in order to process a legal adoption. Such information was found usually to be partial and prejudicial. At the Centre attempts were begun to reopen contact with birth relatives in order to rectify both these limitations. Once they understood the need to reopen contact with the birth family, most adoptive parents were both positive and cooperative. It was often the professional system which was, at that time, harder to convince; the reopening of contact, however limited or tentative, went against conventional practice in adoption. Even though the Children Act had by then been implemented, there was a difference between practice in fostering and practice in adoption where contact was concerned. This difference in practice was in part historical (adoptions had been 'closed' since 1926) and in part structural, in that fostering and adoption teams or practitioners were organized differently in local authorities. Overall, there was a lack of understanding of the significance of information and contact for children who were adopted.

Information and contact in middle childhood

Jane

Jane was eight years old when her parents contacted the Centre. She had been adopted as a baby. The adoptive parents contacted the Centre because the adoptive mother felt that, over the past year, Jane had become more withdrawn and less able to cuddle or to be comforted by her mother. She had reverted to having tantrums and, on occasion, in the context of one of these tantrums, had said such things as, 'You are not my real mother, I don't want to live with you any more.' Prior to this, in early childhood Jane had seemed happy, knew of her adoptive status, and would talk to her parents openly about it. Jane had been told that her birth mother had loved her but could not look after her properly because she had too many children, was tired and often got ill. The reality was that her birth parents both had learning difficulties, and had four children before Jane who were found to be at risk of neglect. There were frequent arguments and hostility between the birth parents, who had separated after Jane's adoption. The other four children had also been adopted; the older two as a sibling pair and the others with two separate families. There was limited contact between the older four children but none with Jane or her adoptive parents. After contact had been made with the birth mother, it transpired that she was now in a new and stable relationship and had a two-year-old child which she and her new partner were parenting successfully.

The process of helping Jane and her parents went through several stages: reviewing what was known, how much of this had been told and the impact this had had on child and parents.

The first stage

To accomplish the first stage both the parents and the child were seen separately and two counsellors were assigned to the family, one to work with the parents, one to work with the child. The issues covered in the parents' session were as follows.

1   *The parents' story*

    – How did they come to adopt?
    – The impact of infertility treatment on their relationship.
    – Miscarriages, stillbirths and the parents' mourning of these explored.
    – Whose idea was it to adopt: his, hers or theirs?

2   *The ideal child*

    – The parents were encouraged to explore with the counsellor their ideal child and compare that fantasy with the reality of the child they adopted.

3   *The parents' reaction to the child's history*

    – What do they know about their child's past?
    – What further information do they require to give cogent and credible explanations of events?
    – What is their genuine reaction to their child's past?
    – What do they feel towards the birth parents?

4   *The impact of further disclosure*

    – What fears or fantasies have the parents about the sort of impact fuller and updated information may have on the child?
    – What are their views on the birth family being contacted for updated information?
    – What degree of contact do they feel would be helpful?

5   *Who should do what*

    – How active do the parents feel they can be in getting further information from social services and the adoption agency?
    – How involved do they wish to be in updating their child's information about their birth family?
    – How involved do they wish professionals to be in the process?

In the sessions with the child the counsellors covered the following areas.

1   *What adoption means to her*
    – Why are children adopted?
    – Is it for ever? Can birth parents come back for you?
    – Does she know the name of her birth parents?
    – Who belongs in her birth family? Why was she adopted?
    – What questions does she have about this?
    – Does she wonder where her birth family is now?

2   *Her fears and fantasies about her birth family*
    This area is not usually accessible to direct questioning. The counsellor will often employ play techniques and creative images to gain access to the child's inner world of fears and fantasies, using drawing, painting or dolls to enact or tell stories about other children who have been adopted. Puppets and other characters can be talked through to gain a picture of how the child perceives their 'two mummies'.

3   *What questions remain to be answered*
    The child was asked to draw up, with the counsellor's help, a list of questions she had about her past and her birth family, such as where are they now, why have they not been in touch, is my birth mother well/alive, what do they look like?

At the end of each session, information about what the child had been exploring was shared with the parents and what the parents had been exploring was shared with the child.

The second stage

Having reached this point, the next stage is for the adoptive parents or foster parents to approach social services for access to the original file information, to provide a more comprehensive and detailed account of the child's pre-placement history. Local authority practice in response to this varies. Some authorities insist on doing a further summary; others attempt to answer the child's specific questions from the file; others give parents direct access to the file. In the latter case, access is given to parents at the office, or sent to the Post-Adoption Centre for the counsellor to share with the parents. In Jane's case, the file information was sent to the counsellor at the Centre to share with the parents. More detailed information emerged about the level of neglect and suspected abuse than the parents had previously been aware of.

A further session with the parents is then often required at this stage so that they can process the new information, the feelings that this evokes and the implications for their child's past, present and future behaviour. Often, what has been considered as a simple 'baby' placement may have involved more trauma for the child than was previously recognized. The parents are then encouraged to share the information with their child by updating the life story book. Often parents are apprehensive at this stage that sharing further more complex or distressing information may disturb their child further. Often parents require considerable reassurance that this is the right thing to do and need support doing it.

In Jane's case, the facts that her birth parents had learning difficulties, were often arguing, and that the birth mother subsequently went on to bring up successfully another child which she kept were shared with Jane. The new knowledge did indeed cause distress. Jane became sad and tearful, and spent a week off school. However, this week was well spent with her mother, who took time off work to be with her, to reassure her. The periodic bouts of crying (mourning) enabled Jane's mother to get closer to her than she had before.

Jane and her family were left to process this new information and its repercussions for a couple of months before a family session (outlined below) was reconvened. (The parents were able to 'check in' at any time with the counsellor.)

The third stage: post-disclosure work

After disclosures, the family is seen, using the same format as before – parents and child together and separately – to review the impact of the new information and the subsequent reaction to it.

In Jane's case, there were still questions she needed to have answers to. She wanted to know what her birth mother looked like; she wanted photos and to know where she was living and what sort of home she lived in. Jane also wanted to know about her siblings. A further plan of work needed to be embarked upon concerning contact with birth parent and siblings.

Reopening contact

In Jane's case she was fortunate, in that social services were still monitoring her birth mother and her new child because of the previous history. Consequently, the birth mother was easy to locate. Social services were cooperative and approached Jane's birth mother with the request for photos and for updated information. Jane's birth mother agreed and was curious to know how Jane and her other siblings were doing. She agreed to cooperate. The contact request had the effect of reviving the birth mother's unresolved feelings of loss, sadness and anger at the loss of the children by her first marriage. Sessions with the social worker helped her process her grief.

In our experience, this is part of the paradox of reopening contact; contact heightens the awareness of loss. It is the sense of loss in the child that often incites the renewed contact, which then resurrects for the birth mother her sense of loss. The ideal resolution of this brings a reduction in the idealization of the lost person and a greater reality-based sense of who they are and what relationship is possible.

Having reached the point where information can be shared, the question arises of what and how this will be done and by whom. It is at this point that counsellors and social workers have to form a genuine partnership with parents. It is now our practice to suggest that birth parents and adoptive parents meet to resolve these questions themselves, with staff at the Centre acting as mediators. Not only in Jane's case, but in about a third of such situations, adoptive and birth parents have agreed to cooperate and to meet.

In our experience the benefits of this approach are:

- that adoptive parents feel in control of the contact process and are therefore less defensive;
- that the birth parent feels they have a more constructive role and feel acknowledged;
- that there is a more positive climate of cooperation around the contact issue for the child. In our view it is important that children do not feel in control and therefore responsible for contact arrangements.

In Jane's case, after some preliminary work with both parties, the adoptive parents met the birth mother and after two sessions the questions of what future information needed to be shared were (a) how this would be done, (b) what names would be used, and (c) how often and when (Christmas, birthdays). These issues were resolved and an exchange of information took place. Though this model has been developed in adoption situations where contact is to be reopened, it has also been used in fostering situations and as a more general practice guide for the establishing of 'letter box' arrangements early on in permanent placements.

With younger children the issue of reopening contact is not just about the needs of the child for information; it is a vehicle for helping children to resolve the adaptive grieving stage. For the birth parents, the reopening of contact is not just about their right to information; it is also a positive way of grieving for their loss of a child while maintaining a positive and significant role in their lives after permanent placement. For the adoptive parents, contact can be a way of reducing difficult or disturbed behaviour in their child and become, as some research suggests, a protective factor in the placement.

In Jane's case, but not in all cases, some time after the exchange of letters was negotiated, a face-to-face meeting was arranged between Jane and her birth mother to meet her emerging needs as an adolescent for a clear sense of her identity.

Reopening contact with older children

Contact issues have arisen in adolescence as a result of 'family crisis' where attachment issues were to the fore and where in middle childhood the child had not resolved the adaptive grieving stage. They may also arise where children have been adopted at a later age and earlier traumatic experiences remain unresolved. For children, having contact via information exchange or direct meetings with birth parents or relatives can be very helpful in enabling them to take on a more integrated and real sense of adult identity during adolescence. The 'genealogical' bewilderment which earlier writers mention (Triseliotis, 1973; Haimes and Timms, 1985) is lessened by more up-to-date and detailed knowledge.

The families with teenagers in crisis who contacted the Centre have tended not to have had any contact of any kind with members of the child's birth family, and the crisis is addressed at the Centre. Both the lack of any kind of comprehensive, up-to-date information and unresolved contact issues are often of central significance. For these young people also the three stages of work outlined for younger children have to be embarked upon. At the post-disclosure stage, the issue of face-to-face contact can be addressed after all parties, adoptive parents, parents and the young person, have had a chance to process their fantasies about personal histories. As with younger children, if reopening of contact is to take place then it should be initiated between the parents (adoptive and birth parents) first. It is important that the birth parents feel that the adoptive parent and the professionals involved want to involve them in a process that will make a positive contribution to their child's development and well-being.

In conclusion, it is hard to talk about contact and reopening contact without establishing a positive partnership with birth parents. For children and young people who have been looked after with the exclusion of their birth families, the same needs, issues and changes in practice apply as for those who were placed in closed adoption. This is the case whether contact has been terminated or lessened over time through lack of support. Rebuilding bridges between the child's family of origin and the family with care of the child can be difficult as the legal process at the time of care proceedings or adoption hearing will often have left birth parents feeling rejected and blamed. We have found that mediation between the adults involved is a very important prelude to forming a sense of partnership.

9 Partnership and contact: issues for management
Brian Waller

The impact during the last 50 years of contrasting policies on the relationship between child care agencies and the parents of children in care makes for depressing reading. Swings between rescue and rehabilitation-centred work have led to professional practices which are very difficult to defend. At one extreme policies have led to the enforced emigration of children and, at the other, to the premature, dangerous and sometimes fatal return of children to families ill-equipped or ill-prepared to receive them.

The recent attention which has been given to the experiences of children who were cut off from their families and sent by respectable child care agencies to Australia, New Zealand and Canada over a period of more than 20 years raises major questions as to how child care professionals could have got it so wrong. The damage and distress caused for these children is graphically described by Margaret Humphreys (1994), a local authority social worker who became aware of the scale and nature of the problems which these policies created for the many thousands of children who were involved.

It is equally distressing to read in a devastating series of more than 50 independent review reports during the 1970s and 1980s of the miserable lives suffered by children such as Maria Colwell, Jasmine Beckford and others at the hands of violent and inadequate parents and carers. During this period it was fashionable for social workers and agencies to consider that, with sufficient support, virtually every child could be maintained at home, irrespective of the quality of care being provided by their parents. It is easy, but probably unwise, to believe that we are no longer making mistakes in the way in which we choose to deal with the relationship between statutory authorities and the parents of children in care. What is obviously the case is that present-day social workers and managers are dealing with the effects of past and probably flawed policies and case work decisions, as the children who have been subject to them grow up in the care system.

This chapter seeks to describe and comment on the steps that currently need to be taken to ensure that a proper balance and partnership is maintained by social work agencies in their dealings with children and their parents, not just to be able to deal with this particular cohort of children, but in order to ensure that children now coming into the care system do not end up, as did so many of their predecessors, as casualties of ill-considered policies and poor social work practice.

Extensive research on the impact on children of these variations in policy and practice has now provided a greatly improved understanding of how children's needs can best be met. This has led to the Children Act 1989, which is based much more extensively on sound research findings than any previous child care legislation. The Act, with its associated volumes of regulations and guidance, now provides a sound legal framework within which agencies and practitioners can provide children and their families with effective services. One of the key principles on which the Act is based is that of continuing parental responsibility (Children Act 1989, s.2). Within the Act, and in the associated government guidance, the importance of both partnership with parents and of parental contact with children in care is specifically emphasized (s.34; DH, 1991c, pp.36–9; DH, 1991d, pp.62–70; Chapter 2 of the present volume).

However, although it is necessary to have well-constructed legislation and guidance, it does not automatically follow that good-quality practice will inevitably occur, especially in this area of social policy where the attitudes and beliefs of professional staff and others, especially foster carers, count for so much. In any event it is unrealistic to expect that even the best constructed government guidance will be able to cover all eventualities or be able to anticipate new issues and subtleties which could not have been anticipated at the time it was being prepared.

Between the expectations set out in the Children Act and the delivery of services to ensure partnership with parents and appropriate contact between individual children and their parents, what agencies need to do is to create a sound framework of local policy and working systems to ensure that front-line practitioners and middle managers are given direction and support. Some of the actions which are described here are applicable to other aspects of child care work, but most are specific to partnership and contact work.

Policy

It is not always widely appreciated how much variation exists between and sometimes within local authorities operating the same legislation. However detailed the law and however prescriptive government guidance might be, there remains in practice wide discretion and room for local interpretation for social service authorities. This is revealed in any set of statistical information where local authority performance is compared and contrasted. Jean Packman's well-known study on the variations in the number of children in care in different authorities revealed that some rural counties had greater proportions of children in care than some city councils dealing with families and communities facing much higher levels of social and economic deprivation (Packman, 1968).

The annual Area Child Protection Committee statistics published by the Department of Health similarly reveal variations between authorities, which can only be explained by local policy differences (DH, 1996). Even within individual local authorities it is very often possible to see differences of interpretation of legislation between one area office and the next, which can only be explained by differences in interpretation by local management about the direction of work to be pursued with families.

There is, of course, room for a proper debate about the extent to which local authority work can and should vary on such significant matters as these. Some see this as evidence of healthy local democracy at work. Others view the variations as indicative of territorial injustice. Clearly, there can be no argument about legitimate variations between authorities facing very different social and economic problems, but it is much harder to justify the manifest variations which do occur between authorities whose populations have similar needs and problems. It is essential, therefore, that authorities make public and explicit their policies on such sensitive areas as prevention, family support and child protection. It may be that there are good and sound reasons for emphasizing a particular local approach to the care of children and to partnerships which the local authority would expect staff to establish with parents. But these need to be identified and spelled out in public documents, which can be examined, discussed and, if necessary, challenged. One reason, for example, that might be acceptable for a local authority to use would be that the historical performance of the council had been too strongly focused on either prevention or protection and that solid research and careful evaluation of past services had demonstrated a need to make adjustments – either way – in the balance of policy and service provision.

What cannot be professionally acceptable is for authorities to be secretive about their local policies or for there not to be any stated policies at all.

Practitioners and managers cannot operate in a vacuum. Both these positions put front-line staff in a difficult position and can lead to poor and variable practice. The impact of local policies can have very significant long-term consequences, both beneficial and harmful, for children and for their families. Authorities have a duty to set out clearly how they intend to go about providing services to children and families under the broad legal umbrella of the Children Act. Better still is for councils to take steps to raise these issues in a way which allows and encourages open public debate and proper consultation. The mechanism now afforded by the requirement for social services authorities to publish annual local children's services plans is one obvious way for this to happen. Few authorities have yet used the opportunity of these plans to try to engage with the wider public on these and a whole range of other issues which are of importance in the delivery of social services to families and children in need.

Although it may be legitimate, for the reasons discussed above, to lay an emphasis on a particular direction for service delivery, it is important to stress the overriding duty which is set out in legislation for each child to be considered as a unique individual. Whatever the local policy position, it is essential that decisions on individual children are based solely on their particular circumstances, interests and needs. It is helpful for this to be made clear by authorities in their policy documents in order to reassure families that there is no question of pre-emptive decision making which does not take full account of the unique circumstances which apply in each case. It is also important to inform front-line staff that, whilst a particular broad policy line such as providing family support to help maintain children with their families was being emphasized on an authority-wide basis, this does not in any way diminish the need in every *individual* case for them to reach decisions which are appropriate for each child considered separately. This is a vitally important safeguard for children and for professional staff, but agency managers and elected representatives can overlook it in their understandable wish to develop an overall strategy and policy direction.

Issues about partnership and contact between children and their families are, of course, closely linked to wider policies about rehabilitation and permanency. There could be a risk, unless this is clarified in the form of agency policy statements or practice manuals, of it being assumed that contact needs to be maintained and encouraged in cases involving rehabilitation but not where children are likely to be in long-term care. For this reason, agencies need to develop local statements which set out their approach to natural parents generally and to contact work in particular, for example by describing the facilities which are available to allow children to meet their parents and other relatives in suitable surroundings.

The changes brought about by the Children Act, which give the issues of partnership and contact a much higher significance than before, place new powers in the hands of the courts for orders to be made regarding contact with parents where children are in public care. Therefore, in putting together local policy and practice manuals and in developing services to facilitate partnership and contact, authorities need to ensure that there is good rapport with the family courts, using the court liaison mechanism which exists for this purpose. The courts, for example when considering social workers' reports dealing with contact matters, will want to be confident that the authority has the necessary facilities to permit contact meetings to take place successfully. The courts will also be interested to know about other local services which have a bearing on ways in which children and parents can best be helped. The role of local authority legal departments in facilitating such links with the courts is very significant here, both in terms of the handling of individual cases coming before the courts and in the establishment of a generally sound working relationship between the courts and the local council. In some areas, social workers feel ill at ease in the court setting, and judges and magistrates have little confidence in their work or knowledge of the services provided by their authority. This situation, while not uncommon, does nothing to help children. Every effort should be made to use the court liaison system to build confidence and trust between social workers, magistrates and judges. Social services department managers and lawyers should be working closely together to achieve this objective.

Review and monitoring

In this as in other aspects of work with children, local authorities need to have effective systems of review and monitoring which will provide information both to front-line staff and to managers to assist in decision making about individual children, in planning for future services and, not least, in complying with specific orders of the court. Local authorities need to know, in overall terms, the numbers and proportions of children in their care who are having satisfactory levels of involvement and contact with parents, relatives and friends, and those who are not.

Many authorities are now using the Department of Health *Looking after Children* (LAC) documentation which provides an age-related assessment and action system for individual children, designed to ensure that their needs are kept under review and followed up with specific actions by the agency. The system operates across seven key dimensions, including health, education, identity, and family and social relationships. In the latter section there are questions about the level of contact between children and their parents, grandparents, siblings and other relatives which prompt the need to consider these points as well as to maintain up-to-date addresses. The assessment section of LAC provides an opportunity to establish whether the contact which children have with members of the family is helpful or not. The section on identity is of special significance for contact work, raising questions about children's knowledge of their extended family history and whether they wish to find out more. These questions are designed to make sure that children know something about their family and culture, that they feel helped to understand and accept why they are being looked after by the local authority, and to help them to feel increasingly confident about themselves. Too many young people in the past have left care ignorant of their backgrounds and insecure as to their identities (see Chapter 4 in the present volume). The LAC system helps to address these issues, although the major responsibility still falls to local authorities and their professional staff to be conscientious and committed in following up the answers to the questions which LAC poses.

The introduction and increasing use of LAC provides a powerful instrument for the better management of relationships and contact between children and their natural families. If used properly, it should prevent partnership and contact issues from being overlooked, as happened so frequently in the past. It can also provide authorities with useful aggregated information, for example about the numbers of children being looked after where contact arrangements are inadequate, and where there may be a need for senior management action to be taken. The LAC system, although applicable to children already in care, has largely been used for new entrants. Its impact, so far as a review–action tool is concerned, will therefore have cumulative rather than immediate benefits for all children in care and authorities need to find other ways in the short term to be able to pick up any partnership/contact issues which are affecting children who have been in care for some time.

Local authorities have a responsibility to review, at intervals of not less than six months, the circumstances of all children for whom they hold responsibility (Children Act 1989, s.26; Review of Children's Cases Regulations 1991). One of the specific issues they are required to consider is the arrangements which exist for contact with children's families, whether these are consistent with the welfare of children, and whether there is any need for changes in the arrangements in order to promote contact with the child's family and others, so long as this is consistent with his welfare (reg. 5). Hence, whether or not LAC is being used, there should be ways in which local authorities make themselves aware of the contact needs of children in their care. Although review systems should provide this safeguard, it is possible that, in practice, contact may not be seen as a priority, especially if there are more immediate concerns in a case needing to be addressed. It is in circumstances such as these that contact can be allowed to drift. Authorities therefore need to have in place a mechanism to monitor the operation of case reviews in order to ensure that contact continues to be given significant consideration. Systems for monitoring case reviews themselves need to be robust and detailed enough to be able to pick up, not just whether a review has taken place, but whether it has adequately covered the specific considerations set out in the regulations.

It is usually more appropriate that monitoring be carried out by staff who have not been involved with the children concerned, either as the social worker or as reviewing officer. Monitoring work could be done by peers or staff from off-line units so that a genuinely fresh view is taken as to whether the review system is working effectively, getting to grips with the changing needs of children and young people, and picking up the important issue of contact with family members.

Training

Any discussion about training people in partnership and contact work needs to deal with *ends* as well as *means*. It is essential to secure a full and genuine appreciation as to *why* contact matters so much as a component of the effective provision of services for children who are looked after. Contact, rather like race and gender, is one of those emotive issues which is not straightforward and 'technical' but which goes to the heart of *how* a local authority needs to undertake its work with children and their families.

It is inevitable that the staff who work with children in local authority care, whether as social workers, residential staff or foster carers, will hold a range of views and beliefs about why the children have come into care and about children's parents and families. These views can be of fundamental importance in determining the outcome and quality of contact work. For staff who have already been through a professional training course, it should be possible to assume some awareness of the importance of contact in relationship both to rehabilitation – if children are going to return to the care of their parents – and to identity issues. For foster carers, especially those whose appointment predates the Children Act, and for unqualified staff, it may be necessary to provide special training to emphasize the significance of links being kept open with families. Many foster carers are, of course, able to handle the conflicting feelings which they are likely to experience in providing day-to-day care for other people's children while also maintaining and facilitating contact with parents and other relatives. On occasions these feelings will be as painful for them as they can be for the children being looked after and for parents. They will need special preparation and support in order to be able to cope with the emotional difficulties which occur even when they fully subscribe to the need for children to maintain and develop their knowledge of, and contact with, their own families. Residential staff, too, especially those who have not gone through professional training, may find it hard to deal with parents as well as with young people whose reactions after contact with their relatives may produce emotional and behavioural problems.

What is really important is that all staff, qualified or not, should be working to a common understanding of the significance of partnership and contact in all its forms for children, and be helped to accept the need for them to establish, with the child, what frequency and kind of relationship and contact is helpful. It can be a recipe for failure if decisions about contacts are made without the full involvement and commitment of all concerned, especially those whose work puts them in daily touch with children and whose influence is of vital significance. All this leads to a conclusion that authorities need to plan very carefully how they go about informing and training staff, including foster carers, about the importance of contact for children being looked after.

As well as ensuring that staff are committed to the *why* of contact, there is also much to be taught about practical ways in which it can be specifically facilitated. This will include the development of communication skills in direct work with children and with families, life story book work, case recording, care planning and report writing, including the preparation of reports for the family courts.

Staffing and resource requirements

Local authorities probably all recognize that work in relation to contact, especially since the advent of the Children Act, is and needs to be more demanding and thoughtful than in the past. However, this recognition must be translated into specific additional budgetary and staffing provision if sufficient attention is to be given by social workers and other staff in dealing with the many issues that have to be addressed. The demands on social worker time are particularly pressing at the beginning of work with children who will eventually enter public care. It is in the period before court orders are made that the kind of contact needed by children can best be established, although it has to be recognized that social workers will at this time be excessively busy in drawing a large volume of other information together into a form which can be considered by the courts. During this initial phase, social workers need to negotiate and agree, where possible, appropriate levels of contact with parents, grandparents and siblings. Adequate budgets and staffing resources must be provided by authorities so that social workers are able to undertake this time-consuming work and also do essential direct work with children. The fashionable notion of the social workers as case managers fails to appreciate the need for social workers to be the key personal link with children. Their work is much more complicated than the case management model implies, and if this is not recognized then direct work with children which is inevitably time-consuming will suffer and decisions will be less well informed than they should be. It may often also be necessary for other staff, social work assistants in particular, to be available to help out in contact visits by, for example, assisting with transport arrangements or helping to supervise meetings, especially if there might be a risk for children in contact with parents who may be upset, aggressive or disturbed.

Authorities also need to identify buildings and rooms which are suitable for contact meetings. These might include rooms in family centres, residential homes and local offices; care and attention must be given to be sure that these venues really are suitable for what is a highly sensitive event for parents, relatives including siblings, and children in care. It is not acceptable to expect contact visits to take place in areas where privacy and confidentiality cannot be guaranteed. When young children are involved, it is very desirable for special rooms to be provided and equipped to enable them and their families to feel relaxed and at ease. Many contact visits will need to take place in the evening or at weekends, and this too should be taken fully into account when rooms or buildings are being designated for contact purposes. It is worth remembering that contact visits can be of extraordinary significance to the families and children involved. Each of the individuals concerned will be anxious and vulnerable, and the location, layout and ambience of the meeting rooms can have an important influence on the outcome.

As well as having direct contact with their parents and other relatives, children can be helped in many other ways to gain an appreciation of their origin and to feel valued and cared for by their natural families, even if it is not possible for them to be at home. Children need to have answers provided to the questions they will have about their birth families and the circumstances of their reception into care. They will also want to have provided to them, at appropriate times, photographs, letters and other documents and objects that enable them to know about their links with their families. Social workers, foster carers and residential staff are particularly well placed to help children maintain these links, but the work involved in direct contact and communication, often over a long period of time, has to be valued and then provided for by authorities in their calculations of the staffing levels needed in quality child care work.

Children who have no contact with their families can be helped by the appointment of independent visitors, whose role is to visit, advise and befriend. Local authorities need to ensure that an independent visiting service is available for all children whose lack of contact make this necessary. The Children Act 1989 makes this a legal obligation (sched. 2, para. 17). The direct financial costs of providing independent visitors are not great, but it is necessary to ensure that independent visitors are carefully selected and trained, and again authorities should not expect to achieve this without making specific provision in their budgets.

Other considerations which should not be overlooked in working out the costs of an effective contact service include the need for transport and escorts to be provided, particularly if siblings are to meet. It will also be necessary to provide additional staff on occasions to help supervise contact meetings where the social worker may not be available. Contact with siblings can sometimes be as or more important for children than contact with their parents and, in those sadly not too unusual situations where children in care have been placed apart from their siblings, or experienced numerous changes of placement or social worker, it can be the most significant event in their lives.

Supervision and management

Partnership and contact work, in all its forms, now occupies a significant position in the spectrum of activities which take place in social services departments and voluntary child care organizations working with looked-after children. Measured in terms of both the time it requires and the demands placed on professional staff, it is a complex and extensive component of what social workers do and how agencies discharge their responsibilities towards looked-after children. The requirements of the Children Act and the scrutiny and oversight from the courts make it imperative that agencies handle this work with a high degree of competence both in regard to individual children and in overall terms. Some of the mechanisms by which authorities go about establishing an effective framework for contact work, including review and monitoring systems, resource allocation, training and so on, have been described above. It is important for these systems to be reviewed overall and for agencies to ensure that the component parts function adequately together in the demonstrable interest of children.

In an increasing number of local authorities there are now organizational arrangements which allow for services for children to be managed as a whole rather than in separate sections or units. This approach can be helpful in locating responsibility for overall management with the designated senior manager and in facilitating an integrated approach. Whatever the particular organizational model which is adopted, and no system will automatically work well, agencies will need to carry out from time to time overall reviews of contact work to check that each of the different elements fits smoothly into the provision of a service which works as a whole. The point may seem obvious, but there is, for example, little purpose in devoting scarce time and resources to training staff to a high level if no facilities exist for contact meetings to take place. Similarly, the best laid plans to help children deal with identity issues can be derailed if foster carers have not been fully involved in the need to help children maintain their links with parents. Senior managers have to take responsibility for ensuring that staff understand the importance of contact work, and they then need to check that there is adequate coordination of activity across the agency.

At the level of work with individual children, the role of the staff supervisor is of critical importance. The supervisor will be the person best placed to ensure that agency policy is adhered to, that work is being coordinated to meet the requirements of court orders and care plans, and that social workers are being supported in this emotionally demanding work. Agencies need to be explicit about their expectations of staff supervision. It needs to be spelled out what supervision is intended to achieve and what it is not intended to do. Supervision should involve ensuring that good-quality services are delivered to children and families by staff who are well motivated and well equipped to do the job. The effective supervisor will, through discussion and by reference to case records, bring an objectivity to bear which can be especially helpful in contact work. It can be both difficult and sometimes unwise for individual staff to be left to decide what kind of contact arrangements are appropriate in a particular case. The experience and wider knowledge of supervisors brings both help and safeguards to bear on the decision-making process. Issues such as race and gender can be sensitive and difficult, and active supervision can be especially helpful here.

The function of the supervisor is most familiar in its application to field social workers, but its use is equally valuable in residential and day-care settings and with foster carers. Group supervision can also be helpful and, while it cannot, of course, be as focused on the work of individual staff, it can be very effective as a mechanism for discussing issues such as agency policy, standard setting and methods of work. When agencies recognize from their internal monitoring systems that there may be generic weaknesses in their work with children and families, group supervision can be a powerful mechanism to help them communicate this to staff and to help bring about changes and improvements in practice.

From the above it will be seen that the development and maintenance of partnership with the families of children being looked after by local authorities need careful management. It cannot be assumed that the apparently simple idea of a working alliance with natural families that will be helpful to children will be easy to achieve in practice. Social service authorities will need to ensure the following:

- that a *published framework of local policy* backed by practice guidance is in place. The annual children's services plans afford the obvious mechanism for enabling policy to be shared and supported;
- that there is careful *training of staff* likely to be in face-to-face contact with parents and children so that there is good understanding about the significance of maintaining children's links with their natural families;
- that there are sound *mechanisms for monitoring and reviewing* work with individual children and their families to ensure that children's knowledge of, and contact with, their parents and wider family are not overlooked;
- that *resources*, including staffing, to enable children to maintain links and contact with their parents are made available and budgeted for;
- that good *systems of supervision* are in place, so that partnership and contact work is properly managed.

Mistakes made in the past have had a devastating effect on generations of children. Now that we do have better knowledge about the need children in care have for links, and often contact, with their parents and wider family, there is an obligation on local authorities to ensure that adequate practical systems such as those described in this chapter are in place to enable these links to be maintained.

10 Searching for lost parents
Annie Pavlovic

This chapter is about searching for family connections and finding lost family members. It is intended as a guide, for social workers in particular, as to how they might take the first steps towards establishing working relationships with parents whose children are in public care, and where all contact between them and the local authority and their children has been lost. Such working relationships, or lack of them, can have a very significant impact on a young person's developing sense of self and their individual, familial, cultural and ethnic identity. However, practitioners are often ignorant of the resources available and the processes involved which would enable them to begin to forge such partnerships. It is hoped that the information provided here will help to bridge some of the gaps in both knowledge and identity needs.

The chapter is divided into two complementary parts. The first relates to and draws upon the 'working in partnership with "lost" parents' research project. In the research study, tracing lost parents was often identified by social workers as the first barrier to establishing a working relationship with 'lost' parents and hence to promoting contact between children and their families. The second part of this chapter outlines the sources of information available and the appropriate techniques for using these in relation to conducting such a search. A list of useful addresses is included in the appendix.

Re-establishing links with lost parents

The social workers in the study did not usually know how to begin to locate lost parents and, although most were fascinated and enthused by the training provided by the project in relation to tracing, many were denied either the time or the resources necessary to carry out what, at managerial level, was not considered to be a legitimate social work activity. Along with many practitioners, we would challenge that view. Where the social workers were not able to undertake the tracing work, the project did so with the assistance of Ariel Bruce, a tracing consultant and former social worker.

Most of us draw our knowledge of ourselves, family members and family events from family photographs, stories and so forth. Most of the children and young people in the study had no such resources. Their only sources of familial identity were their hazy memories, their social work case file and their life story book. Sadly, these sources were often limited and selective in content. Whilst case files often reflected traditional social work practices of marginalizing parents or constructing family members in negative ways, life story books sometimes began, artificially, with an account of entry to care, elaborated only in terms of subsequent placements. The project team were surprised at the paucity of information about the child. Favourite colours, likes and dislikes, first words, what day of the week or time of the day the child was born, who had visited on that day and so forth were frequently omitted, as was any mapping of family trees. Grandparents, aunts, uncles and even siblings often went unacknowledged or were referred to by only the most elementary reference to name or age. Many children and young people in care have no record of what their grandmothers were called, how many siblings either of their parents have, where their parents or grandparents have worked, where they have lived, whether family members are still living or how or when they might have died. Much of this information, of course, is lost along with parents and contributes to the gaps in identity that create crises later in life.

Balancing short-term and long-term needs presents continuing dilemmas in social work practice. Fullness of recording in case files and life story books can go some way towards redressing imbalances, if not resolving the dilemmas, and help to build the bridges of dynamic life stories. Official documents such as birth, marriage and death certificates record a wealth of information relating to family names, locations, occupations and so on. This form of information can go some way towards meeting identity needs in the absence of family contact, since it locates individuals within a familial, historical, geographical and cultural context. It can also help preparation for direct contact with estranged family members. Yet these sources of information were rarely available in case files or life story books; very often even the birth certificate of the child or young person to whom the file related was absent. For some children the social services department's information was at variance with that recorded on the birth certificate. For example, one young woman's father was said to be unknown, but his name was recorded on her birth certificate, which had apparently not been seen by her social worker. The routine inclusion of official documentation in the short term might help alleviate the crises people often encounter in the long term and/or facilitate contact with estranged family members in both pragmatic and sensitive ways.

Practitioners are not unusual in their lack of awareness of the tracing process. In the course of the study, the research team were approached by 10 individuals who were seeking help in relation to tracing estranged family members or their own identity. It was impossible to refuse some assistance, knowing that alternative sources of help were rarely available to those without substantial resources. That so many people approached (and continue to approach) a research team located in a university for help is testimony to the enduring gap in both individual identities and social work activity in this area. It is hoped that the information provided here will help to fill some of these gaps.

Case studies

The project team conducted what were sometimes extensive searches for parents on practitioners' behalf. Drawing on this work and using three case studies based on examples from the research, the sources of information available from public records are outlined and explained. These three cases effectively demonstrate how a diversity of sources of information were employed to fill some of the gaps in young people's histories, and to identify family members. Using this information, social workers were enabled to attempt to re-establish working relationships with parents and even contact between parent and child. Names and some personal details have been changed in these examples.

Ian Fairway

Ian was aged 18 years at the time of the study. He had been received into care when he was only a few weeks old and had been placed with the same foster carers throughout most of his care career.

The bulk of Ian's social work case file had been lost and this meant that the reasons for his reception into care and for his long-term stay were unclear, but these were thought to relate to Ian's mother's ill-health. No contact between the local authority and Ian's parents had been recorded; there was only an entry, written when Ian was a year old, stating that the family did not visit Ian, nor did they contact the department for information about him. There was no record of any contact between Ian and his family; a case recording two years later noted that 'Ian may need considerable help in the future to understand how he had arrived in care.'

There were no further entries on the existing file relating to Ian or to his family for a further 11 years, when a reference was made to Ian in the context of a review relating to another child placed with Ian's carers; a social worker noted that Ian was 'fine'. One month later, a review relating to Ian recorded that he was well settled with his foster carers; the placement subsequently continued until Ian was aged 18, and left home. He obtained a job that involved working abroad and needed his birth certificate to obtain a passport. The certificate revealed that, while Ian had been born locally, his parents were of a different nationality. This discovery created an identity crisis for Ian. His social worker recorded that Ian was saying that he did not want actively to pursue information about his past but he was beginning to ask a lot of questions. Ian's social worker agreed to Ian's request to find out as much information as possible and to leave it on his file so that he could have access to it when he felt ready.

The social worker consulted Ian's long-term carer, whose account of the circumstances in which Ian was received into care was consistent with the report on the file that Ian's mother suffered health difficulties. The carer also recalled that some contact had been maintained between the department and Ian's mother during the first year of Ian's life, and that Ian's mother had requested photographs of Ian, but there had been no direct contact between him and any member of his family. Ian's carer believed that there were two older children of the family.

There was exceptionally little information about Ian's family and nothing recent. The last known address relating to Ian's parents – recorded at the time of initial intervention and on Ian's birth certificate – had long been demolished and the whereabouts of his parents were unknown. Nor was there any recorded information relating to any other members of the family. Ian's identity was a blank page in an out-of-print book!

The search that followed initially concentrated on obtaining information, rather than tracing people. Ian's social worker consulted social services archives in an attempt to locate Ian's file, or any file relating to his siblings or to his mother, in the hope that they would contain the missing links in Ian's identity. No records relating to any member of the family were found.

Following consultation with the research project, the search was shifted to official public records. Ian had been born in 1976. His parents were named on his birth certificate as Clive Victor and Maria Anna Fairway (maiden name Bates). This was inconsistent with the case file records, which stated that Ian's father's sole first name was Victor. Knowing from Ian's birth certificate that his parents were married at the time of his birth, I embarked on a search for their marriage certificate and consulted the marriage index in the Family Records Centre in London. Working backwards from 1976, when Ian was born, I searched the marriage indexes for every quarter of every year to 1960, but found no trace of a Bates marrying a Fairway. Knowing, again from Ian's birth certificate, that neither of his parents had been born in England, I requested the General Register Office in their country of origin to conduct a similar search for their marriage. Again, no positive trace was found.

Transferring the search back to London, I made a sideways shift and attempted to locate the births of Ian's siblings, searching the birth indexes backwards from 1976 for any children born under the surname of Fairway, mother's maiden name Bates. Two corresponding entries were found, one relating to Barbara, born in 1963, and the other to Brian, born in 1961. The details recorded in full on the birth certificates of Barbara and Brian Fairway revealed that they were, indeed, Ian's siblings.

The discovery that Ian's parents had a son born to them in 1961 prompted me to take up the search for their marriage again, looking to earlier records. Searching backwards from where I had left off I discovered that the marriage of a Clive Victor Fairway to a Maria Bates had taken place in England in 1958. Ian's mother was named as Maria Anna Fairway (formerly Bates) on his birth certificate. This was not truly reflected in the marriage index (which listed the bride as merely Maria) but other details – such as geographical location – did correspond with the information known from Ian's birth certificate and I felt certain that the full marriage certificate would reveal that the marriage entry related to Ian's parents. The certificate confirmed this to be the case.

The cumulative information revealed through the marriage certificate of Ian's parents and the birth certificates of his siblings gave a much fuller picture of Ian's familial identity and enabled Ian's social worker to begin compiling a family tree. We now had the following information.

- Ian's father, Clive Victor Fairway, married Ian's mother, Maria Bates in 1958.
- Clive was 28 years of age and Maria 22 years at the time of their marriage.
- At that time, Clive Victor worked as a clerk and Maria as a machinist. Clive Victor was the son of Peter Fairway. Ian's paternal grandfather had worked as a saddler and was deceased at the time of Ian's parents' marriage.
- Maria was the daughter of a general labourer called Martin Bates, also deceased at the time of her marriage. Maria had been formerly known as Mary Anna.

- Clive Victor and Maria Fairway had been married for three years when their first son, Brian, was born. Maria registered her son's birth and stated his father's name as Victor (dropping the Clive) and his occupation still as clerk.
- Two years later Ian's sister, Barbara, was born. Barbara was given the middle name Anna, reflecting the original name of her mother. Barbara's father registered the birth, stating his name as Clive Victor Fairway but signing himself simply 'V. Fairway', indicating that this is what he was known as. His occupation remained that of clerk.
- Ian was born 13 years later. His father registered the birth, stating himself to be Clive Victor Fairway and signing as 'C.V. Fairway'.
- Working with the information from the marriage certificate of Ian's parents, this means that his father was 46 and his mother 40 when Ian was born, and that they had been married for 18 years.

This developing pen picture raised as many questions as it addressed. Ian's social worker decided that we should continue the search but did not plan, at this stage, to approach any family members unless Ian (who was still working abroad) specifically instructed her to do so. This position both presented and reflected something of a contradiction; there was obviously a limit to how much could be discovered and left on file 'for when he was ready to know' without actually approaching any family members.

I returned to the records office in London and conducted a search for the marriage of either or both of Ian's siblings with the dual aims of following the family tree and obtaining more recent information of the whereabouts of family members. No trace was found of Ian's brother, Brian, but Ian's sister, Barbara, was found to have married in 1987. I checked the electoral register for the address she gave at the time of her marriage. Both Clive and Maria Fairway were listed at the address on the 'current' electoral roll. Ian's family had been located.

Adam

Adam was received into care following the sudden death of his mother when he was about six months old. No contact with his father or extended family members had taken place since Adam was a year old and his father requested that he be placed for adoption. Adam was never adopted, but remained with the same foster carer through to adulthood. Although Adam grew up with the knowledge that his mother had died, no identity or life story work was conducted until, aged 16 years, he indicated at a review that he wished to know more about his past and about his father.

Adam's case file contained little information about his own family and the reasons why he had remained in long-term care. There was no indication on the file of any efforts to facilitate contact or of Adam's father being told that his son had not been adopted. The search for Adam's father began, as always, with the information that *was* recorded and, in the event, proved relatively straightforward.

The name and age (although not exact date of birth) of Adam's father were recorded on file, as was his address at the time of Adam's entry to care. The electoral register was consulted via the library local to this last known address. This confirmed that Adam's father had been listed there at the time but was no longer registered at that address. Directory enquiries confirmed that someone of the same name as Adam's father was listed in the area, but that his telephone number was ex-directory. A further telephone call to the local town hall electoral services department (which differs from the electoral register at the library) revealed a local address for someone of the same name as Adam's father.

There was no way of knowing, at that point, whether this person was actually Adam's father or merely someone of the same name, but a carefully worded letter from the social worker evoked a positive response that confirmed that the right person had been located. The direct work that followed had to address the sensitive issues of why Adam had not been adopted and why his father had not been informed. This work was made even more difficult by the opposition of Adam's long-term carer on the one hand, and Adam's father's difficult personal circumstances on the other.

It transpired that Adam's father had always believed that his son had been adopted and therefore had never contacted the department. He had remarried but had no other children. Adam's father did, however, want to know about Adam and to support Adam in his need to know about his family. With the help of his wife, who knew nothing of Adam and of the social worker, Adam's father compiled a pen-picture of himself and Adam's mother. He outlined the events of their meeting, her becoming pregnant with Adam and the tragic circumstances of her death. He passed on a photograph album and a 'baby book' containing photographs of Adam as a baby with the parents he had never known. He wrote notes, describing when and where the photographs had been taken. Some of the photographs had captions in Adam's mother's own handwriting. One such photograph of Adam in his mother's arms stated: '*My beautiful baby*'.

At the conclusion of the study, no direct contact had taken place between Adam and his father, although exchange of letters and photographs continued. The value of this form of contact should not be underestimated, although it is difficult to quantify or describe how much it means to both Adam and his father.

Jill

Jill's lone mother, Theresa, had disabilities, and her family were unsupportive. The decision to remove Jill from her mother at birth was made without any prior discussions with Theresa. The case file recorded contact between Jill and her mother up to the age of three years and periodic visits by Theresa to the district office to find out about Jill's progress and development. This was discouraged; no attempts were made to work with Theresa. Jill's father's identity was not known to social services.

Jill was 14 at the onset of the study and had been placed with the same foster carers since her initial reception into care. Theresa had contacted social services about a year earlier and requested contact with Jill. Jill told her social worker that she did not want direct contact at this time but would very much like to have a photograph. This exchange of photographs never took place; Theresa failed to keep a follow-up appointment and the social worker had no current address for her.

Jill's case file recorded Theresa's full name and date of birth, and the name of her maternal grandfather, John. This information was sufficient to obtain a copy of Theresa's birth certificate, by post, from the General Register Office at Southport. This confirmed Jill's grandfather was John and showed her grandmother to be Mary. In consultation with Jill's social worker, I embarked on a search for John and Mary in the hope that they would know Theresa's whereabouts. Although information on the case file listed their address in 1989, the electoral register at the local library indicated that they no longer lived there. Having no obvious way forward, the search had to retrace John and Mary's steps.

I requested that the General Register Office at Southport conduct a search for the marriage of John and Mary. Their daughter, Theresa, had been born in 1950 and was thought to have two older siblings. On the basis of this, I requested that Southport conduct a five year search for John and Mary's marriage, from 1941 to 1945 inclusive. The marriage certificate disclosed that John and Mary had married in a Catholic church in 1942 and stated their respective ages at time of marriage as 19 and 17 years. The information relating to religion came as a surprise to Jill's social worker. The information relating to ages enabled me to obtain copies of John's and Mary's birth certificates from the General Register Office. A copy of each certificate was sent to the National Health Service Register, also based at Southport, with a request that they search their records to establish whether they had received notification of the death of either John or Mary, or whether they were currently registered with a general practitioner in this country. The response, six weeks later, confirmed that Jill's grandfather was registered with a doctor but that, sadly, her grandmother had died two years previously. The next step was to obtain a copy of Mary's death certificate.

The person who registers a death, the informant, has to state details of themselves and their relationship to the deceased. Mary's daughter, Stella, had registered Mary's death. Stella's address was recorded on the certificate. Directory enquiries confirmed that Stella was still listed at the same address and gave me her telephone number, which was passed to Jill's social worker.

The search for Jill's family had been somewhat lengthy and had drawn on a range of sources; it had confirmed some and revealed many other aspects of Jill's identity. Certificates containing information relating to family and geographical connections, occupations and religion, record aspects of who we are. In a pragmatic sense, the certificates in this example provided the stepping stones that enabled Jill's social worker to re-establish connections with Jill's mother and extended family.

Writing the letters to 'lost' parents

Obtaining information was the first step towards bridging some of the gaps in identity and locating lost parents. The next step was for the social worker to initiate contact with the parent or other family member. This apparently straightforward act of making the first contact is in practice more likely to be the most difficult step towards the re-establishment of a working relationship with a parent.

A 'lost' parent has a degree of unreality which is challenged once a worker, who may never have met a child's parent, starts to think about making contact with them. Having some understanding of the ways in which parents become lost may be a crucial aspect of the process of restoring a working relationship and this is explored in greater detail by Masson and Harrison in Chapter 6 of this volume. Little may be known about a parent, and what is recorded may be very negative; a worker may be unclear about why a child came into care or stayed in care. There may be anxieties about raising expectations on the part of children or their parents, causing grief, having to convey difficult information, or finding out that a parent has died. There are implications in finding out that a parent's life has become more difficult or, conversely, that a parent's life has improved considerably. There is a consciousness that there are no neutral facts and that information has implications which for either parents or children may be far-reaching and sometimes difficult to evaluate.

Many of the social workers in the study found initiating contact with 'lost' parents a difficult issue. They sometimes appeared reluctant to take the next step. In spite of the meticulous tracing process, the initial letter from the social worker to a parent remained a 'leap in the dark'. The social worker could not be absolutely certain that the letter would be received by the correct person. The intended recipient's circumstances were not known and their response could not be predicted. The possibilities of a successful outcome were often overshadowed by fears of a negative response or of no response at all.

Initiating contact in these circumstances has implications for the confidentiality of each party. Parents may want to know more than children and young people wish to convey at this point. Social workers need to balance obtaining information for children and young people with responding to requests for information from parents who have often been marginalized in the past. Deciding what to say is only half the story; there is also the question of how to say it, what tone to adopt, what language to use and so forth. In addition, those contacted may need support in relation to renewing working partnerships and in other aspects of their lives and histories; it may not be clear that support will be available for dealing with difficulties which do not relate directly to the child's needs. Although writing letters is immensely difficult and generates considerable anxiety for social workers and young people, it is, perhaps, the only way of gaining access to people who hold the information that children need to make sense of their lives.

Workers are not without some example and guidance, in taking this first step (see Chapter 8 of the present volume). The field of post-adoption contact is particularly relevant to situations in which current social workers are contemplating making an approach to a parent where there has been no working relationship for a long period of time, where a foster placement has become a de facto adoption or where, from case records, it appears possible that a parent may believe that a child had been placed for adoption. In these and other circumstances it is important to bear in mind that a letter may be read by someone other than the intended recipient and the writer must therefore take great care about its content. Drawing on work undertaken by Diana Reich of the Post-Adoption Centre, the following suggestions may be helpful for practitioners writing a first letter to a newly found parent:

- write in a clear and concise style;
- write in a way which will be understood by the recipient and which clearly identifies the child, without giving information which assumes or implies that they are the child's parent;
- respect the integrity of the individual child and parent, by neither giving nor demanding specific information;
- make no assumptions or judgments about the parent's history or the reasons for the child coming into the public care;
- make clear that initial discussions can be confidential and that no information will be conveyed without a parent's or a child's consent;
- be tentative in tone and keep as many doors open as possible;
- give the receiver of the letter as much 'space' and control as possible; do not make them feel guilty if they do not feel able to respond immediately;
- acknowledge within the letter that the contact may be unanticipated and allow for a parent taking some time to respond;
- include some information about the child or young person, as long as this is agreed with them;
- give suggestions for support and information about relevant agencies and organizations;
- indicate clearly how and when you can be reached and make sure that nothing obstructs this;
- include a translation if you know that English is not the parent's first language;
- follow up after a period of time;
- share the content of the letter with the child or young person whenever possible.

The following is the kind of letter which might result:

Dear Angela Evans,

I am a social worker in touch with a young woman called Elaine Evans who was born on 31 May 1983 and who has been in the care of the local authority since 27 November 1985.

Elaine has now reached the age of 15 and like many young people in her situation has little information about her family background. The local authority is trying to make sure that young people have as much knowledge as possible about their lives and this can be very helpful to them.

I am contacting you because I am trying to gather together some information and family history for Elaine. I wondered if you would feel able to meet me to discuss this. Our discussions would be confidential and no information would be recorded or passed on without your agreement.

Elaine is well and looking forward to going on holiday with her school in August.

I understand that this letter may have come as a surprise to you and you might like a little time to think about it. I have enclosed a leaflet which gives the names and addresses of organizations you might like to know about and which you could contact if you would like advice.

My telephone number is [..........] and I am available on each of the following mornings if you want to contact me directly [...................] if you would rather, you could write to me using the enclosed self-addressed envelope.

I do hope you will feel able to meet me and I will contact you again by letter in three weeks' time.

There are also situations in which workers have some knowledge or where there has been more recent contact and a slightly more direct approach is possible. The selection of letters below does not necessarily relate to the case examples in the previous section, but does reflect some of the dilemmas social workers faced and the cautious ways in which they managed them.

Dear Mrs Davenport,

I hope all is well with you. I am writing on behalf of your daughter, Tracy. She would very much like to have contact with you via an exchange of letters.

Tracy has told me that you have moved. She acknowledges that you may not wish to divulge your address. However, an exchange of letters may take place using this office if you wish, or through someone of your choice.

Tracy would also love to have a recent photograph of her brother and to know you are both well.

This year, Tracy will be sitting her GCSE exams. Her school reports are very good. Tracy is thinking of pursuing a nursing career.

I hope you will feel able to exchange letters with Tracy.

Dear Mr Fielder,

I am a social worker currently working with a young man who needs to have more information about his past. I wondered if it would be possible for you to contact me in order that I could explain this matter further, as I think you may be able to help.

I look forward to hearing from you.

Dear Christine,

I am the social worker working with your daughter Karen and I was wondering if you would like to know how she is getting on. She does talk about you and I told her that I would try and find out how you were and how you were managing. If you would like to write a letter to Karen or to send an up-to-date photo, please feel you can do so. Perhaps you could drop me a brief letter at the above address as a first step.

I look forward to hearing from you soon.

The ethics and politics of tracing

The case studies and letters depicted here demonstrate that the tracing process involves *people* and not merely information. It emanates from individual needs and affects the lives of all those involved, with possibly far-reaching consequences. It is a political process in that the searcher, who controls the process, has access to knowledge and strategies that the person searched for has no awareness of or control over. These two central parties to the process are also unequal in terms of the support and preparation they receive for potential reunion or refusal of contact. The impact of being found also differs from that of finding: a social worker is available to mediate for a young person in the public care and can provide some emotional support; the person who has been found often has to cope alone and may have to give explanations to their family. The searcher or their social worker and the person searched for are not the only people involved: the tracing process and reunion or refusal of contact can impinge upon other people in their lives. Some people do not wish to be found and feel threatened and/or exposed by the initial contact. Some of the previously unknown information revealed through the search may be unwelcome or unsettling to the person being located. For example, beliefs about one's parents and oneself may be shaken by finding that they have mental health problems, or a criminal conviction, or even that they are caring for other children.

The search and the management of issues arising from or relating to it inevitably become another component in the life stories and identities of the parties involved. The strategy that I have adopted in searches has been to compile a file of the search itself, comprising copies of all documents obtained, letters sent and notes of telephone calls received. I have made a copy of this available to both the searcher and the person searched for. The social worker then has a record of what avenues have been tried on behalf of the young person. Those searched for know the process through which they were located. In providing such information about the search, care must always be taken to respect the wishes of those who do not want their current whereabouts disclosed. Those conducting searches must always be aware that there are good reasons why some people feel the need to disappear. One of the mothers in the study had resorted to such extreme measures in her flight from domestic violence. There is a danger that, unless carefully thought through, the whole tracing process will reflect and compound the discrimination experienced by parents of looked-after children and increase their feelings of powerlesness. There are obligations to consider the impact of giving information to or withholding it from parents and their need for support in handling the conflicts that may be generated through the process.

Sources of information

There is a wealth of information available in relation to each of us. What the reader may find surprising is that very often the details we perhaps regard as private and/or confidential are, in reality, public information that anyone can obtain in relation to anyone else. This public information provides the basis from which to conduct a search.

The sources described here relate to England and Wales. Variations of these sources are to be found in Scotland, Northern Ireland and Eire. I have disaggregated these sources here for ease of reference. In practice, however, the process of searching rarely progresses in a linear way and involves using these sources in conjunction with one another.

Birth, marriage, death and adoption certificates

Birth, marriage and death certificates provide information relating to family and social context that proves invaluable when conducting a search. Compiled for official purposes, this information records both continuities and discontinuities in people's lives. It enables us to distinguish any individual from others of the same name and facilitates the searching process. It provides some insight into the individual's life and circumstances, ultimately enabling the searcher to approach the person being searched for in a way that is sensitive to that person's circumstances. These official sources of information not only provide the stepping stones of the tracing process but can help to bridge gaps in identity.

Whenever a birth, marriage or death takes place the event has, by law, to be registered, at a local registrar's office. After registration the information is passed to the Registrar General at the Office of National Statistics. The Registrar General maintains records relating to births, marriages and deaths registered in England and Wales and births and deaths at sea since 1 July 1837, when the Registration Act 1836 came into operation. Similar records are available in relation to Scotland, Northern Ireland and the Republic of Ireland.

All records represent separate events and are not linked together in family formations. The registers themselves are not open to inspection, but there are indexes held at the Family Records Centre in London, through which individual entries can be traced. The indexes give only very limited information; this is not sufficient to enable a search for any individual to be conducted. However, full copies of birth, marriage or death certificates can be obtained through the use of the indexes. To conduct a search it is therefore necessary to be familiar with the information recorded on certificates and to know how to use the indexes to identify the required certificates.

Birth certificates

For most purposes individuals use the short form of their birth certificate which contains only their name, sex, date and place of birth and is issued free at birth registration. A full certificate of birth (see copy, on next page) also gives details of parentage and the person who registered the birth, the informant. The mother and the father (provided he is married to the mother) are qualified to be informants; normally one of them must register the birth. The information given on a full certificate has changed from time to time. Since 1995 it has been as follows:

1 Child's date and place of birth;
2 Child's name and surname;
3 Child's sex;
4 Father's name and surname;
5 Father's place of birth;
6 Father's occupation;
7 Mother's name and surname;
8 Mother's place of birth;
9 (a) Mother's maiden surname and
   (b) surname at marriage if not her maiden surname;
10 Mother's usual address;
11 Informant if not mother or father;
12 Informant's qualification;

DH 853804

CERTIFIED COPY of an ENTRY OF BIRTH
Pursuant to the Births and Deaths Registration Acts, 1836 to 1947.

B. Cert.
R.B.D.

Registration District _____

Birth in the Sub-District of _Carlisle_ In the COUNTY BOROUGH OF CARLISLE

1953

No.	When and Where Born	Name, if any	Sex	Name and Surname of Father	Name and Maiden Surname of Mother	Rank or Profession of Father	Signature, Description and Residence of Informant	When Registered	Signature of Registrar	Baptismal Name if added after Registration of Birth
419	Sixth July 1953 City Maternity Hospital U.D.	Christine	Girl	John Simpson	Muriel Johnson Simpson formerly Smith	Drug Samples of 65 Lancaster Street, Carlisle U.D.	J. Simpson Father 65 Lancaster Street, Carlisle.	Fourth July 1953	J. Sim Registrar	

I, _____, Registrar of Births and Deaths for the Sub-District of _____ in the _____ COUNTY do hereby certify that this is a true copy of the Entry No. 419 in the Register Book of Births for the said Sub-District and that such Register Book is now legally in my custody.

WITNESS MY HAND this 6th day of July, 1953.

_____ Registrar of Births and Deaths.

13 Usual address of informant if not mother's address;
14 Informant's signature;
15 Date of registration.

The registration district is stated at the top of the birth certificate.

Some of the boxes or columns on the certificate may be scored through. For example, if the child has not been given a name at time of registration, section 2 will be scored through. A name may be given or changed after registration has taken place and this will be inserted and will appear on any copies of the certificate that are obtained subsequently. Unmarried mothers cannot name the father for the purpose of the birth certificate unless he is present at registration, has sworn a declaration of paternity, or a court order has been obtained proving paternity. In these cases sections 4, 5 and 6 will be scored through. There are some variations in birth certificates; for example, the parents' place of birth has not always been recorded.

The detailed information on a birth certificate makes it possible to distinguish two individuals of the same name. Two Jane Smiths, for example, even if they are born on the same date in the same hospital, are unlikely to have parents with the same names or occupations or, even if these coincide, to have mothers who also share a common maiden name.

Some of the information on birth certificates is duplicated on certificates relating to other life events. Occupation is included on death certificates. Age at time of marriage, father's name and occupation are recorded on marriage certificates; where the father is not named on the birth certificate, he is also omitted on a person's marriage certificate and consequently this becomes identifying information in itself.

Some details from the original birth certificate (date and place of birth) remain intact on the adoption birth certificate. Nor does the change in legal identity via adoption ever eliminate the original birth certificate from the records held by the Registrar General. Those who have been adopted may, when they are adults, apply for a copy of their original birth certificate; help is available from adoption agencies, and leaflets explaining the provisions have been produced by the Department of Health (DH, 1991f).

For further details of records on adoption, see Stafford (1993).

Marriage certificates

Marriage certificates comprise eight columns of information, as follows:

1 when married;
2 name and surname of each party;
3 age of each party at time of marriage;

P S 982336

CERTIFIED COPY of an ENTRY OF MARRIAGE.
Pursuant to the Marriage Act 1949.

Registration District _Robert + Leonjor Jon_

Marriage solemnized at _St. Mary the Virgin_
in the _Kings_ in the Parish _of Wombeter_
of _St. Mary the Virgin_

No.	When married	Name and surname	Age	Condition	Rank or profession	Residence at the time of marriage	Father's name and surname	Rank or profession of father
88	27th March 1955	Reginald Leonard Kenny	30	Bachelor	Antomotic Operator	43 Wombery Cottages	Ernest Nelson Kenny	Grocer Foreman
	1955	Victoria Mary Elizabeth Hoff	25	Spinster	Typist	113 Thompson La Lithgow	Sydney William Ernest Hoff	Stage Hand

Married in the _Parish church_ according to the rites and ceremonies of the _Established Church_ by _matter Licence_ by me, _A. H. Jordan, Vicar_

This marriage was solemnized between us: { Reginald Leonard Kenny / Victoria Mary Elizabeth Hoff } in the presence of us: { Herbert Thomas Kenny / Betty Kathleen Kenny }

WITNESS MY HAND this 27th day of March 1955, in the twenty of November 1955. in the Register Book of Marriages of the said Church.

A. H. Jordan, Vicar

I hereby certify that this is a true copy of the Entry No. 88 in the Register Book of Marriages of the said Church.

CAUTION:—Any person who (1) falsifies any of the particulars on this Certificate, or (2) uses it as true, knowing it to be falsified is liable to Prosecution.

4 condition of each party at time of marriage (that is, whether bachelor, spinster or previous marriage dissolved);
5 rank or profession of each party at time of marriage;
6 address of each party at time of marriage;
7 father's name and surname of each party to the marriage;
8 rank or profession of father.

Details of place of marriage, registration district and the names of the witnesses to the marriage are also shown on the certificate (see copy, opposite).

The continuity of detail on marriage certificates locates individuals within both their own familial relationships and those being newly forged. These are invaluable to the tracing process. Addresses and details of occupations provide colour to the outline provided as well as directly assisting a search. The names of witnesses to the marriage, who are usually friends or relatives of the marriage parties, may provide another link if the search reaches a dead end.

Death certificates

Death certificates (see copy, on next page) comprise nine columns, as follows:

1 date and place of death;
2 name and surname of deceased;
3 sex of deceased;
4 age of deceased;
5 occupation of deceased;
6 cause of death;
7 name and surname of informant (that is, person registering the death); qualification of informant (that is, relationship to deceased); usual address of informant;
8 date of registration;
9 signature of the registrar.

Death is often registered by a family member or close friend of the deceased; the information on death certificates in relation to the deceased is only as accurate as the knowledge of this informant, who may not have had access to other documentation relating to the deceased. For this reason, some of the details on a death certificate, such as full name or occupation, may not correspond with the information recorded on the birth or marriage certificates of the deceased. Although the knowledge of the death of a family member is an important piece of information in relation to familial identity, and the cause of death may have implications for genetic identity,

IY 519286

D. Cert.
R.B.D.

CERTIFIED COPY of an ENTRY OF DEATH
Pursuant to the Births and Deaths Registration Act, 1953

Registration District

1961 Death in the Sub-district of SYDENHAM in the METROPOLITAN BOROUGH OF LEWISHAM

No.	When and where died	Name and surname	Sex	Age	Occupation	Cause of death	Signature, description, and residence of informant	When registered	Signature of registrar
333	Fifteenth December 1961 20 Betgrave Road Ladywell	George Warren	Male	80 years	Caretaker nun retired	1(a) cerebral thrombosis 11 Chronic bronchitis emphysema Certified by T.V. Meredith M.R.C.S.	D.W. Warren Son in law 2 Summerley Villas Hunstead Avenue Shortlands Kent	Eighteenth December 1961	K.m. Payne Deputy Registrar

I, KATHLEEN MAY PAYNE, DEPUTY, Registrar of Births and Deaths for the Sub-district of SYDENHAM, in the METROPOLITAN BOROUGH OF LEWISHAM, do hereby certify that this is a true copy of Entry No. 333 in the Register Book of Deaths for the said Sub-district, and that such Register Book is now legally in my custody.

WITNESS MY HAND this 18th day of December, 1961.

K.m. Payne Deputy Registrar of Births and Deaths.

CAUTION:—Any person who (1) falsifies any of the particulars on this certificate, or (2) uses a falsified certificate as true, knowing it to be false, is liable to prosecution.

it is through details of the informant, rather than the deceased, that death certificates can play a crucial role in the tracing process. The informant's name, address and relationship to the deceased often build the last bridge to family members being found.

Thus information contained in birth, marriage and death certificates is invaluable in relation to both individual identity and the search for lost relatives. It represents a starting point in more ways than one. But before you can utilize this information you have to know how to obtain it.

Using the birth, marriage and death indexes

Applications for the certificates outlined above can be made by post to the Office of National Statistics (ONS) or in person, at the Family Records Centre in London, where the indexes may be consulted. Postal applications for certificates are convenient for the purchase of the document when relatively full information is already available. For example, if you want to obtain the birth certificate of Jane Smith and you already know her father's name, or that he was not named, or her place of birth, or her mother's maiden name, but you are not certain of her exact date of birth, it is possible to make a postal application and request that a search (usually limited to a five-year period) be conducted. However, where the need to trace arises in the context of a lack of information, this process often involves obtaining a series of certificates. The cost of searches and certificates can make this an expensive process.

Personal searches at the Family Records Centre can be more effective, particularly where the search involves tracing a number of people about whom little is known, as in the case of Ian Fairway. The indexes at the Family Records Centre are organized like a large library, along rows of shelves in separate sections for each life event. The index binders are colour-coded for ease of reference. Births are red, marriages green and deaths black. Individual volumes are arranged alphabetically for each yearly quarter, based on the date of registration. The alphabetical order of the index relates to the surname of the person who has been born, married or died and, within this, to their first name(s). In relation to marriages there are two separate entries, each corresponding to the surname of one party.

The date of registration usually differs from the date of a birth or a death. Deaths may not be registered until a few days after the event. Births can be registered at any time during the six weeks following the event. Given that the indexes are arranged quarterly (March, June, September, December) and yearly, this means that an entry of a birth or death may not appear until the following quarter or even the year following the date of the event. A baby born on 1 December 1985, for example, may not be registered until six weeks later, on 12 January 1986 and so will appear in the March index of 1986. Marriages are always registered in the quarter when the event took place. It takes some time to produce the indexes; consequently, records will not be available for events occurring during the last 12 months.

Birth index

The birth index lists:

- name of child (in alphabetical ordering of last and then first names);
- mother's maiden name;
- place where birth was registered;
- reference number.

Where a mother is unmarried and the birth of her child is registered in her maiden surname, this name will appear in the first and second columns in the birth index.

It is not necessary to know all of the details of a registration in order to use the birth index or to obtain a copy of a birth certificate, but the more information available the easier it will be to identify the correct entry in the index. Knowledge about geographical connections, for example, can compensate for lack of knowledge about mother's maiden name by enabling the searcher to distinguish a Jane Smith known to have been born in Coventry from other Jane Smiths. Similarly, where mother's maiden name is known but place of registration is not, the required entry can be identified. The exact date of birth does not appear in the index and the record may appear in the index for the next quarter to that in which the birth took place.

Where the year of birth is unknown it is necessary to consult the index for every quarter of every year, but approximate age can usually be determined from broader family histories, so a five- or 10-year search will often serve to locate the entry sought. This sounds arduous, but a 10-year search usually takes about an hour, depending upon how common the name is and, thus, the number of entries. A search for Jane Smith will take much longer than a search for Jane Pavlovic or for Anita Smith, whereas a search for Jane C.B. Smith will be more straightforward than one for her singularly named sister!

Be aware of different spellings of names before you embark upon a search: Jane Smith might be Jayne or Jaine Smyth and will be located in a different part of the alphabetically ordered index accordingly.

> To search for the birth of someone called Angela Allen, born 25 June 1954, place of birth and mother's maiden name unknown.

Consult the red birth index for the June quarter of 1954 under the surname Allen. Everyone registered under that name at that time will be listed alphabetically according to their first names, thus:

Name	Mother's maiden name	Registration district
Allen		
Agatha B.	Smith	Portsmouth
Aileen	Anderson	Coventry
Alan	Bell	Liverpool
Andrew	Allen	Hackney
Angela	Pickard	Nuneaton
Angela	Harrison	Bromsgrove
Anita J.	Allen	Birmingham

There are two possible entries in the 1954 June quarter index that correspond to the known details of the Angela Allen in question. Either or neither of these may relate to the Angela Allen that you seek. Her birth may have been registered six weeks later and, if so, it will appear in the next quarter; this volume should also be checked. Make a note of all of the possible corresponding entries, including those with a middle name – unless you are certain, for example from seeing the short birth certificate, that Angela Allen has no middle name. Even if Angela uses a middle name, do not disregard entries in the index without one because many people acquire a middle name in adulthood!

The exact details of the index (year and quarter) and the reference numbers that appear alongside the entry should be noted for use when applying for the certificate.

Marriage index

Marriage indexes are in green binders. Up to 1983, they were compiled alphabetically in yearly quarters. From 1984 onwards, they are arranged solely in alphabetical order for the full year. Entries in the marriage index are listed thus:

| Full name | surname of spouse | registration district | ref. no. |

As with the birth index, the information is very limited, but it is not necessary to know all the details in order to locate the entry you seek. You may be able to use some known details that do not appear in the index as 'checking information' when applying for marriage certificates.

> You wish to search for an entry relating to a Simon George Whittaker. You know very little about him, other than that he originates from the Bournemouth area and was thought to be aged about 18 years when his daughter was born in 1978. You are not even certain whether Simon George Whittaker ever married. Therefore you do not know the name of his spouse or the district in which a marriage may have taken place. You do know the name of Simon George Whittaker's father (to use as checking information on your application form).

Begin by looking at what you do know. If Simon George Whittaker was aged 18 in 1978, he must have been born in approximately 1960. This means that he was not old enough to marry legally until 1976.

Begin a search of the marriage indices from about 1974, to allow for error. Search each quarter for each year under W for Whittaker and under S for Simon. Make a note of every entry that might possibly be the Simon George Whittaker you seek. Pay particular attention to every Simon G. Whittaker, but do not disregard other variations or 'plain' Simon Whittaker. Pay particular attention to any entries that relate to the registration district of Bournemouth, but do not disregard entries relating to a Simon Whittaker in other areas.

Name	Surname of spouse	District
Whittaker		
Simon	Crawford	Bournemouth
Simon	Stevens	Doncaster
Simon A.	Hodgson	Canterbury
Simon A.M.	Flamson	Ampthill
Simon B.	Huggins	Yns Mon
Simon F.	Anderson	Coventry
Simon G.	Hannon	Bristol
Simon G.	Scott	Bournemouth

Any of these entries might relate to the Simon George Whittaker you seek, since the information you have about him is very limited and has not been verified by other sources (such as his birth certificate or a close family member). Adopt a strategic process of elimination and begin with what you know. In the first instance, apply for the certificate relating to Simon G. Whittaker who married Scott in Bournemouth, since two of these details correspond: middle initial and district. Then apply for the certificates relating to Simon Whittaker who married Crawford in Bournemouth and the certificate relating to Simon G. Whittaker who married Hannon in Bristol, since in each case one of the details corresponds: geography in the first and middle initial in the second. The entries should be cross-referenced against the alphabetical index listing the name of the spouse. Check that the reference numbers for each entry correspond. The entry for the spouse will list her full name and this should be noted for the purpose of completing the application form for the marriage certificate. You may find that the full details on any certificate obtained automatically eliminate it from your search; it may be, for example, that the marriage certificate relating to Simon G. Whittaker and Hannon who married in Bournemouth reveals that they were aged 42 and 37 years, respectively, at the time of their marriage in 1982 and, therefore, cannot be the person(s) you seek. If, however, this certificate reveals Simon George Whittaker to be aged 22 years at time of marriage in 1982, there is a strong possibility that this is the Simon George Whittaker that you are seeking.

The certificate will reveal his address at time of marriage, his occupation, the name of his father (which may allow you to obtain Simon's birth certificate) and his father's occupation. All of this information can be followed through, verified or eliminated via other sources. The section relating to the father of the bride or groom usually states whether they are retired or deceased. If the latter is the case, consult the death indices next, working backwards through the quarters and years from the date of the marriage (when he was known not to be alive).

Death index

Death indexes are in black binders that list:

- name of deceased (in alphabetical order of last and then first names);
- district in which the death was registered;
- age at death, or date of birth (differs according to date of index);
- reference number.

Like births, deaths which occurred in one quarter of a year may be registered in a subsequent quarter and will thus be found in a later index. As with the indices relating to births and marriages, it is not necessary to be familiar with all of the details in order to conduct a search of the index or to obtain a copy of the death certificate. Known details that do not appear in the index may be used as 'checking information' when applying for certificates. A note of caution: since the deceased themselves cannot register their own death, the information recorded is only as accurate as the knowledge of the informant registering the death.

To search for an entry relating to the death of Maria May Pope.

Maria's exact age or date of birth is unknown but it is known that she married Richard Pope in 1946. Maria must have been aged at least 16 at her marriage; therefore she was born in or before 1930.

Maria and Richard Pope are known to have been living in Coventry in 1976. Their whereabouts since then are unknown and it is not known for certain that Maria has actually died. Maria was aged 46 years when she was last known to be alive. It is unlikely, though not impossible, that she died at this young age. It might, therefore, be better to commence the search by consulting the most recent death indices that correspond to Maria's later years, and working backwards to 1976.

Consult each quarter for each year under P for Pope and then M for Maria, paying particular attention to Marias with the middle initial also M. (for May), but not ruling out 'plain' Marias. Pay particular attention to any Maria Pope who died in Coventry, but do not rule out other districts (it is not known whether Maria remained in Coventry after 1976 and, even if she did, she may have died while away from home). Finally, focus on any Maria M. Pope whose date of birth is recorded as being 1930 or before. Make a note of every entry that might relate to the one you seek.

The search reveals five entries that might relate to the Maria May Pope that you seek:

1	1992	–	Maria M.	–	Coventry	–	born 12/6/29
2	1989	–	Maria	–	Lewisham	–	born 1/4/27
3	1989	–	Maria M.	–	York	–	born 15/1/20
4	1988	–	Maria	–	Liverpool	–	born 6/8/30
5	1986	–	Maria M.	–	Leicester	–	born 2/9/31

You might need to obtain all of the certificates in a process of elimination and verification, but you should begin with the most likely. In this instance, entries 1, 3 and 5 correspond most closely to the known name. Districts in which the deaths were registered are limited in their helpfulness but 1 corresponds with the last known whereabouts. Obtain the certificate for entry 1 first because it corresponds most closely to known details relating to Maria May Pope. If it is known that Maria remained married to Richard, you should state on the application form that she is the wife or widow of Richard Pope for checking purposes. Full details on the death certificate will reveal whether this is the same Maria May Pope you are seeking.

Applying for certificates

Application forms for birth, marriage, death and adoption certificates can be completed and submitted at the Family Records Centre. Always apply for 'full', rather than 'short', certificates since the latter do not give comprehensive details. Where all of the details requested on the form cannot be completed, this does not usually prevent the application being processed. Some details that may be unknown to you – parents' full names, for example – will not appear in the index, but will be requested on the application form. Where these details are known, they can be used as 'checking information': so, for example, a certificate can be requested 'only if mother's full name is Rosa Alice'. All of the entries you refer to will still be checked, but a reduced rate will be charged for entries that do not correspond to the checking information.

The certificate(s) ordered will arrive by post four working days later, or you can collect them from the Family Records Centre in person the following day for an increased fee. The certificates will show the details outlined above. Combining these with other family documents and with other sources of public information, detailed below, develops a picture of the child's family and may assist in tracing parents or other relatives.

The National Health Service Register

The name of every person in England and Wales who is, or has been, registered with a general practitioner is placed on the National Health Service Register. The register is kept by the Office for National Statistics at Southport. The NHS register is not open to the public and ONS cannot divulge addresses relating to any persons. However, ONS may be able to assist in re-establishing contact through the two-tier service which is provided. Firstly, on receipt of full details (such as a copy of a birth certificate) ONS may be able to confirm whether a person is currently registered with a doctor in England or Wales, or whether notification of death has been received. In the case of notification of death, ONS will disclose details of when the death occurred and where it was registered. Information of deaths is available through the NHS register before it appears in the index at the Family Records Centre. Secondly, ONS provides a 'mediation' service and can pass a letter on to any person currently registered with an NHS doctor. Access to this service may be gained by writing to the National Health Service Register at the Office of National Statistics. It is subject to the following strictly enforced criteria:

- Contact must be to the advantage of the person being sought.
- ONS cannot assist in cases where an adoption is involved, in tracing former husbands and wives, or where contact may, in the opinion of ONS, disrupt personal or domestic circumstances. A letter in an unsealed envelope should be submitted for ONS to pass on to the person being sought.
- The letter will be held for up to three months while attempts at contact are made.
- If a positive response is received, ONS will notify you that the letter has been forwarded. Otherwise, your letter will be returned to you.
- ONS reserves the right to refuse applications or to cease processing at any time without explanation.
- No guarantees can be given.

Electoral registers

A list of electors, the Electoral Roll, is compiled in every area. The register is compiled by addresses and lists the names of persons able to vote at every address in the area. Electoral registers can be used either to confirm that a named person is residing at a known address or to trace how long they lived at a known address, with whom, or when they appear to have left. This information can be helpful in relation to the search for or approach to family members or for the death or marriage of family members.

Current and recent electoral registers are kept in local libraries and are open to the public. Old electoral registers are usually kept in district council archives and are accessible via the archivist. Most libraries and councils can be consulted by telephone and can provide copies of electoral registers, although there are local variations in service and fees. Electoral registration departments located within local district councils deal with all issues relating to the organization of electoral data. Computerized systems potentially enable electoral registers to be compiled and/or used according to names, rather than addresses. There is no universal policy, but local authorities can use their discretion in responding to requests for information relating to a named person's whereabouts in their area.

Like other sources of information, however, the electoral register is only as reliable as the information submitted; its reliability can vary for all sorts of personal and/or political reasons. For example, many people did not place themselves on the electoral register during the 'poll tax' era, but this does not necessarily mean that they did not reside at a particular address.

The Salvation Army

The Salvation Army offer a 'Family Tracing Service' that was first established under the title 'Mrs Booth's Enquiry Bureau' about a century ago. The service can offer support to those involved in searching for relatives throughout the United Kingdom and in many countries overseas. Access to the service can be gained by contacting the Salvation Army.

'There are certain enquiries with which the tracing service does not normally become involved, for example those to do with: friends, alleged fathers of non-marital children, young people under 16/17 years, former husbands or wives, spouses for divorce purposes, estate or similar business matters, genealogies' (The Salvation Army Family Tracing Service).

The service can be reached by contacting the Salvation Army at the address set out in the appendix.

Appendix: useful addresses

The Family Records Centre
1 Myddleton Street
Islington
London EC1R 1UW

General Register Office (Eire)
Joyce House
8-11 Lombard Street East
Dublin 2

Office for National Statistics
General Register Office (England and Wales)
Smedley Hydro
Trafalgar Road
Birkdale
Southport
PR8 2HH

General Register Office (Scotland)
New Register House
Edinburgh EH1 3YT

Office for National Statistics
National Health Service General Register
Smedley Hydro
Trafalgar Road
Birkdale
Southport
PR8 2HH

The Salvation Army
Family Tracing Service
105–109 Judd Street
London WC1H 9TS

Bibliography

Adams, R. Dominelli, L. and Payne, M. (1998) *Social Work: Themes, Issues and Critical Debates* (Basingstoke: Macmillan).
Ahmad, B. (1990) *Black Perspectives in Social Work* (Birmingham: Venture Press).
Aldgate, J. (1989) *Using Written Agreements with Children and Families* (London: Family Rights Group).
Amit-Talai, V. (1995) *Youth Cultures: a Cross-cultural Perspective* (London: Routledge).
Arnstein, S.R. (1969) 'A ladder of citizen participation', *Journal of the American Institute of Planners*, 35 (4) 216–24.
Arnstein, S.R. (1971) 'Eight rungs on the ladder of citizen participation', in E.S. Cahn and B.A. Passett (eds), *Citizen Participation: Effecting Community Change* (London: Praeger).
Association of Directors of Social Services (1997) *The Foster Care Market: A National Perspective* (Ipswich: Suffolk Social Services).
Audit Commission (1994) *Seen but not heard: co-ordinating community child health and social services for children in need* (London: HMSO).
Banks, M., Bates, I., Breakwell, G., Bynner, J., Emler, N., Jamieson, L. and Roberts, K. (1992) *Careers and Identities* (Buckingham: Open University Press).
Banks, N. (1992) 'Techniques for Direct Identity Work with Black Children', *Adoption and Fostering*, 16 (3) 19–24.
Barn, R. (1993) *The Black Child in the Public Care* (London: Batsford).
Barn, R., Sinclair, R. and Ferdinand, D. (1997) *Acting on Principle: An Examination of Race and Ethnicity in Social Services Provision for Children and Families* (London: BAAF).
Bebbington, A. and Miles, J. (1989) 'The background of children who enter local authority care', *British Journal of Social Work*, 19, 349–68.

Bell, M. (1996) 'An account of the experiences of 51 families involved in an initial child protection conference', *Child and Family Social Work*, 1 (1) 43–55.
Beresford, P. and Croft, S. (1986) *Whose Welfare?* (Brighton: Lewis Cohen Urban Studies Centre).
Berger, J. (1980) *About Looking* (London: Winters and Readers).
Bernard, J. (1973) *The future of marriage* (London: Souvenir Press).
Berridge, D. (1995) 'Families in need: crisis and responsibility', in H. Dean (ed.), *Parents' Duties, Children's Debts: The Limits of Policy Intervention* (Aldershot: Ashgate).
Berridge, D. (1997) *Foster Care: A Research Review* (London: Stationery Office).
Berridge, D. and Brodie, I. (1998) *Children's Homes Revisited* (London: Jessica Kingsley).
Berridge, D. and Cleaver, H. (1987) *Foster Home Breakdown* (Oxford: Blackwell).
Berridge, D., Brodie, I., Porteous, D., Ayre, P., Barrett, D., Burroughs, L. and Wenman, H. (forthcoming) *Planning, Family Support and the Use of Residential Care for Children and Young People* (Luton: University of Luton).
Biehal, N. (1993) 'Changing Practice: participation rights and community care', *British Journal of Social Work*, 23, 443–58.
Biehal, N. and Sainsbury, E. (1991) 'From Values to Rights in Social Work', *British Journal of Social Work*, 21, 245–57.
Biehal, N., Clayden, J., Stein, M. and Wade, J. (1992a) *Prepared for Living?* (London: National Children's Bureau).
Biehal, N., Clayden, J., Stein, M. and Wade, J. (1995) *Moving On: Young People and Leaving Care Schemes* (London: HMSO).
Biehal, N., Fisher, M., Marsh, P. and Sainsbury, E. (1992b) 'A Framework of Rights for Social Work', in A. Coote (ed.), *The Welfare of Citizens* (London: Rivers Oram Press).
Bilson, A. and Barker, R. (1995) 'Parental Contact with Children Fostered and in Residential Care after the Children Act 1989', *British Journal of Social Work*, 25, 367–81.
Blasi, A. (1988) 'Identity and the development of the self', in D.K. Lapsley and F. Clark Power (eds), *Self, ego and identity: integrative approaches* (New York: Springer Verlag).
BMA, GMSC, HEA, Brook Advisory Centres, FPA and RCGP (1995) *Confidentiality and people under 16* (London: Health Education Authority).
Booth, T. and Booth, W. (1994) *Parenting Under Pressure; Mothers and Fathers with Learning Difficulties* (Buckingham: Open University Press).
Brandon, M., Thoburn, J., Lewis, A. and Way, A. (1999) *Safeguarding Children with The Children Act 1989* (London: Stationery Office).

Brannen, J., Dodd, K., Oakley, A. and Storey, P. (1994) *Young People, Health and Family Life* (Buckingham: Open University Press).
Broad, B. (1997) *Young People Leaving Care: Life After the Children Act 1989* (London: Jessica Kingsley).
Brodie, I. and Berridge, D. (1996) *Exclusion from School: Research Themes and Issues* (Luton: University of Luton).
Brodzinski, D., Singer, L. and Braff, A. (1984) 'Children's understanding of adoption', *Child Development*, 55 (3) 869–78.
Brown, C. (1984) *Child Abuse Parents Speaking* (Bristol: School of Advanced Urban Studies).
Buchanan, A. (1994) *Partnership in Practice* (Aldershot: Avebury).
Bullock, R., Little, M. and Millham, S. (1993a) *Going Home* (Aldershot: Dartmouth).
Bullock, R., Little, M. and Millham, S. (1993b) *Residential Care for Children: A Review of the Research* (London: HMSO).
Burkitt, I. (1991) *Social Selves: Theories of the Social Formation of Personality* (London: Sage).
Burman, E. (1994) *Deconstructing Developmental Psychology* (London: Routledge).
Butler, I. and Williamson, H. (1994) *Children Speak: Children Trauma & Social Work* (Harlow: Longman/NSPCC).
Butler-Sloss, Lord Justice E. (1988) *Report of the Inquiry into Child Abuse in Cleveland 1987*, 1988 Cmnd 412 (London: HMSO).
Chambers, C., Funge, S., Harris, G. and Williams, C. (1996) *Celebrating Identity: a Resource Manual for Practitioners Working with Black Children and Young People Including Black Children of Mixed Parentage* (Stoke on Trent: Trentham).
Cheetham, J. and Kazi, M.A.F. (1998) *The Working of Social Work* (London: Jessica Kingsley).
Children Act Advisory Committee (1997) *Final Report* (London: Lord Chancellor's Department).
Children's Rights Development Unit (1994) *U.K. Agenda for Children* (London: CRDU).
Chodorow, N. (1978) *The Reproduction of Mothering: Psychoanalysis and the Sociology of Gender* (Berkeley: University of California Press).
Clarke, J. (1996) 'After Social Work?', in N. Parton (ed.), *Social Theory, Social Change and Social Work* (London: Routledge).
Cleaver, H. and Freeman, P. (1995) *Parental Perspectives in Cases of Suspected Child Abuse* (London: HMSO).
Cloke, C. and Davies, M. (eds) (1995) *Participation and Empowerment in Child Protection* (London: Pitman Publishing).

Coleman, J. (1992) 'The Nature of Adolescence', in J. Coleman and C. Warren-Adamson (eds), *Youth Policy in the 1990s* (London: Routledge).
Coleman, J.C. and Hendry, L. (1990) *The Nature of Adolescence* (London: Routledge).
Colton, M., Drury, C. and Williams, M. (1995) *Children in Need* (Aldershot: Avebury).
Coombe, V. and Little, A. (1986) *Race and Social Work* (London: Tavistock).
Coote, A. (ed.) (1992) *The Welfare of Citizens* (London: Rivers Oram Press).
Cretney, S. and Masson, J. (1997) *Principles of family law* (London: Sweet and Maxwell).
Crosskill, D. (ed.) (1994) *The Black Family Within Us: a Report of the Black Social Workers' Residential Conference* (London: CCETSW).
Daniel, P. and Ivatts, J. (1998) *Children and Social Policy* (Basingstoke: Macmillan).
Dartington Social Research Unit (1995) *Child Protection: Messages from Research* (London: HMSO).
Davies, M. and Cloke, C. (1995) 'Participation and Empowerment in Child Protection' in C. Cloke and M. Davies (eds), *Participation and Empowerment in Child Protection* (London: Pitman Publishing).
Dean, H. (ed.) (1995) *Parents' Duties, Children's Debts: The Limits of Policy Intervention* (Aldershot: Ashgate).
De'Ath, E. and Pugh, G. (1985–6) *Partnership Papers* (London: National Children's Bureau).
Dennehy, A., Smith, L. and Harker, P. (1997) *Not to be Ignored; Young People, Poverty and Health* (London: Child Poverty Action Group).
DH (1989a) *The Care of Children: Principles and Practice* (London: HMSO).
DH (1989b) *An Introduction to the Children Act* (London: HMSO).
DH (1991a) *Patterns and Outcomes: Child Placement* (London: HMSO).
DH (1991b) *Children Act 1989 Guidance and Regulations Volume 1, court orders* (London: HMSO).
DH (1991c) *The Children Act Guidance and Regulations Volume 2* (London: HMSO).
DH (1991d) *Children Act 1989 Guidance and Regulations Volume 3, family placements* (London: HMSO).
DH (1991e) *Working Together under the Children Act 1989* (London: HMSO).
DH (1991f) *Children Act Guidance and Regulations, Volume 9, adoption issues* (London: HMSO).
DH (1993) *Children Act Report 1992*, Cmnd 2144 (London: HMSO).
DH (1995) *The Challenge of Partnership in Child Protection* (London: HMSO).
DH (1996) *Children and young people on child protection registers* (London: Department of Health).

DH (1997) *Children's Homes at 31 March 1997 England* (London: Department of Health).
DH (1998) *Quality Protects* (London: Department of Health).
DH *Personal social services records – disclosure of information to clients*, Circular LAC (83) 14 (London: Department of Health).
DH *Data Protection Act 1984 Social work etc orders: individual's right of access to information*, Circular LAC (87) 10 (London: Department of Health).
DH *Data Protection Act 1984 Social work etc orders: individual's right of access to information*, Circular LAC (88) 16 (London: Department of Health).
DH *Personal social services: confidentiality of personal information*, Circular LAC (88) 17 (London: Department of Health).
DH *Access to personal files Act 1987 Access to personal files (social services) regulations: Guidance notes*, Circular LAC (89) 2 (London: Department of Health).
DHSS (1985) *Social Work Decisions in Child Care: Recent Research Findings and their Implications* (London: HMSO).
Dobash, R. and Dobash, R. (1992) *Women, Violence and Social Change* (London: Routledge).
Eichenbaum, L. and Orbach, S. (1982) *Outside in–Inside out: women's psychology – a feminist psychoanalytical approach* (Harmondsworth: Penguin).
Eichenbaum, L. and Orbach, S. (1985) *Understanding Women* (Harmondsworth: Penguin).
Erikson, E. (1968) *Identity: Youth and Crisis* (New York: Norton).
Erikson, E. (1977) *Childhood and Society* (London: Paladin).
Family Rights Group (1986) *Promoting Links: keeping children and families in touch* (London: Family Rights Group).
Family Rights Group (1991) *The Children Act 1989: Working in Partnership with Families* (London: HMSO).
Fanshel, D. and Shinn, E. (1978) *Children in Foster Care: A Longitudinal Investigation* (New York: Columbia Press).
Farmer, E. and Owen, M. (1995) *Child Protection Practice: Private risks and public remedies* (London: HMSO).
Farmer, E. and Parker, R. (1991) *Trials and Tribulations* (London: HMSO).
Fisher, M., Marsh, P. and Phillips, D. with Sainsbury, E. (1986) *In and Out of Care: The Experiences of Children, Parents and Social Workers* (London: Batsford/BAAF).
Fletcher-Campbell, F. (1997) *The Education of Children who are looked after* (London: NFER).
Forder, C. (1995) 'Legal establishment of the parent–child relationship: constitutional principles', PhD thesis, University of Maastricht.
Foreman, A. (1977) *Femininity as Alienation: Women and the Family in Marxism and Psychoanalysis* (London: Pluto).

Fox Harding, L. (1991) *Perspectives in Child Care Policy* (London: Longman).
Fratter, J. (1996), *Adoption with contact* (London: BAAF).
Fratter, J., Rowe, J., Sapsford, D. and Thoburn, J. (1991) *Permanent Family Placement* (London: BAAF).
Freeman, P. and Hunt, J. (1998) *Parental Perspectives on Care Proceedings – Evaluating the Children Act* (London: Stationery Office).
Gardner, R. (1987) *Who says? Choice and Control in Care* (London: National Children's Bureau).
Geerz, C. (1979) 'From the natives' point of view: On the nature of Anthropological Understanding', in P. Rabinow and W.M. Sullivan (eds), *Interpretive Social Science* (Berkeley: University of California Press).
Gibbons, J., Gallagher, B., Bell, C. and Gordon, D. (1995) *Development after physical abuse in early childhood: a follow-up study of children on child protection registers* (Norwich: University of East Anglia).
Gilligan, C. (1982) *In a different voice: psychological theory and women's voice* (Cambridge, Mass. and London: Harvard University Press).
Gittens, D. (1998) *The Child in Question* (Basingstoke: Macmillan).
Goldstein, J., Freud, A. and Solnit, J. (1973) *Beyond the Best Interests of the Children* (New York: Free Press).
Graham, H. (1994) *Hardship and Health in Women's Lives* (Hemel Hempstead: Harvester Wheatsheaf).
Greenwood, J. (1994) *Realism, Identity and Emotion: Reclaiming Social Psychology* (London: Sage).
Grimshaw, R. and Sinclair, R. (1997a) *Planning to Care: Regulation, Procedure and Practice Under the Children Act 1989* (London: National Children's Bureau).
Grimshaw, R. and Sinclair, R. (1997b) *Planning and Reviewing under the Children Act 1989: research messages for local authorities* (London: National Children's Bureau).
Haimes, E. and Timms, N. (1985) *Adoption, identity and social policy* (Aldershot: Gower).
Hamilton, C. and Hopegood, L. (1997) 'Offering children confidentiality: law and guidance', *Childright*, 140, 1–8.
Harris, N. (1993) *Law and Education* (London: Sweet and Maxwell).
Harrison, C. and Masson, J. (1994) 'Working in partnership with "lost" parents; issues of theory and practice', *Adoption and Fostering*, 18 (1), 40–44.
Harrison, C. and Pavlovic, A. (1996) 'Working in partnership with "lost" parents', in H. Argent (ed.), *See You Soon: Contact With Children Looked After by Local Authorities* (London: BAAF).
Hendrick, H. (1994) *Child Welfare England 1972–1989* (London: Routledge).
Hester, M. and Radford, L. (1996) *Domestic violence and child contact arrangements in England and Denmark* (Bristol: Policy Press).

Hill, M. and Tisdall, K. (1997) *Children and Society* (Harlow: Longman).
Hooper, C.A. (1992) *Mothers Surviving Sexual Violence* (London: Routledge).
Howe, D. (1992) 'Theories of helping, empowerment and participation', in J. Thoburn (ed.), *Participation in Practice – Involving Families in Child Protection* (Norwich: University of East Anglia).
Howe, D., Sawbridge, P. and Hinings, D. (1992) *Half a million women* (London: Penguin).
Humphreys, M. (1994) *Empty cradles* (London: Doubleday).
Humphries, B. (1994) 'Empowerment and social research: elements for an analytical framework', in B. Humphries and C. Truman (eds), *Re-thinking Social Research* (Aldershot: Avebury).
Hunt, J. and Macleod, A. (1998) *The Last resort: Child protection, the courts and the Children Act, 1989* (London: Stationery Office).
Ince, L. (1998) *Making it alone: A study of the Care experience of young black people* (London: BAAF).
Ingleby, D. (1986) 'Development in Social Context', in M. Richards and P. Wright (eds), *Children of Social Worlds* (Cambridge: Polity Press).
Jenkins, S. and Norman, E. (1972) *Filial Deprivation and Foster Care* (New York: Columbia University Press).
Jenks, C. (1996) *Childhood* (London: Routledge).
Johnston, J. (1973) *Lesbian Nation and the Feminist Solution* (New York: Simon & Schuster).
Jolly, S. (1994) Cutting the ties – the termination of contact in care, *Journal of Social Welfare and Family Law*, 3, 299–311.
Jones, G. (1987) 'Leaving the parental home: an analysis of early housing careers', *Journal of Social Policy*, 16 (1) 49–74.
Kahan, B. (1994) *Growing Up in Groups* (London: HMSO).
Katz, I. (1995) 'Approaches to Empowerment and Participation in Child Protection' in C. Cloke and M. Davies (eds), *Participation and Empowerment in Child Protection* (London: Pitman Publishing).
Kelly, L., Wingfield, R. and Burton, S. (1991) *An Explanatory Study of the Prevalence of Sexual Abuse in a Sample of 16–21-year-olds* (London: Child Abuse Studies Unit, North London Polytechnic).
Kelly, L., Wingfield, R., Burton, S. and Regan, L. (1995) *Splintered Lives* (London: Barnardo's).
Kirk, D. (1964) *Shared Fate* (New York: Free Press).
Kitzinger, C. (1987) *The Social Construction of Lesbianism* (London: Sage).
Kitzinger, C. (1989) 'Liberal Humanism as an Ideology of Social Control: the Regulation of Lesbian Identities', in J. Shotter and K.J. Gergen (eds), *Texts of Identity* (London: Sage).
Kitzinger, C. (1993) *Changing our Minds: Lesbianism Feminism and Psychology* (London: Only Women Press).

Kroger, J. (1989) *Identity in Adolescence: the Balance Between Self and Other* (London: Routledge).
Laming, H. (1998) *Social Services Facing the Future: The Seventh Annual Report of the Chief Inspector, Social Services Inspectorate 1997/1998* (London: Stationery Office).
Langan, M. (ed.) (1992) *Women, Oppression and Social Work* (London: Routledge).
Langan, M. and Clarke, J. (1994) 'Managing in the mixed economy of care', in J. Clarke, (ed.), *A Crisis in Care? Challenges to social work* (Milton Keynes: Open University Press).
Lansdown, G. (1995) 'Children's Rights to Participation: a Critique', in C. Cloke and M. Davies (eds), *Participation and Empowerment in Child Protection* (London: Pitman Publishing).
Law Commission (1988) *Guardianship and custody*, Report No 172 (London: HMSO).
Leonard, P. (1984) *Personality and Ideology: Towards a Materialist Understanding of the Individual* (London: Macmillan).
Lewis, A. (1992) 'An overview of research into participation in child protection work', in J. Thoburn (ed.), *Participation in Practice – Involving Families in Child Protection* (Norwich: University of East Anglia).
Lewis, A. (1994) *Chairing Child Protection Conferences* (Aldershot: Avebury).
Lewis, A., Shemmings, D. and Thoburn, J. (1992) *Participation in Practice: A Reader* (Norwich: University of East Anglia).
Lister, R. (1990) *The Exclusive Society: Citizenship and the Poor* (London: Child Poverty Action Group).
Loughran, G. and Riches, P. (1996) *Working in Partnership with Stepfamilies* (London: National Stepfamily Association).
MacLeod, M. and Saraga, E. (1988) *Child Sexual Abuse: Towards a Feminist Professional Practice* (London: PNL Press).
Mama, A. (1989) *The Hidden Struggle: Statutory and Voluntary Section Responses to Violence Against Women in the Home* (London: Race and Housing Research Unit).
Marsh, P. and Crow, G. (1998) *Family Group Conferences in Child Welfare* (Oxford: Blackwell Science).
Marsh, P. and Fisher, M. (1992) *Good Intentions: Developing partnership in social services* (York: Joseph Rowntree Trust).
Martin, F. (1998) 'Tales of transition: self narrative and direct scribing in exploring care leaving', *Child and Family Social Work*, 3 (1) 1–12.
Martin, J. (1989) *Modern Equity* (London: Stevens).
Masson, J. (1990) 'Contact between parents and children in long-term care: the unresolved dispute', *International Journal of Law and the Family*, 4 (1) 97–122.

Masson, J. (1992) 'Implementing Change for Children: Action at the Centre and Local Reaction', *Journal of Law & Society* 19 (3) 320-38.
Masson, J. (1997) 'Maintaining contact between parents and children in public care', *Children & Society*, 11 (4) 222-30.
Masson, J. and Harrison, C. (1993) 'Contact point', *Inside* (a supplement) *Community Care*, 28 October, pp.5-6.
Masson, J. and Winn Oakley, M. (1999) *Out of Hearing* (Chichester: John Wiley).
Masson, J., Harrison, C. and Pavlovic, A. (1997) *Working with Children and 'Lost' Parents: Putting Partnership into Practice* (York: York Publishing Services).
Maxime, J.E. (1986) 'Some psychological models of black self-concept' in S. Ahmad, J. Cheetham and J. Small (eds), *Social Work with Black Children and Their Families* (London: Batsford/BAAF).
Mayall, B. (1996) *Children, Health and the Social Order* (Buckingham: Open University Press).
Millham, S., Bullock, R., Hosie, K. and Halle, M. (1986) *Lost in Care* (Aldershot: Gower).
Millham, S., Bullock, R., Hosie, K. and Little, M. (1989) *Access disputes in child-care* (Aldershot: Gower).
Milner, J. (1993), 'A disappearing act: the differing career paths of fathers and mothers in child protection investigations', *Critical Social Policy*, 38 (Autumn).
Mitchell, J. (1974) *Feminism and Psychoanalysis* (Harmondsworth: Penguin).
Monaco, M. and Thoburn, J. (1987) *Self-help for parents with children in care* (Norwich: University of East Anglia).
Moore, S. and Rosenthal, D. (1993) *Sexuality in Adolescence* (London: Routledge).
Morris, J. (1995) *Gone Missing? A Research and Policy Review of Disabled Children in Residential and Foster Care* (London: Who Cares? Trust).
Morris, S. and Wheatley, H. (1994) *Time to Listen: the Experiences of Children and Residential and Foster Care* (London: Childline).
Morss, J.R. (1996) *Growing Critical: Alternatives to Developmental Psychology* (London: Routledge).
Mullender, A. (ed.) (1991) *Open adoption: the philosophy and the practice* (London: BAAF).
Mullender, A. (1996) *Rethinking Domestic Violence* (London: Routledge).
Mullender, A. and Kearn, C. (1997) *I'm here waiting: birth relatives' views on part 11 of the Adoption Contact Register for England and Wales* (London: BAAF).
Mullender, A. and Morley, R. (1994) *Children Living with Domestic Violence* (London: Whiting and Birch).

Mullins, A. (1997) *Making a Difference: Practice Guidelines for Professionals Working with Women and Children who Experience Domestic Violence* (London: NCH Action for Children).

National Foster Care Association (1997) *Foster Care in Crisis* (London: National Foster Care Association).

Owen, M. (1992) *Social Justice and Children in Care* (Aldershot: Avebury).

Packman, H. (1975) *The Child's Generation* (Oxford: Basil Blackwell and Martin Robertson).

Packman, J. (1968) *Childcare needs and numbers* (London: Allen & Unwin).

Packman, J. (1986) *Who Needs Care?* (Oxford: Basil Blackwell).

Packman, J. and Hall, C. (1995) *The Implementation of Section 20 of the Children Act 1989: Report to the Department of Health* (Totnes: Dartington Social Research Unit).

Packman, J. and Hall, C. (1998) *From care to accommodation. Evaluating the Children Act* (London: Stationery Office).

Packman, J. and Jordan, B. (1991) 'The Children Act: looking forward, looking back', *Children & Society*, 21 (4) 315–27.

Pahl, J. (1989) *Money and Marriage* (London: Macmillan).

Palmer, S. (1992) 'Including birth families in foster care: a Canadian–British comparison', *Children and Youth Services Review*, 14 (5) 407–25.

Parker, R., Ward, H., Jackson, S., Aldgate, J. and Wedge, P. (1991) *Looking After Children: Assessing Outcomes in Child Care* (London: HMSO).

Parsloe, P., Daines, R. and Lyins, K. (1990) *Aiming at Partnership* (London: Barnardo's).

Parton, N. (1991) *Governing the Family: Child Care, Child Protection and the State* (Basingstoke: Macmillan).

Parton, N. (1996) 'Social Theory, Social Change and Social Work: an Introduction', in N. Parton (ed.), *Social Theory, Social Change and Social Work* (London: Routledge).

Platt, D. and Shemmings, D. (eds) (1996) *Making Enquiries into Allegations of Child Abuse: Partnership with Families* (Chichester: John Wiley).

Prosser, H. (1978) *Perspectives on Foster Care* (London: National Children's Bureau).

Quinton, D., Rushton, A., Dance, C. and Mayes, D. (1997) 'Contact between children placed away from home and their birth parents: research issues and evidence', *Clinical Child Psychology and Psychiatry*, 2 (3) 393–413.

Rees, S. (1991), *Achieving power: practice and policy in social welfare* (Sydney: Allen & Unwin).

Rich, A. (1981) *Compulsory Heterosexuality and Lesbian Existence* (London: Only Women Press).

Richards, M. (1996) 'Addressing the needs of children and adults at separa-

tion and divorce', in J. Walker and J. Hornick (eds), *Communication in Marriage and Divorce* (London: BT Forum).
Richards, M. and Light, P. (eds) (1986) *Children of Social Worlds* (Cambridge: Polity Press).
Robinson, L. (1998) 'Social work through the life course', in R. Adams, L. Dominella and M. Payne (eds), *Social Work: Themes, Issues and Critical Debates* (Basingstoke: Macmillan).
Rodgers, B. and Pryor, J. (1998) *Divorce and separation: the outcomes for children* (York: Joseph Rowntree Foundation).
Rowe, J., Hundleby, M. and Garnett, L. (1989) *Child Care Now* (London: BAAF).
Ryan, J. (1992) 'Psychoanalysis and women loving women', in H. Crowley and S. Himmelweit (eds), *Knowing women: Feminism and Knowledge* (Cambridge: Polity Press in association with Open University Press).
Ryburn, M. (1992) *Adoption in the Nineties: Identity and Openness* (Leamington: Leamington Press).
Ryburn, M. (1994) *Contested Adoptions* (Aldershot: Arena).
Schaffer, R. (1990) *Making Decisions About Children* (Oxford: Basil Blackwell).
Schšn, D. (1983) *The Reflective Practitioner: How Professionals Think in Action* (Aldershot: Arena).
Select Committee on Health (1998) *Report: Children Looked after by Local Authorities*, HCP 247 (London: Stationery Office).
Sellick, C. and Thoburn, J. (1996) *What Works in Family Placement?* (Barkingside: Barnardo's).
Seve, L. (1978) *Man in Marxist Theory and the Psychology of the Person* (Brighton: Harvester).
SFLA (1997) *Guide to good practice for solicitors acting for children*, 4th edn (London: Solicitor's Family Law Association).
Sharland, E., Jones, D., Aldgate, J., Seal, H. and Croucher, M. (1996) *Professional Intervention in Child Sexual Abuse* (London: HMSO).
Shemmings, D. (1996) *Children's Involvement in Child Protection Conferences* (Norwich: UEA Social Work Monographs).
Shemmings, D. (1998) *In on the Act: Involving Young People in Family Support and Child Protection* (Norwich: University of East Anglia).
Shotter, J. and Gergen, K.J. (eds) (1989) *Texts of Identity* (London: Sage).
Sinclair, I. and Gibbs, I. (1998) *Children's Homes: A Study in Diversity* (Chichester: John Wiley).
Sinclair, R. (1984) *Decision Making in Statutory Reviews on Children in Care* (Aldershot: Gower).
Sinclair, R. (1998) *The education of children in need: a research overview* (London: National Children's Bureau).

Sinclair, R. and Grimshaw, R. (1997) 'Partnership with parents in planning the care of their children', *Children & Society*, 11, 231–41.
Slugoski, B. and Ginsberg, G. (1989) 'Ego identity and explanatory speech', in J. Shotter and K.J. Gergen (eds), *Texts of Identity* (London: Sage).
Squire, C. (1989) *Significant Differences: Feminism in Psychology* (London: Routledge).
SSI (1995) *Moving goal posts* (London: Department of Health).
SSI (1996) *For children's sake: an SSI inspection of local authority fostering services* (London: Department of Health).
SSI (1997) *Responding to Families in Need: Inspection of Assessment, Planning and Decision-Making in Family Support Services* (London: Department of Health).
Stafford, G. (1993) *Where to find adoption records* (London: BAAF).
Stein, M. and Carey, K. (1986) *Leaving care* (Oxford: Blackwell).
Steinberg, D. and Epstein, D. (1997) *Policing the Boundaries of Heterosexuality* (London: Routledge).
Stevenson, O. (1992) 'Social work intervention to protect children: aspects of research and practice', *Child Abuse Review*, 1, 19–32.
Thoburn J. (1985) 'What kind of permanence?' *Adoption and Fostering*, 9 (4) 29–34.
Thoburn, J. (1990) *Success and failure in permanent family placements* (Aldershot: Gower).
Thoburn, J., Brandon, M. and Lewis, A. (1997) 'Need, risk and significant harm', in Nigel Parton (ed.), *Child Protection and Family Support: Tensions, contradictions and possibilities* (London: Routledge).
Thoburn, J., Lewis, A. and Shemmings, D. (1995) *Paternalism or Partnership? Family involvement in the child protection process* (London: HMSO).
Thoburn, J., Murdoch, A. and O'Brien, A. (1986) *Permanence in Child Care* (Oxford: Blackwell).
Triseliotis, J. (1973) *In search of origins* (London: Routledge).
Triseliotis, J. (1985) 'Adoption with contact', *Adoption and Fostering*, 9 (4) 19–24.
Triseliotis, J. (1989) 'Foster care outcomes: a review of key research findings', *Adoption and Fostering*, 13 (3) 5–17.
Triseliotis, J. and Russell, J. (1984) *The Outcome of Adoption and Residential Care* (London: Gower).
Triseliotis, J., Sellick, C. and Short, R. (1995) *Foster Care: Theory and Practice* (London: Batsford).
Triseliotis, J., Shireman, J. and Hundleby, M. (1997) *Adoption Theory, Policy and Practice* (London: Cassell).
Tunnard, J. (1991) 'Setting the scene for partnership', in Family Rights Group

(ed.), *The Children Act 1989: Working in Partnership with Families* (London: HMSO).

United Nations High Commissioner for Refugees (1994) *Refugee children: guidelines for protection and care* (Geneva: UNHCR).

Utting, W. (1991) *Children in the public care* (London: HMSO).

Utting, W. (1997) *People like us* (London: Stationery Office).

Van Bueren, G. (1995) *The international law on the rights of the child* (London: Martinus Nijhoff).

Ward, H. (1995) *Looking after Children: Research in Practice* (London: HMSO).

Warner, M. (1994) *Fear of a Queer Planet: Queer Politics and Social Theory* (Minneapolis: University of Minnesota Press).

Weeden, C. (1987) *Feminist Practice and Post-Structurist Theory* (Oxford: Blackwell).

Whisman, V. (1996) *Queer by Choice: Lesbians, Gay Men and the Politics of Identity* (London: Routledge).

Who Cares? Trust (1993) *Not Just a Name* (London: National Consumer Council).

Williams, F. (1994) 'Social Relations, Welfare and the Post-Fordist Debate', in R. Burrows and B. Loader (eds), *Towards a Post-Fordist Welfare State* (London: Sage).

Wilson, M. (1993) *Crossing the Boundary: Black Women Survive Incest* (London: Virago).

Woodhead, M., Light, R. and Carr, R. (1991) *Growing up in a Changing Society* (London: Routledge).

Wozniak, R.H. (ed.) (1993) *Worlds of Childhood Reader* (New York: Harper Collins).

Young, L. and Bagley, C. (1975) 'Self esteem, self concept and the development of black identity: a local ethical overview', in G. Verma and C. Bagley (eds), *Race and Education Across Cultures* (London: Heinemann).

Index

abuse 12, 98
  access to information 38
  Cleveland cases 91
  emotional 74
  'single issue' families 54
  within care system 39, 76–7
Access to Personal Files Act 1987 35, 36
Access to Personal Files (Social Services) Regulations 1989 36
access to records 2, 34–40, 47–8, 72, 140
action research 3, 8–25
'acute distress' families 54
adaptive grieving 148
adolescence
  see also young people
  adoption information 148, 154
  identity 65–90, 121
  research study 17
adoption xiv, 145–54
  ascribed identity 72–3
  birth certificate 183
  contact process 176
  family loss 116
  'letterbox' services 44
  research study 14
Adoption and Fostering 9
advocacy 32
after care *see* leaving care
age, returning home relationship 129–30
anti-discriminatory practice 23, 67, 70–3
Area Child Protection Committee 157

Arnstein, S.R. 55, 137
Arrangements for the Placement of Children Regulations 1991 112
ascribed identity 72–3
assessment 159–60
Association of Directors of Social Services 99
attachments 8

Ballard, Barbara xv
barriers
  to contact 113
  to partnership 105, 108, 116–24
  to practice xiii, xv, 23
behavioural difficulties 12
Berridge, David xi, xiii, 91–103
Biehal, Nina xi, xiv, 127–43
birth certificates 168–9, 170, 180–3, 187, 189
birth index 171, 181, 187–9
black children *see* ethnicity
Brandon, M. 53
Brodzinski, David 147–8
Bruce, Ariel 168
Burnell, Alan xi, xiv, 145–54
Butler, I. 90

care orders 4, 29, 32–3, 36
care system
  abuse within 39, 76–7
  entering 14, 145
  files/reviews 80–1

identity development within 74
termination of contact 106
young people's attitudes towards 75–8
case management 163
case studies
  access to information 37, 38
  adoption 149–54
  confidentiality 38, 41–2
  gender prejudice 110–11
  letter contact 45
  parental role re-evaluation 123–4
  reviews 43
  tracing process 169–75
  transracial placements 3–4
  welfare 31–2, 33
chairing child protection conferences 58
The Challenge of Partnership in Child Protection (DH, 1995) 56, 60
Child Care Act 1980 34
child liberation 94
child protection x, xi, 13, 49
  conferences 50, 51–3, 57–9
  confidentiality 40
  priority of 115
  research 51–6
  state paternalism 93
Child Protection: Messages from Research (Dartington Social Research Unit, 1995) 53, 56
child rescue 109, 118
children
  see also adolescence; looked after children
  adoption issues 145–54
  cognitive development 147–8
  confidentiality 40–2, 47–8
  consultation 59
  identity 66, 160
  impact of loss 106, 116
  indirect contact 163–4
  interests 27
  interpretation of events 124–5
  legal status 30, 135
  long-term planning 22
  loss of family contact 107–8
  maintaining status quo 117
  numbers in care 1, 157
  research study 12–15, 20
  rights 28, 94–5, 120, 135, 136, 137
  time in care 97
  welfare 28, 31
Children Act 1989 ix, xii, xiii, 156
  child protection 49–50
  children's rights 94–5
  contact arrangements 44, 47
  court powers 159
  decision making 136
  identity 66
  implementation 2–3
  independent visiting service 164
  local authority obligations x, 27–8, 31, 34, 136
  parental responsibility 2, 28, 29–30, 92, 128, 135
  parental rights to information 36–40
  partnership 4–5, 91, 102
  planning process 97
  refusal of contact 106
  reviews 43
  termination of contact 113
citizenship rights 135
Cleaver, H. 53, 54
Cleveland abuse cases 91
Cleveland Report 51
coercion of parents 50, 54, 60
cognitive development 147–8
Community Care 9
complaints 33–4
compulsory orders 36
conferences
  child protection 50, 51–3, 57–9
  family group 97–8
  confidentiality 34, 35, 136, 176
  children's right to 38, 40–2
  partnership-based practice 61
conflict
  parent/social worker 60
  'rebellious' youth 70
  social worker role 22, 23
confusion 88
consultancy 11, 21
consultation
  children 59
  decision making 136, 137
  parental rights 30, 39
  planning process 97
  public 158
consumerism 127, 133–4

contact
  adoptive care 147–54
  after care 128, 129, 130–3, 137–8
  assessment/review systems 160–1
  barriers to partnership 116, 119–20, 122
  Children Act obligations 92
  court powers 159
  erosion of 113–14
  family 1–2, 7–8
  foster care 101
  initiating 175–9
  legal issues 44–7
  management issues 164–5
  orders for refusal of 106
  paradigms of 94
  parental role re-evaluation 124
  research 13, 17–18, 19, 96, 97
  residential care 95, 101–2
  staff training 161–2
  termination of 1–2, 13, 37, 46, 106, 112–13, 119
  visits 163
  young people's attitudes 81–4
Contact Regulations 1991 46
continuity 94, 117
correspondence 44, 45
counselling, adoption 150–1
court liaison system 159
court orders 29, 46
cross-cultural studies 8

Dartington Social Research Unit 53, 56, 96, 98
data collection 8–11
Data Protection Act 1984 35
death certificates 175, 180–1, 185–7, 193
death index 181, 187, 191–3
decision making
  child protection conferences 52, 59
  legal instruments 28
  parental involvement 92
  parents' rights 135, 136
  participation 128, 136, 137, 141–2
  research 96
deemed care order 4
Department of Health
  access to information 35
  Area Child Protection Committee 157
  child protection research 51, 53, 56, 60

foster care 99
  guidance on consultation 39
  identity 66–7
  LAC (Looking After Children)
    documentation 7, 35–6, 66–7, 159–60
  practice guidance 28
  quality of care 7
  research programme 95–6
deterrence model of contact 94
developmental psychology 69, 70, 73
direct contact 17, 83, 163, 164
disability 7, 15
disclosure of information, right to 35, 36
discrimination
  black identity 73
  female identity 71–2
  legal rights against 28
  multiple disadvantage 6
  parents xi, xv, 109, 123, 125
  step-families 99
  stigmatization 79
  welfare services 74
disruption model of contact 94
domestic violence 50, 84, 107, 110, 125
drug use 50

'effective helping' 61
Eichenbaum, L. 71
electoral register 173, 174, 194–5
emotions 7, 69
empowerment 3, 8, 141–2
Erikson, Erik 69, 70, 72
ethics of searching 179–80
ethnicity
  after care 85
  contact with family 83
  identity 73
  loss of community contact 107
  racism 4, 6, 73, 79, 83, 85
  transracial placements 4, 14
Eurocentricity 73, 110
European Commission of Human Rights 35
European Convention on Human Rights 28, 35, 41, 44
European Court of Human Rights 28
exclusion 71, 79
'exclusion clauses' 52
extended families 97–8, 131, 138

family
  see also siblings
  after care contact 128, 129, 130–3, 137–8, 141
  child protection process 52, 53, 55, 57–9
  contact 1–2, 7–8, 81–4, 95, 102, 160
  continuity of relationships 96
  fostering with relatives 100–1
  loss of contact 107–8
  parenthood 108–9
  partnership-based practice 60–1
  reconciliation 130–1, 137, 138–9
  step-families 98–9
  support services 2, 49, 58, 59, 94, 98
family group conferences 58, 97–8
Family Records Centre, London 171, 181, 187, 193
Family Rights Group 137
family trees 168
Farmer, E. 53
fathers 13, 15, 92, 107, 111
feminism 6, 71–2
files 80–1, 114–15, 168
filial deprivation 7, 111
'former' parents 4
foster care xiii
  adoptive care comparison 146–7, 149
  differential treatment 76–7
  exclusion of parents 113–14
  family ideology 111–12
  maltreatment within 77–8
  partnership approaches 95
  placements 99–101
  research study 14
  residential care comparison 78
foster carers
  abuse by 76–7
  barriers to partnership 117–18
  contact orders 113–14
  family ideology 111–12
  reviews 43–4
  support workers 63
  training 161–2
Fox Harding, L. 93–4
Freeman, P. 53, 54
Freud, Sigmund 71

Gaskin, Graham 35
Gaskin v. U.K. (1990) 35

gender
  division of labour 109–11
  identity development 71–2
General Registrar Office 174
gift sending 45, 88, 92, 115–16
'Gillick competency' 30, 40–1, 135
Gilligan, Carol 71
Ginsberg, G. 68, 71–2
grieving, adaptive 148
group supervision 165–6
guardian ad litem 46, 112

Hall, C. 50, 60
Harrison, Christine ix–xvi, 1–25, 65–90, 105–25
heterosexuality 72
homophobia 72
homosexuality 72
Howe, D. 60
Human Rights Act 1998 28
Humphreys, Margaret 155

identity xiii, 120, 125
  adolescence 65–90, 121
  adoption issues xiv, 146
  LAC assessment 160
'inclusive permanence' 100
independent visiting service 164
indexes
  birth 171, 181, 187–9
  death 181, 187, 191–3
  marriage 171, 181, 187, 188, 189–91
indirect contact 92, 163–4, 173–4
  see also letter contact
individual
  society dichotomy 68, 70, 73
  uniqueness of the 158
inequalities, structural 71, 93–4
information
  adoption issues 72–3, 147, 148, 149–52
  child protection conferences 57–8
  exchange of 83–4
  exclusion of fathers 111
  files 80
  personal identity 66, 87–9
  reviews 20
  right to 34–40, 47–8
  searching for parents xv, 168, 169, 179–80
  sharing 137, 139–40

sources of 180–95
institutions, social order 70
interests, parent/child dichotomy 27, 135–6
intrapsychic processes 70, 71
Iqbal, Nihid xvi

Jenkins, S. 7
Jenks, C. 65
Jolly, S. 94
Joseph Rowntree Foundation ix, xv

knowledge, young people's identity 66, 87–9

LAC (Looking After Children) documentation (DH, 1995) 7, 35–6, 66–7, 159–60
'ladder of citizen participation' 55, 93, 137
laissez faire approach 93
learning disability 50
leaving care xiv, 7–8, 84–5, 102, 127–43
legal aid 46–7
Legal Aid Board 113
legal issues xii, 27–48, 112–14, 159
letters
    indirect contact 17, 44–5, 88, 92, 115–16, 153, 163
    initiating contact with parents 175–9
Lewis, A. 51
life story work 66, 67, 89, 162, 168
local authorities
    care order instigation 32–3
    complaints against 33–4
    court liaison system 159
    delegation of parental responsibility 29, 32
    disclosure of information 36, 38–40, 42
    management approaches 165, 166
    obligations under Children Act 1989 x, 27–8, 31, 34, 136
    policy variations between 157–8
    pre-placement histories 151
    restoring contact 45–7
    reviews/monitoring 159–61
    staff/resource requirements 162–4
lone parent families 98–9
long-term care x, 6, 101, 115, 117, 119

long-term planning 22, 125
looked after children
    adopted children comparison xiv
    identity 66
    leaving care 132–3, 137
    longer term 49–50
    numbers in care 1, 157
    partnership-based practice 95–103
    research study 9, 10
    review meetings 58
loss
    adaptive grieving 148
    identity issues 76, 87
    reopening contact 153
Lost in Care (Millham et al, 1986) 1
lost parents ix–xv, 16–18, 36–7, 89, 105–16, 167–95

maltreatment xii, 50, 53, 76–7, 155
management
    lost parents 115
    partnership issues 58, 155–66
    research study 11, 24
marginalization 71, 106, 109
marriage certificates 171, 174, 180–1, 183–5, 191
marriage index 171, 181, 187, 188, 189–91
masculinity 71
Masson, Judith ix–xvi, 1–25, 27–48, 105–25
maturity 30
mediation xiv, 139, 142, 154
medical treatment, parental consent 30
mental health difficulties 50
Millham, S. 1, 46, 106
monitoring 159–61, 166
Morris, S. 15
mothers, division of labour 109–11
multiple disadvantage xiii, 6

National Foster Care Association 99
National Health Service Register 175, 193–4
needs, defining 141
negotiation 62–3
Norman, E. 7

Office of National Statistics (ONS) 181, 187, 193–4

oppression 6, 70–1, 72, 73, 74
  see also discrimination; racism
Orbach, S. 71
organizational culture 23
organizational factors xiv–xv, 16, 22, 25, 90, 114–15
Owen, M. 53

Packman, Jean 50, 60, 157
'paradox of personal identity' 68
paramountcy principle 136
parental responsibility 92, 127, 128, 135
  legal issues 29–32, 34, 36, 38–9, 42, 44–5
  mother/father distinction 109
parenthood 29, 108–9
parents
  access to information 34–40, 47–8, 140
  adoptive 150–2, 153, 154
  after care contact 129, 130–3, 137–8
  barriers to partnership 23, 116–20, 121–2
  child protection process 51–6, 57, 58
  complaints by 33–4
  conflicts of interest 135–6
  contact 44–7, 83–4, 92, 94, 101–2, 103
  discrimination against xi, xv, 109, 123, 125
  filial deprivation 7, 111
  foster care placements 100–2
  initiating contact with 175–9
  lost ix–xv, 16–18, 36–7, 89, 105–16, 167–95
  negotiation with 62–3
  participation in decision making 128, 136, 137, 141–2
  planning for leaving care 140–1
  poor social work practices 96–7
  power 134–5
  problem groups 50
  re-evaluation of role 123, 124, 125
  'rebellious' youth 70
  reconciliation 130–1, 137, 138–9
  research study 15, 16–20, 25
  residential care 95
  reviews 43–4
  rights 29, 30, 48, 93–4
  roles 27
  value of xii–xiii
  welfare agencies relationship x

willingness to participate in partnership 60
participation
  child protection process 52–3, 55–6
  decision making 128, 136, 137, 141–2
  ladder of citizen 55, 93, 137
paternalism
  practice 60
  state 93
patriarchy 71, 93
Pavlovic, Annie ix–xvi, 8, 167–95
peer relationships 146
permanency planning 7
personal identity 65–90, 120, 121, 125, 146, 160
placements
  adoption 145, 146
  extended family 98
  foster care 99–101, 111–12, 113–14, 117–18
  residential care 101–2
  transracial 4, 14
planning
  leaving care 140–1, 142
  long-term 22, 125
  process 97
Platt, D. 57
'play fair' practice 60
policy xiv, 157–9, 166
  barriers to partnership xv
  child protection 56–9
  ill-considered 155–6
Post-Adoption Centre, London 147, 151, 154, 176
poverty 71, 84, 110
power
  imbalances of 23, 134–5
  'ladder of participation' 93
  sharing of 55
practice
  barriers xiii, xv, 23
  child protection 51–6
  guidance relationship 156
  oppressive 109
  partnership-based xii, 56–63, 95–103
  research relationship 23–5
practitioners xii, 16, 23
  see also professionals; social workers; staff
privacy, partnership-based practice 60

professionals
    see also practitioners; social workers; staff
    attitudes xiii
    child protection conferences 52, 57
    information sharing 40
psychoanalysis, identity formation 69
psychosocial development 69, 71
psychotherapy, feminist 71
public records
    Family Records Centre, London 171, 181, 187, 193
    General Registrar Office 174
    National Health Service Register 175, 193–4
    Office of National Statistics (ONS) 181, 187, 193–4

Quality Protects (DH, 1998) 7
Quinton, D. 103

R. v. Derbyshire County Council ex parte K. (1994) 36
racism 4, 6, 73, 79, 83, 85
rape 76–7, 84
'rebellious' youth 70
reconciliation 130–1, 137, 138–9
records
    see also information; public records
    access to 2, 34–40, 47–8, 72
    gaps in files 114–15
refugees 106
Registrar General 181
regulations
    local authority obligations 27
    reviews 43
rehabilitation 14, 94, 106, 119, 158
Reich, Diana 147, 176
rejection 131–2
relationships
    impact of care 85–6
    leaving care 130, 133, 137, 138, 141
    maintaining 90
    peer 146
    with social workers 86–7
    young people's identity 76
relatives, fostering 100–1
removal at birth 12–13
research xi–xii, 1–25
    child protection cases 50–7

evidence 103
foster care 99–101
partnership approaches 95–9
residential care 101–2
young people's identity 67, 75–89
residential care xiii, 14
    embarrassment about 79
    foster care comparison 78
    maltreatment within 77
    partnership approaches 95
    placements 101–2
    staff training 162
resources 115, 162–4, 166
responsibility
    parental 92, 127, 128, 135
    legal issues 29–32, 34, 36, 38–9, 42, 44–5
    mother/father distinction 109
retrospective implementation, Children Act 1989 xii, 2
Review of Children's Cases Regulations (1991) 43
reviews 19–20, 43–4, 106, 159–61, 166
Rich, Adrienne 72
rights
    children's 94–5, 120, 135, 136, 137
    identity 65–6
    to information 34–40, 47–8
    legal instruments 28
    parental 29, 30, 48, 93–4
Rowe, J. 49
Ryburn, M. 108

Salvation Army 195
school, stigmatization 79
searches xv, 21, 167–95
self-concept 68
self-esteem 67, 68, 73
service delivery, local authority variations 157–8
service provision, consumerism 127, 133–4
sexuality
    female identity 71
    homosexuality 72
Sharland, E. 53
Shemmings, D. 57, 59
siblings
    contact with 81–3, 102, 164
    emotional support 131, 138

loss of contact 13, 107–8
'significant harm' families 50, 53–4, 62
'single issue' families 54
Slugoski, B. 68, 71–2
social context, identity 70–1, 73–4
social disconnectedness 102
social learning theory 69
social order 70, 72
social services
   exclusion of parents 109, 112–13, 121–2
   management 166
   parent-initiated contact 107, 121
   partnership principles 133
   public debate 158
social workers
   see also practitioners; professionals; staff
   allocation of 58
   attitudes 20–3
   barriers to partnership xiii, 116, 119–21, 122–3
   challenges to 3
   contact letters 175–9
   coordination of services 134
   demands on 98
   exclusion of parents 112
   family issues 139
   finding answers 89
   maintaining status quo 117
   management issues 11, 24, 58, 115, 155–66
   negotiation 62–3
   parental involvement 20
   parents' mistrust of 32, 54
   participation in research xi, xvi, 5, 9–11, 12, 23–4
   partnership-based practice x, 59–61
   poor practice 96–7, 109, 156
   power 134–5
   re-evaluation of parental role 124
   restoring parental contact 46, 47
   searching for lost parents 167–8
   staff turnover 11, 24, 106–7, 114
   staffing resources 162–4
   supervision 165
   support for substitute care 112
   young people's attitudes towards 86–7, 90
society, individual dichotomy 68, 70, 73

SPSS (Statistical Package for the Social Sciences) 11
staff
   see also practitioners; professionals; social workers
   professional attitudes xiii
   resources 162–4, 166
   supervision 164–6
   training 161–2, 166
   turnover 11, 24, 106–7, 114
state
   conceptual approaches to child care 93–4
   philosophy of care 118
status 30, 135
status quo, maintaining the 116, 117–18
statutory provisions 27
step-families 98–9
stereotyping 99
stigmatization 74, 79, 108, 146
'strategic practice' 60
stress, adolescence 69
structural inequalities 71, 93–4
supervised contact 163, 164
supervision 164–6
support
   family 2, 49, 58, 59, 94, 98
   from social workers 86
   leaving care 129, 130, 131, 138, 140, 142

termination of contact 1–2, 13, 37, 46, 106, 112–13, 119
Thatcher, Margaret 91
Thoburn, June xi, xii, 49–63
tracing process xv, 21, 167–95
training 161–2, 166
transracial placements 4, 14
trauma 145
Tunnard, J. ix, 92–3

UN Convention on the Rights of the Child 28–9, 65–6, 120
unemployment 134

values 25, 128
violence, domestic 50, 84, 107, 110, 125
visits 163, 164
voluntary care 50, 108
voluntary sector services 133, 134

Waller, Brian xi, xiv, 155–66
welfare
 conflict of duties 31
 consumerism 127, 133–4
 contact issues 46
 maintaining status quo 117
 reviews 160
 rights relationship 120
 safeguarding 136
 UN Convention on the Rights of the Child 28–9
welfare service, discrimination within 74

Williamson, H. 90
women
 fear of violence 84
 removal of child at birth 12–13
 sexual identity 71
 social expectations 110–11
 Working Together under the Children Act 1989 (DH, 1991) 51

young people
 see also adolescence
 identity 65–90
 leaving care 127–43